Legal Writing and Legal Skills for Foreign LL.M. Students

ESL Workbook

∎ ∎ ∎

Karen Lundquist
Assistant Professor of ESL and Legal Skills
University of Minnesota Law School

The publisher is not engaged in rendering legal or other professional advice, and this publication is not a substitute for the advice of an attorney. If you require legal or other expert advice, you should seek the services of a competent attorney or other professional.

© 2017 LEG, Inc. d/b/a West Academic
　　444 Cedar Street, Suite 700
　　St. Paul, MN 55101
　　1-877-888-1330

West, West Academic Publishing, and West Academic are trademarks of West Publishing Corporation, used under license.

Printed in the United States of America

ISBN: 978-1-68328-762-9

TABLE OF CONTENTS

SECTION I

Unit 1. Damages 1

    Soucek v. Banham, 524 N.W.2d 478 (Minn. Ct. App. 1994). 1

    State v. Weber, No. A07-1218, 1995 WL 238940 (Minn. Ct. App. April 25, 1995). 5

    State v. Graham, No. C1-02-887, 2003 WL 282470 (Minn. Ct. App. Feb. 11, 2003). 8

    Jensen v. Walsh, 623 N.W.2d 247 (Minn. 2001). 11

Unit 2. Apparent Authority 14

    Edinburg Volunteer Fire Co. v. Danko Emergency Equipment Co., 867 N.Y.S.2d 547 (N.Y. App. Div. 2008) . . 14

    Merrell-Benco Agency, LLC v. HSBC Bank USA, 799 N.Y.S.2d 590 (N.Y. App. Div. 2005). 18

    Hallock v. State of New York, 474 N.E.2d 1178 (N.Y. 1984). 22

    Greene v. Hellman, 412 N.E.2d 1301 (N.Y. 1980). 26

    Regency Oaks Corp. v. Norman-Spencer McKernan, Inc., 12 N.Y.S.3d 398 (N.Y. App. Div. 2015). 30

Unit 3. Contract Formation and Promissory Estoppel. 33

Contract Formation. 33

    Cleveland Wrecking Co. v. Hercules Construction Corp., 23 F. Supp. 2d 287 (E.D.N.Y. 1998) 33

    International Business Machines Corp. v. Johnson, 629 F. Supp. 2d 321 (S.D.N.Y. 2005). 37

    Trademark Properties, Inc. v. A&E Television Networks, 422 Fed. Appx. 199 (4th Cir. 2011). 40

    Kowalchuk v. Stroup, 61 A.D.3d 118 (N.Y. App. Div. 2009). 43

    Bazak International Corp. v. Tarrant Apparel Group, 378 F. Supp. 2d 377 (S.D.N.Y. 2005). 46

Promissory Estoppel 49

    Goff-Hamel v. Obstetricians & Gynecologists, P.C., 588 N.W.2d 798 (Neb. 1999). 49

    Maxell, Inc. v. Kenney Deans, Inc., No. A-98-930, 1999 WL 731846 (Neb. Ct. App. Sept. 21, 1999). 51

    deNourie & Yost Homes, LLC v. Frost, 854 N.W.2d 298 (Neb. 2014). 54

    168th and Dodge LP v. Rave Reviews Cinemas, LLC, 501 F.3d 945 (8th Cir. 2007). 58

Unit 4. Trespass and Nuisance 61

Trespass 61

Public Service Co. of Colorado v. Van Wyk, 27 P.3d 377 (Colo. 2001). 61

Hoery v. United States, 64 P.3d 214 (Colo. 2003). 66

Cook v. Rockwell International Corp., 273 F. Supp. 2d 1175 (Colo. 2003). 69

Miller v. Carnation Co., 516 P.2d 661 (Colo. App. 1973). 71

Cobai v. Young, 679 P.2d 121 (Colo. App. 1984). 74

Nuisance 78

Wernke v. Halas, 600 N.E.2d 117 (Ind. Ct. App. 1992).. 78

Owens v. Phillips, 73 Ind. 284 (Ind. 1881). 82

Bonewitz v. Parker, 912 N.E.2d 378 (Ind. 2009). 86

Davoust v. Mitchell, 257 N.E.2d 332 (Ind. Ct. App. 1970). 89

Hendricks v. Tubbs, 92 N.E.2d 561 (Ind. 1950). 94

SECTION II

Unit 1. Negligence/Duty to Warn 98

Lundgren v. Fultz, 354 N.W.2d 25 (Minn. 1984). 98

Bjerke v. Johnson, 742 N.W.2d 660 (Minn. 2007). 101

Patzwald v. Krey, 390 N.W.2d 920 (Minn. 1986).. 104

Udofot v. Seven Eights Liquor, No. A10-431, 2010 WL 5071313 (Minn. Ct. App. March 15, 2011).. 108

H.B. ex rel. v. Whittemore, 552 N.W.2d 705 (Minn. 1996). 110

Wood on Behalf of Doe v. Astleford, 412 N.W.2d 753 (Minn. Ct. App. 1987). . . 118

Unit 2. Defamation 122

Herlihy v. The Metropolitan Museum of Art, 633 N.Y.S.2d 106 (N.Y. App. Div. 1995). 122

Baldwin v. Shell Oil Co., 419 N.Y.S.2d 752 (N.Y. App. Div. 1979). 129

Buckley v. Litman, 443 N.E.2d 469 (N.Y. 1982). 132

Byam v. Collins, 19 N.E. 75 (N.Y. 1888). 135

Van Wyck v. Aspinwall, 17 N.E. 190 (N.Y. 1858). 138

Unit 3. Constitutional Right to Privacy 142

State v. Boland, 800 P.2d 1112 (Wash. 1990). 142

State v. Sweeney, 107 P.3d 110 (Wash. Ct. App. 2005)......................147

State v. Graffius, 871 P.2d 1115 (Wash. Ct. App. 1994)......................150

State v. Rodriguez, 828 P.2d 636 (Wash. Ct. App. 1992)......................153

Unit 4. LLC/Partnership Dispute 155

Anest v. Audino, 773 N.E.2d 202 (Ill. App. Ct. 2002)......................155

Gifford v. Gallano Farms, LLC, Nos. 2-10-0055, 2-10-0355, 2011 WL 10109462 (Ill. App. Ct. May 18, 2011)...159

Azulay, Horn and Seiden, LLC v. Horn, 2013 Il App. (1st) 1120625 (Ill. App. Ct. Aug. 1, 2013)...............163

Shrock v. Meier, 2012 IL App (1st) 111408-U (Ill. App. Ct. Mar. 19, 2012)......................167

Tully v. McLean, 948 N.E.2d 714 (Ill. App. Ct. 2011)......................170

SECTION III

Unit 1. Restrictive Covenants and Preliminary Injunctions 174

Reed, Roberts Associates, Inc. v. Strauman, 353 N.E.2d 590 (N.Y. 1976)......................174

BDO Seidman v. Hirshberg, 712 N.E.2d 1220 (N.Y. 1999)......................178

Kanan, Corbin, Schupak, Aronow, Inc. v. FD International, Ltd., 797 N.Y.S.2d 883 (N.Y. Sup. Ct. 2005)....182

Veramark Technologies, Inc. v. Bouk, 10 F. Supp. 3d 395 (W.D.N.Y. 2014)......................186

Scott, Stackrow & Co. v. Skavina, 780 N.Y.S.2d 675 (N.Y. App. Div. 2004)......................190

Merrill Lynch, Pierce, Fenner & Smith v. Dunn, 191 F. Supp. 2d 1346 (M.D. Fla. 2002)......................193

Lucente v. International Business Machines Corp., 310 F.3d 243 (2nd Cir. 2002)......................196

Zellner v. Conrad, 589 N.Y.S.2d 903 (N.Y. App. Div. 1992)......................201

Ashland Management, Inc. v. Altair Investments NA, LLC, 869 N.Y.S.2d 465 (N.Y. App. Div. 2008)........206

Unit 2. Personal Jurisdiction and the Internet 210

Atkinson v. McLaughlin, 462 F. Supp. 2d 1038 (D.N.D. 2006)......................210

Mink v. AAAA Development, Inc., 190 F.3d 333 (5th Cir. 1999)......................216

Carrot Bunch Co., v. Computer Friends, Inc., 218 F. Supp. 2d 820 (N.D. Tex. 2002)......................219

Ford v. Mentor Worldwide, LLC, 2 F. Supp. 3d 898 (E.D. La. 2014)......................222

Gatte v. Ready 4 A Change, LLC, No. 2:11-CV-2083, 2013 WL 123613 (W.D. La. Jan. 13, 2013)...........225

The Kelly Law Firm, P.C. v. An Attorney For You, 679 F. Supp. 2d 755 (S.D. Tex. 2009)......................228

Percle v. SFGL Foods, Inc., 356 F. Supp. 2d 629 (M.D. La. 2004)......................231

Tempur-Pedic International, Inc. v. Go Satellite, Inc., 758 F. Supp. 2d 366 (N.D. Tex. 2010)......................235

Unit 3. Title VII of the Civil Rights Act of 1964 and Religious Accommodations 238

American Postal Workers Union v. Postmaster General, 781 F.2d 772 (9th Cir. 1986) 238

Anderson v. General Dynamics Convair Aerospace Division, 589 F.2d 397 (9th Cir. 1978) 242

Bhatia v. Chevron U.S.A., Inc., 734 F.2d 1382 (9th Cir. 1984) 244

Burns v. Southern Pacific Transportation Co., 589 F.2d 403 (9th Cir. 1978) 247

EEOC v. AutoNation USA Corp., 52 Fed. Appx. 327 (9th Cir. 2002) 249

EEOC v. Townley Engineering & Manufacturing Co., 859 F.2d 610 (9th Cir. 1988) 253

International Association of Machinists & Aerospace Workers v. Boeing Co., 833 F.2d 165 (9th Cir. 1987) . . . 256

Proctor v. Consolidated Freightways Corp. of Delaware, 795 F.2d 1472 (9th Cir. 1986) 259

Slater v. Douglas County, 743 F. Supp. 2d 1188 (D. Or. 2010) 262

Tiano v. Dillard Department Stores, Inc., 139 F.3d 679 (9th Cir. 1998) 264

EEOC Consent Decree EEOC v. Razzoo's, L.P., No. 3:05-cv-00562 (N.D. Tex. June 16, 2006) 267

Unit 4. Premises Liability 270

Statutes 270

M.G.L.A. 186 § 15 and § 19 270

Cases 274

Young v. Garwacki, 402 N.E.2d 1045 (Mass. 1980) 274

Humphrey v. Byron, 850 N.E.2d 1044 (Mass. 2006) 280

Monterosso v. Gaudette, 391 N.E.2d 948 (Mass. App. Ct. 1979) 284

Bishop v. TES Realty Trust, 942 N.E.2d 173 (Mass. 2011) 287

Chausse v. Coz, 540 N.E.2d 667 (Mass. 1989) 290

The Great Atlantic and Pacific Tea Co. v. Yanofsky, 403 N.E.2d 370 (Mass. 1980) 292

Index 296

Legal Writing and Legal Skills for Foreign LL.M. Students

ESL Workbook

SECTION I

Unit 1 Damages

Soucek v. Banham,
524 N.W.2d 478 (Minn. Ct. App. 1994).

Vocabulary and Legal Terminology

Compensatory damages: Damages recoverable for the precise injury sustained; damages that make an injured party whole as opposed to punitive, nominal, or exemplary damages. Compensatory damages include medical expenses, pain, mental suffering, and injury to one's reputation.[1]

Intrinsic: Being an essential or natural characteristic of something.

To get loose: To break free, such as a dog that was on a leash or a rope and the leash came off, allowing the dog to roam freely.

To spot: To see or notice, especially something that is hidden or hard to see.

Municipal animal warden: A city employee whose job it is to catch dogs and cats that are running freely.

To impound: To take legal custody of something such as a dog or a car.

Contravention: Contradiction.

Fireproofing materials: Materials that are applied to make an object resistant to flames.

Asbestos: A heat and fire-resistant material used for insulation. Asbestos can cause serious diseases of the lungs when people breathe its dust.

Tortfeasors: Those who commit a tort or a civil wrong.

Tortious conduct: Actions or behavior that can form the basis for a tort claim.

Fortuitous: Happening by chance or with luck.

---

[1] *Damages*, GILBERT'S POCKET SIZE LAW DICTIONARY (3rd ed. 2014).

Pre-Reading Questions

Before you begin reading, skim the caption and the procedural posture, overview and outcome paragraphs. Answer the following questions:

1. Is the case in federal or state court?
2. At which level of the court system was this case decided (i.e. at the trial court, court of appeals, supreme court)?
3. Who are the parties to the case?
4. What claim(s) did the plaintiff bring?
5. What happened procedurally at the trial court?
    a. The plaintiff filed a motion for punitive damages, and the trial court granted the motion. The court then reversed its own decision to allow Soucek to seek punitive damages. Why?
    b. How did the case conclude at the trial court?
6. Who appealed and on what grounds?
7. What did the appellate court decide and why?

Comprehension Questions

With a general idea of the case in your mind, you can now read the case. As you are reading and after you finish reading, answer the following questions:

1. State the issue before the court.
2. Describe the "apparent conflict" between the two Minnesota Supreme Court cases, Keene and Wilson, one of which allowed punitive damages when the plaintiff suffered only property damages and one which did not.
    a. Why did the court in Wilson allow the award of punitive damages?
    b. What public policy arguments did the court make in that ruling?
    c. In contrast, what public policy arguments were used in Keene to deny the recovery of punitive damages?
3. How does the court in the Soucek decision reconcile this conflict?
4. What damages is Soucek limited to recovering in light of this decision?
5. The plaintiff argued "persuasively" that policy reasons exist for allowing the recovery of damages to more than the fair market value of a pet when it is killed. What policy arguments can you think of for limiting damages to the fair market value of the animal?
6. Is this case useful for our case? Why or why not?
7. What type of damages did Park suffer: property or personal injury?
8. Based on what you know so far about the law, what advice will you give her?

Language Focus – The Subjunctive in English

When we talk about verbs, we talk about the verb tense, which indicates time: past, present, future, present continuous, past perfect, and so on. We also talk about the voice of the verb, which can be passive or active. We might even talk about verb endings, such as *–ing*, *-ed* or the third-person singular *–s*. Another characteristic of verbs is the *mood* of a verb. In English, we have four moods for verbs: indicative, imperative, infinitive, and subjunctive. Unlike a verb tense indicating time, mood indicates a state of being; the subjunctive mood expresses what is imagined or desired.

This might all seem irrelevant to you as a law student, but before you turn the page and forget about verb moods all together, examine the following sentence from the Soucek decision. Pay particular attention to the subject and verb of the relative clause (the part of the sentence following the relative pronoun *that*).

> Soucek also requested that the measure of compensatory damages include the intrinsic value of his dog as a pet.

Grammatically, what is strange in this sentence? If you aren't sure, first identify the subject of the relative clause. Is it singular or plural? Now identify the verb of that same relative clause. What tense is it? Is it past, present or future?

You've probably caught on by now! In the relative clause, the subject — measure of compensatory damages — is singular. Don't be fooled by *of compensatory damages*, which is plural. That is not the subject. That is a prepositional phrase that modifies or describes measure, the singular subject. But the verb is neither past nor present. If it were present tense, it would be *includes*, as measure is third-person singular. And if it were past tense, it would be *included*. What's going on?

This sentence, specifically the verb *include*, is an example of the subjunctive mood in English. The verb doesn't have a past or present tense (because it is subjunctive), and the verb form is the same for all persons. There is no past tense *–ed* and no third-person singular *–s*. You use just the verb root (the infinitive minus *to*).

What determines when you use the subjunctive is the verb of the main sentence, here *requested*. We use the subjunctive after the following verbs and the following expressions:[2]

to advise (that)	It is best (that)
to ask (that)	It is crucial (that)
to command (that)	It is desirable (that)
to demand (that)	It is essential (that)
to desire (that)	It is imperative (that)
to insist (that)	It is important (that)
to propose (that)	It is recommended (that)
to recommend (that)	It is urgent (that)
to request (that)	It is vital (that)
to suggest (that)	It is a good idea (that)
to urge (that)	It is a bad idea (that)

---

[2] *Subjunctive*, ENGLISHPAGE.COM, http://www.englishpage.com/minitutorials/subjunctive.html (last visited May 4, 2016).

Here are a few examples. The main verb and the verb in the subjunctive are highlighted for you.

- The senior partner **demanded** that I **be** present at the hearing, even though the deadline for another brief was looming.
- *It is imperative* that a new attorney **take** an active role in the law firm.
- They **are asking** that we **be** quiet.
- Opposing counsel **has urged** his client that he **settle** the matter before going to court, but the client has refused.

State v. Weber,
No. A07-1218, 1995 WL 238940 (Minn. Ct. App. April 25, 1995).

Vocabulary and Legal Terminology

Antipathy: Strong feelings of dislike.

Insulation: Material used to prevent heat loss in a house, placed in the attic (above the ceiling) or in the walls.

Deputy: An assistant to the sheriff, with authority to act in the sheriff's place when he or she is absent.

Sheriff: In the United States, an elected official at the county level, responsible for enforcing the law.

Carcass: Dead body of an animal, often one slaughtered for food.

To get back at someone: To take revenge; to do something to hurt someone after he has done something to hurt you.

Dispositive: Something that brings about the conclusion or the settlement of a legal dispute or case.[3]

To restrict: To limit.

Pre-Reading Questions

Before you begin reading, skim the caption and the procedural posture, overview and outcome paragraphs. Answer the following questions:

1. Is the case in federal or state court? Is it a civil or criminal matter?
2. Why was the defendant arrested and charged with a crime?
3. What crime was he charged with?
4. What happened at the trial court?
5. What did the defendant argue on appeal?
6. Who appealed?
7. What did the court of appeals decide?

Comprehension Questions

With a general idea of the case in your mind, you can now read the case. As you are reading and after you finish reading, answer the following questions:

1. What is the issue before the court?
2. How does the court reason and use precedent to conclude that Minnesota case law does not allow punitive damages when the plaintiff suffers property damage?
3. What did the court determine was appropriate for restitution and on what basis?

---

[3] *Dispositive*, Gilbert's Pocket Size Law Dictionary (3rd ed. 2014).

4. State v. Weber is a criminal case, and our matter with Pamela Park is a civil case. Is this case still useful to your understanding of the issue of damages in our case? Why or why not?

Language Focus — Are They Really Synonyms?

In the State v. Weber case, it is stated that "[t]he deputy brought the dog's carcass back to the Dohrmanns for identification."

In the Vocabulary and Legal Terminology section, you learned that a carcass is the dead body of an animal. A synonym for carcass is dead body. But as you can see, carcass is much more specific than a dead body as the term describes specifically the body of a dead animal, especially (but not only) one slaughtered for food. In a thesaurus listing for carcass, you will find other words listed as synonyms, including *remains, cadaver* and *corpse*. What's the difference between these words and do they really have the same meaning?

Below you will find four sentences, each of which uses one of the above nouns that is a synonym for carcass, but with a subtle difference in meaning. Read each sentence and analyze it, identifying how the meaning of the sentence changes with the use of the different bolded and italicized noun.

After the four sentences, you will find the nouns, with a blank space to write the definition. Use a dictionary if you are unsure. After you have found and written the meaning of the word in the blank, write a sentence that shows your understanding of the word.

Carcass vs. Remains vs. Cadaver vs. Corpse

1. After receiving a complaint from neighbors, city employees entered the abandoned home and were horrified when they found **carcasses** of cats and dogs that had died of starvation.
2. Unidentified **remains** of the victims of the September 11 terrorist attacks were moved to the memorial that now stands at what was the site of the World Trade Center.
3. During the first semester of medical school, most students are nervous the first time that they see and have to dissect a **cadaver**.
4. Rita's family members were inconsolable when they saw her **corpse** at the morgue, where she had been brought following the car accident that she was a victim of.

Carcass: _____

Remains: _____

Cadaver: _____

Corpse: _____

Now try the same exercise with these five verbs, some of which you are likely familiar with through your studies in your LL.M. program.

To rob vs. to burglarize vs. to raid vs. to steal vs. to shoplift

1. Many victims are **robbed** while walking alone late at night, often absorbed by their cell phone so they are unaware of their surroundings.
2. When Pablo and Norma returned home after a weekend at the sea, they immediately knew that something had happened while they were away. The front door had been kicked in, evidence that their home had been **burglarized**.
3. Police officers **raided** the home of a suspected drug dealer, hoping to arrest him and find evidence of his criminal activities.
4. The young woman **stole** her mother's iPad, sold it and used the money to buy drugs.
5. The young woman's friend instead **shoplifted** an expensive Hermes purse and sold it on eBay to then use the money to buy drugs.

To rob: _____

To burglarize: _____

To raid: _____

To steal: _____

To shoplift: _____

State v. Graham,
No. C1-02-887, 2003 WL 282470 (Minn. Ct. App. Feb. 11, 2003).

Vocabulary and Legal Terminology

Within the province (of someone): In someone's authority.

Purebred: An animal such as a dog that is of one breed, as opposed to a mutt or a mixed-breed.

Speculative: Based on speculation, or guesses or ideas, rather than on facts.

Clear error: A mistake in application of law or in matters of fact made by a trial court that when reviewed by the court of appeals is obviously wrong.[4]

To flush out: To make something leave a hiding place.

Game prey: Animals that are hunted such as deer, bear, duck and wild turkey (as well as many others, depending on the part of the country or the world where you live).

Pre-Reading Questions

Before you begin reading, skim the caption and the overview and outcome paragraphs. Answer the following questions:

1. Is the case in federal or state court?
2. At which level of the court system was this case decided (i.e. at the trial court, court of appeals, supreme court)?
3. What happened procedurally at the trial court?
4. Who appealed and on what grounds?
5. What did the appellate court decide and on what grounds?

Comprehension Questions

With a general idea of the case in your mind, you can now read the case. As you are reading and after you finish reading, answer the following questions:

1. What is the issue before the court?
2. What happened that led to the defendant being charged with cruelty to animals?
3. Both the state and the defendant had their own expert witness. Why?
4. The expert witnesses presented conflicting opinions on the value of the dog. How does the court decide which expert to believe?
5. Why did the state's expert testify that the dog, Gypsy, that was shot and killed had a fair market value of $2,000? Doesn't that seem like a lot for a dog?

---

[4] *Error*, GILBERT'S POCKET SIZE LAW DICTIONARY (3rd ed. 2014).

6. Is this case useful for our client matter with Pamela Park? Why or why not?
7. How can you use these facts and apply them to Park's matter? Will the decision help her potentially recover more money for Honey's death? Why or why not?

Language Focus – What's the Difference?

Look at these three sentences from the cases in this Unit and examine the highlighted words.

> We therefore *find* that the restitution award must be restricted to the $500 which compensated Dohrmann for the market value of his dog.

> [In Soucek] this court affirmed the trial court's restriction of damages to the replacement cost of the dog, [and ***held***] that the intrinsic value of a pet to its owner is not currently included in damages that may be recovered for intentionally killing a pet.

> The State appealed the trial court's ***ruling*** to the Court of Appeals.

It might be easy to think that we can say *the court finds, the court holds* and *the court rules* interchangeably, and that the verbs are synonyms. But they aren't, and each word is used in a specific context and to describe a specific action that a court takes. What do you think the difference is between *to find, to hold* and *to rule*? Try to define the three verbs on your own before looking at the dictionary definitions provided below.

To find: To decide on issues of fact.[5]

To hold: (of a court) To reach a final decision in a case.[6]

To rule: To decide the law; to require a certain action.[7]

Here are some exercises so you can practice your understanding of these three verbs. Circle the correct verb in the sentences. Once you have chosen the verb you think is correct, state the reason for your choice.

1. The trial court ***found/held/ruled*** that the evidence that the plaintiff wanted to introduce at trial was inadmissible because it was overly prejudicial to the defendant and lacked probative value.
2. In 2015, the Supreme Court ***found/held/ruled*** that laws that denied a same-sex couple the right to marry violated the individuals' constitutional right to equal protection.
3. We are waiting for the court to decide on a motion that we filed last week. If the court ***finds/holds/rules*** in our favor, the case will be dismissed.
4. It is surprising that in most employment discrimination cases, the court ***finds/holds/rules*** that the defendant is not liable and has not violated any laws.

---

[5] *Finding,* Gilbert's Pocket Size Law Dictionary (3rd ed. 2014).
[6] *Holding,* Gilbert's Pocket Size Law Dictionary (3rd ed. 2014).
[7] *Rule,* Gilbert's Pocket Size Law Dictionary (3rd ed. 2014).

5. Most criminal defendants are ***found/held/ruled*** guilty by a jury of their peers.
6. The Court of Appeals must uphold the trial court's ***findings/holdings/rulings*** of fact unless they are clearly erroneous.
7. The Supreme Court's ***finding/holding/ruling*** in the Dred Scott decision, which denied blacks (called negroes in the decision) citizenship, is one of the most shameful decisisons of U.S. Supreme Court history.
8. When the State appeals a pretrial order, it must show clearly and unequivocally (1) that the district court's ***finding/holding/ruling*** was erroneous and (2) that the ***finding/holding/ruling*** will have a "critical impact" on the State's ability to prosecute the case.
9. The district court ***found/held/ruled*** that the plaintiff's own conduct was a contributing factor to the accident, thus barring her from any recovery.

Jensen v. Walsh,
623 N.W.2d 247 (Minn. 2001).

Vocabulary and Legal Terminology

En banc: (French) In full bench. Term refers to situation where all qualified judges of a court take part in a case. Note that the pronunciation is /en **bangk**/ *or* /on **bongk**/, with the stress on *banc*.[8]

Houseboat: A boat that can be parked (or moored, as explained below) and used as a home.

Bitter dispute: A heated and angry argument. See the Language Focus for additional information on the use of the word bitter in this and other expressions.

Channel: A narrow body of water that connects two seas or larger bodies of water, such as the English Channel that separates France and England.

Moored: Parked, but for a boat.

Writ of attachment: A writ is a formal written command or authorization of the court issued to an officer, directing him to act in some way, and a writ of attachment orders the taking of property to be held as security by the court for the purpose of satisfying an anticipated judgment.[9]

To execute: (here) To perform or carry out an order, such as serving a writ on a defendant.

Calf (plural calves): (here) Baby cow.

Backdrop: Background.

Pre-Reading Questions

Before you begin reading, skim the caption, the first paragraph and the syllabus. Answer the following questions:

1. Is the case in federal or state court?
2. Who are the parties to the case and what is the relationship between them?
3. What claims did the plaintiff bring?
4. What happened procedurally at the trial court?
   a. What motion was filed?
   b. Who filed the motion and was it granted?
5. What did the court of appeals decide and on what grounds?
6. What did the supreme court hold and what was the disposition?
7. After reading the holding, are you surprised after reading the other three cases in this Unit? Why or why not?

---

[8] *En Banc*, Gilbert's Pocket Size Law Dictionary (3rd ed. 2014).
[9] *Writ*, Gilbert's Pocket Size Law Dictionary (3rd ed. 2014); *Attachment*, Gilbert's Pocket Size Law Dictionary (3rd ed. 2014).

Comprehension Questions

With a general idea of the case in your mind, you can now read the case. As you are reading and after you finish reading, answer the following questions:

1. Restate in your own words the issue in this case.
2. This case deals with a heated dispute between neighbors.
    a. What thoughts or personal reaction did you have when you read the details of what Walsh and his business associate did to the Jensen family?
    b. What do you think drives neighbors to file a lawsuit against another neighbor? Do you have an opinion, whether good or bad, about neighbors who sue neighbors?
    c. How would a dispute like this, between neighbors, be resolved in your home country? Through the courts? In another way?
3. Summarize in your own words the common law rule of punitive damages in Minnesota.
4. How did statute §549.20 change the common law? _____
   _____
   _____
   _____
   _____
5. What had been happening that led the legislature to pass this statute?
6. This case deals with and discusses public policy. Explain what public policy and what interests must be considered and balanced when dealing with punitive damages.
7. How does the Jensen case change Minnesota law regarding punitive damages?
8. Explain the evolution of the law regarding punitive damages.
9. Do you agree with this decision? Why or why not?
10. Is this case useful for our fact pattern? Why or why not?
11. How does the decision affect the advice that you will give Pamela Park about the damages that she could recover for Honey's death?

Language Focus – Adjectives and Idiomatic Expressions

The court vividly describes the relationship between the parties in the Jensen v. Walsh case: They were engaged in a **bitter** dispute. We often use the adjective *bitter* to describe food that we eat or beverages that we drink. Bitter foods include unsweetened cocoa, coffee (without sugar), celery, olives, beer and marmalade. The opposite of bitter is sweet.

We also use the word bitter in a figurative sense, such as to describe the dispute between the parties in the Jensen case. Here, the word means full of anger and hatred. In this case, the opposite of a bitter battle would not be a sweet battle, but rather peace and harmony!

Bitter is also used in different idiomatic expressions:

A bitter pill to swallow _____
To the bitter end _____
To take the bitter with the sweet _____
The bitter fruits _____

Can you guess what these expressions mean? If you aren't familiar with them, look them up in a dictionary and write the meaning on the space following the expression. Idiomatic expressions are difficult to understand because their meaning is never literal.

Interestingly enough, English also has different idiomatic expressions with sweet. Do you know the meanings of these expressions? If you don't, look them up in the dictionary. Then write a sentence using the idiomatic expression. After writing a sentence in English that demonstrates your understanding of the expression, determine how you express these same expressions in your mother tongue. Do you have the same or a similar idiomatic expression, or do you have to translate the idea behind the expression instead?

To keep it short and sweet _____
To have a sweet tooth _____
To sweet talk someone _____

Unit 2 Apparent Authority

Edinburg Volunteer Fire Co. v. Danko Emergency Equipment Co.,
867 N.Y.S.2d 547 (N.Y. App. Div. 2008).

Vocabulary and Legal Terminology

Negligent hiring: A tort claim brought by an injured person against an employer, alleging that the employer was negligent in hiring an individual who then injured the person. To be liable, the employee must have been acting in the scope of employment when injuring the person, and the employer must know or should have known that the employee would have injured someone while carrying out his job.

To forge: To copy something such as a signature or a banknote for fraudulent purposes.

To abscond: To depart secretly and hide.

To recoup: To regain something lost, often money.

To assert: To claim.

To imbue: To permeate or fill with a feeling or emotion.

To contemplate: To consider or think about.

Pre-Reading Questions

Before you begin reading, skim the caption and the synopsis and holding paragraphs and answer the following questions:

1. Is the case in federal or state court?
2. At which level of the court system was the case decided (i.e. at the trial court, court of appeals, supreme court)?

Edinburg Volunteer Fire Co. v. Danko Emergency Equipment Co., 867 N.Y.S.2d 547 (N.Y. App. Div. 2008)

3. Who are the parties to the case?
4. Who sued whom, and what causes of action did the plaintiff bring?
5. What happened procedurally at the trial court?
   a. Was there a trial?
   b. Was a motion filed?
   c. Did one party win? Who?
6. Who appealed?
7. What was the disposition of the appellate court? On what grounds?

Comprehension Questions

With a general idea of the case in your mind, you can now read the case. As you are reading and after you finish reading, answer the following questions:

1. Identify the actors:
   a. Who is the principal? _____
   b. Who is the agent? _____
   c. Who is the third party? _____

2. Look at the paragraph on the first page that begins "Because plaintiff failed to prove that Fahd had apparent authority…"
   a. Identify the rules of apparent authority that are stated in that paragraph.
   b. How many rules are there?
   c. Rephrase the rules into your own words:
      1) _____
      2) _____
      3) _____

3. What facts does the court use in its analysis when determining that Fahd, the defendant, did not have apparent authority to bind the principal?
   a. _____
   b. _____
   c. _____
   d. _____
   e. _____
   f. _____

4. For apparent authority to be found, the belief that the agent can bind the principal must be "reasonable."
   a. In this case, did the court think that the plaintiff's belief was reasonable?
   b. What facts did the court use to reach that conclusion?

c. Do you think that a reasonable businessman would have acted differently than the plaintiff did? Why or why not?

5. The decision seems harsh to the plaintiff, especially given the fact that Fahd committed suicide and the plaintiff has no one else to recover his money from.
   a. Does this seem fair and do you think that the court decided correctly?
   b. Why or why not?
   c. Should sympathy for the plaintiff be part of the court's reasoning?

6. Is this case useful for our fact pattern?
   a. Why or why not?
   b. Is it more useful for SDA or for Canopy? Why?

Language Focus — Predictive vs. Persuasive Language

When we think about the type of writing or speaking that lawyers do, we often conjure up in our mind a lawyer in court, persuading a judge or a jury about her client's case. In fact, lawyers often do need to write or speak in a persuasive way, which means that the lawyer tries to move the judge or jury to a belief or position (that his client is innocent, for example) or a course of action (to dismiss a complaint) by argument.

But sometimes, a lawyer doesn't need or want to persuade a client, a judge or jury, or another lawyer, but simply inform him or her about the law. A client often wants to know whether he will win or lose if he sues or is sued, or a senior attorney or partner at a law firm wants to know the same when making a strategic decision about whether to take a case, choose a certain strategy, or recommend that a client pursue litigation. In these situations, a lawyer makes a prediction about how a court might decide a case if it were litigated. We call the type of writing that a lawyer does in these situations predictive writing. Predictive writing is objective, while persuasive writing is not.

Look at this paragraph from the Edinburg Volunteer Fire Co. case and the revised version below.
- Read the paragraphs and decide which one is persuasive and which one is predictive.
- Underline the language choices (vocabulary, grammar, construction) that indicate which paragraph is persuasive and the other predictive.
- What can you identify about the language choices that make them more persuasive or predictive?

Version #1 (from the Edinburg Volunteer Fire Co. case):

Plaintiff should have been, and actually was, suspicious of some aspects of the prepayment arrangement. Although the proposal listed the purchase price, the prepayment was not credited nor even mentioned in any document. Several documents, including the order checklist, specifically stated that no prepayment was contemplated. Plaintiff's treasurer even inquired of Fahd as to why the prepayment check was being made payable to his personal company rather than defendant, but blindly accepted his answer without contacting defendant to confirm this unusual arrangement. No receipt was given or requested for the $55,000 prepayment. Defendant's literature listed a toll-free telephone number for customer inquiries, yet plaintiff did not even place a call to verify Fahd's authority. Under the circumstances, plaintiff failed to establish that Fahd had apparent authority to act on defendant's behalf in accepting the prepayment check.

Version #2 (revised):

Plaintiff should have been, and actually was, suspicious of some aspects of the prepayment arrangement. The prepayment was not credited or mentioned in the documents, although the proposal listed the purchase price. Some documents and the order checklist stated that no prepayment was contemplated. Plaintiff's treasurer asked Fahd why the check was being made payable to his personal company rather than defendant, but accepted his answer without further inquiry. Plaintiff did not receive a receipt for the prepayment or call the defendant's toll-free number for customer inquiries to verify Fahd's authority. Under these circumstances, plaintiff has not established that Fahd had apparent authority to act on defendant's behalf in accepting the prepayment check.

Merrell-Benco Agency, LLC v. HSBC Bank USA,
799 N.Y.S.2d 590 (N.Y. App. Div. 2005).

Vocabulary and Legal Terminology

Bench trial: A trial without a jury and with the judge acting as the fact-finder.

Unfettered: Unrestrained.

To clothe with something: (here, authority) To provide with or give a certain quality.

Declaratory judgment: A statement of the court declaring the rights and duties of the parties in a case or stating an opinion on a question of law without awarding relief. This judgment is binding whereas an advisory opinion is not.[10]

Fraud: Deception, deceit; trickery.[11]

Misappropriation: Wrongful or unauthorized use of property or funds (e.g., using trust funds other than for the beneficiary of the trust).[12]

Condonation: The pardoning or forgiving of past misconduct.

Pre-Reading Questions

Before you begin reading, skim the caption and the synopsis/holding paragraphs as well as the first paragraph of the case. Answer the following questions:

1. Is the case in federal or state court?
2. At which level of the court system was the case decided (i.e. at the trial court, court of appeals, supreme court)?
3. Who are the parties to the case?
4. Who sued whom, and what causes of action did the plaintiff bring?
5. What happened procedurally at the trial court?
    a. Was there a trial?
    b. Was a motion filed?
    c. Did one party win? Who?
6. Who appealed?
7. Why were there three causes of action and three judgments? Were there three separate trials (you might have to read the case to find the answer to this question)?

---

[10] *Judgment*, Gilbert's Pocket Size Law Dictionary (3rd ed. 2014).
[11] *Fraud*, Gilbert's Pocket Size Law Dictionary (3rd ed. 2014).
[12] *Misappropriation*, Gilbert's Pocket Size Law Dictionary (3rd ed. 2014).

Merrell-Benco Agency, LLC v. HSBC Bank USA, 799 N.Y.S.2d 590 (N.Y. App. Div. 2005)

Comprehension Questions

With a general idea of the case in your mind, you can now read the case. As you are reading and after you finish reading, answer the following questions:

1. Identify the actors:
   a. Who is the principal?_____
   b. Who is the agent? _____
   c. Who is the third party (or parties)? _____
2. What did Cohen do that led to the lawsuits being filed?
3. Who brought the lawsuits and on what grounds?
4. What arguments did Merrell-Benco make as to its liability for Cohen's actions?
5. Did the court agree with Merrell-Benco's arguments? Why or why not?
6. Did Cohen have apparent authority to bind Merrell-Benco?
7. What facts did the court use to reach its decision regarding Cohen's authority and whether he had apparent authority or not?
8. Does this case give us any idea of whether an agent's title is important in determining whether apparent authority exists? Why or why not?
9. Identify the rules of apparent authority that are stated in the case.
   a. How many rules are there?
   b. Rephrase the rules into your own words:
      1) _____
      _____
      _____
      2) _____
      _____
      _____
      3) _____
      _____
      _____
10. The court says that "condonation of control is critically relevant to the appearance of apparent authority."
    a. What is "condonation of control?"
    b. Why is the condonation of control "critically relevant" in the analysis of apparent authority?
    c. Does our case have a "condonation of control?"
11. Is this case useful for our fact pattern?
    a. Why or why not?
    b. Is it more useful for SDA or for Canopy? Why?

Grammar Review — Adverbs

Examine the use of adverbs in these sentences from the Merrell-Benco case.

> Although Bauer placed certain limits on Cohen's authority, such limits were **woefully** inadequate and of **remarkably** short duration.

The new owner attended periodic staff meetings and **intentionally** portrayed the agency as a continuation of the prior agency.

[W]e recognize the deference **rightfully** accorded to Supreme Court when it conducts a full and fair trial.

Adverbs are words that modify an adjective, as in the first example, a verb, as in the second and third example, or another adverb (*he speaks remarkably quickly*).

Most adverbs are formed by taking the adjective and adding the suffix *-ly*.

woeful	→	woefully
rightful	→	rightfully
remarkable	→	remarkably
intentional	→	intentionally

Note the spelling changes! Adjectives that end in "l" have a double "l" in the adverb, and adjectives that end in "e" drop the "e" and add "ly."

The spelling of other adjectives stays the same:

bad	→	badly
quick	→	quickly

Or change by changing "y" to "i":

easy	→	easily

Some adverbs stay the same as the adjective, such as "*We worked hard*," or "*She always drives very fast*."

Adverbs are very descriptive, and the use of an adverb can drastically change the sense of a sentence. As a general rule, in predictive writing, we try to avoid descriptive adverbs that color or characterize the sentence. Adverbs are often more suited to persuasive writing, but still must be used cautiously as an excessive use of adverbs can make your writing fall into *hyperbole*, or extravagant exaggeration.

It is best to follow the suggestion of legal writing expert Bryan Garner, who admonishes legal writers against adverbs: "[A]dverbs often weaken verbs. Think of the best single word instead of warming up a tepid one with a qualifier."[13]

And if you don't want to follow Garner's advice, listen to what Supreme Court Justice Anthony Kennedy, in an interview with Garner, says about the use of adverbs in legal writing:

> I think adverbs are a cop-out. They're a way for you to qualify, and if you don't use them, it forces you to think through the conclusion of your sentence. And it forces you to confront the significance of your word choice, the importance of your diction.[14]

---

[13] Bryan A. Garner, The Elements of Legal Style 363-364 (2nd ed. 2004).

[14] Interview by Bryan A. Garner of Anthony M. Kennedy, Senior Associate Justice of the United States Supreme Court, http://www.lawprose.org/bryan-garner/garners-interviews/supreme-court-interviews/justice-anthony-kennedy-supreme-court-of-the-united-states-part-3/.

Look at this example of an introduction to a memorandum of law. As you read the paragraph, pay attention to the use of adjectives and adverbs. Once you are finished, analyze the paragraph and determine whether or not the paragraph and the use of adverbs are effective and why. If you determine that the paragraph is not effective, edit and improve it.[15]

> This case . . . is about a strip club's blatantly flagrant misclassification of its entertainers as independent contractors. Rick's Cabaret ("Rick's NY" or "the Club") is a strip club in New York, which is owned and operated by the three Defendants in this case. Through the managers and staff who work at Rick's NY, Defendants exercise extreme control over the entertainers who faithfully work there. On a daily basis, Defendants dictate the minutiae of their entertainers' work through rules governing absolutely everything from the heel height of their shoes and length of their dresses to the order and timing by which entertainers must remove their clothing. What is more, Defendants threaten and impose extremely high monetary fines for violations of their rules. Despite this control, which often vastly exceeds that found in a typical employment relationship, and despite their clear awareness that their misclassification has clearly violated the law, Defendants have continuously classified all of their entertainers at the club as independent contractors. In self-serving reliance on this misclassification, Defendants pay their entertainers no wages whatsoever and instead repeatedly charge them "house fees" as a condition of employment and fines for violating Defendants' rules.

---

[15] This paragraph, from pleadings filed in the case, Hart v. Rick's Cabaret International, Inc., is the same as that used for an exercise in the Additional Online Resources. That exercise is to help you differentiate between predictive and persuasive legal writing. This paragraph is from the plaintiffs' memorandum in opposition to the defendants' motion for summary judgment. Pls' Memo. Opp. Summ. J. 10, Hart v. Rick's Cabaret Int'l, Inc., No. 09-CV-3043 (S.D.N.Y. 2013).

Hallock v. State of New York,
474 N.E.2d 1178 (N.Y. 1984).

Vocabulary and Legal Terminology

Rescission: The abrogation or voiding of a contract, removing all obligations of the parties, and restoring them to their original positions.[16]

Eminent domain: A government's power to take, or authorize others to take, private property for a public purpose provided that just compensation is paid for it.[17]

Dam: A barrier built to prevent the flow of water.

To appropriate: To take or use something, usually without permission.

Tract: A defined area of land.

Full fee interest: An entire interest in real property that is not subject to any encumbrances such as an easement or covenant.[18]

Easement: The right to use, or limit the use of, part of the land owned by another for a special purpose.[19]

To remit: To send back (here, to the lower court for trial).

To reconvey: To restore or return something.

Retention: The act of keeping something.

To vacate: To cancel; annul; set aside; rescind.[20]

Plenary action: Plenary means "full or complete." Plenary action means a decision taken by all the judges of the appellate court.

To foreclose: To preclude; to prevent someone from doing something.

Collusion: A secret agreement between two or more persons to commit a fraudulent act; term especially applies to manufacturing evidence to obtain a divorce.[21]

Misfeasance: The improper or wrongful performance of some lawful act.[22]

To relegate: To move or put someone in a lower position; here *relegate to relief* means to prevent recovery.

---

[16] *Rescission*, Gilbert's Pocket Size Law Dictionary (3rd ed. 2014).
[17] *Eminent Domain*, Gilbert's Pocket Size Law Dictionary (3rd ed. 2014).
[18] New Jersey Sea Grant Consortium, http://www.njseagrant.org/njcoastalaccess/coastal_access_toolkit/glossary_a_h.html (last visited April 29, 2016).
[19] *Easement*, Gilbert's Pocket Size Law Dictionary (3rd ed. 2014).
[20] *Vacate*, Gilbert's Pocket Size Law Dictionary (3rd ed. 2014).
[21] *Collusion*, Gilbert's Pocket Size Law Dictionary (3rd ed. 2014).
[22] *Misfeasance*, Gilbert's Pocket Size Law Dictionary (3rd ed. 2014).

Hallock v. State of New York, 474 N.E.2d 1178 (N.Y. 1984)   23

Pre-Reading Questions

Before you begin reading, skim the caption and the first paragraph. Answer the following questions:

1. Is the case in federal or state court?
2. At which level of the court system was this case decided (i.e. at the trial court, court of appeals, supreme court)?
3. Who are the parties to the case?
4. Who was asking that a settlement agreement be vacated or found void?
5. From the synopsis paragraph, can you get an idea of the arguments that the landowners made to convince the court to vacate the agreement? What are those arguments?
6. What happened procedurally at the trial court?
7. What happened procedurally at the appellate court?
8. What did the court of appeals (i.e. the highest court) decide?

Comprehension Questions

With a general idea of the case in your mind, you can now read the case. As you are reading and after you finish reading, answer the following questions:

1. Summarize the facts that led to the dispute.
2. The court tells us that when an attorney represents a client, the attorney has authority to make "certain procedural or tactical decisions," but that authority is not without limits. Compare that authority to the authority that attorneys have in your legal system to make decisions on behalf of clients.
    a. What decisions can an attorney make without consulting his or her client?
    b. What decisions must the client make?
    c. What happens if an attorney makes a decision that should be made by the client?
3. What policy reasons support the court's ruling that the settlement agreement should not be vacated?
4. When will a court make an exception and find a settlement agreement void?
5. What facts does the court use to show that Quartararo had apparent authority to accept the settlement agreement for his clients?
6. What facts did the court use to show that Phillips could not challenge the settlement agreement?
7. What facts did the court use to show that Hallock could not challenge the settlement agreement either?
8. Does this decision seem fair to you? Why or why not?
9. Is this case useful for our fact pattern?
    a. Why or why not?
    b. Is it more useful for SDA or for Canopy? Why?

Language Focus — Paraphrasing Complex Sentences

There is no way around it: the cases that you read for your LL.M. program are sometimes very difficult to understand. Unusual legal terminology, abstract concepts, and complex sentences are part of what makes reading cases so difficult.

While your initial tendency when you encounter such sentences might be to translate into your mother tongue to grasp the sense, that can actually be counterproductive as you are robbing yourself of the challenge of rephrasing into English. It is like using a bilingual dictionary instead of a monolingual one. While a bilingual one might be easier since you see the translation and immediately understand the meaning of an unfamiliar word, you lose the challenge of reading the definition in English and understanding the sense of the new word.

When you encounter a particularly difficult case or sentence within a case, one method you can put into practice to help you understand is paraphrasing. By paraphrasing, you are forced not only to make sense of the difficult passages (because you can't paraphrase what you don't understand) but you also challenge your language skills as an English speaker as you must find other ways of expressing what you read. Paraphrasing is also helpful to avoid plagiarism.

Take these sentences from the Hallock case and rephrase them into your own words and into more understandable English.

1. Phillips cannot be heard to challenge the settlement.
   ➤ *Cannot be heard* uses the verb "to hear" in an unusual way. What does the court mean?

   Your rephrase _____
   _____
   _____

2. Action was brought seeking rescission of settlement agreement entered in eminent domain proceeding on behalf of landowners whose land was appropriated by State.
   ➤ Here, to rephrase the sentence, it can be helpful to change the passive voice (action was brought) into an active verb. To do so, you must identify the subject of the verb.

   Your rephrase _____
   _____
   _____

This sentence is from another New York apparent authority case, Wen Kroy Realty Co. v. Public National Bank & Trust Co. of New York, 183 N.E. 73 (N.Y. 1932). The case is not included in your materials but provides an excellent example of a sentence that can create problems of comprehension unless you parse it apart.

> An agent in charge of a branch store, having been granted power to make a general indorsement of checks due the principal, although instructed to deposit all proceeds of the same in a particular bank, who indorses and transfers a check to an innocent purchaser and uses the proceeds of the check for his own purposes, nevertheless transfers good title to the check.

First identify what in the sentence makes it hard to understand. Grammar? Sentence structure? Unfamiliar vocabulary?

1. Try to parse apart the sentence to identify its parts:
   a. Who is the subject (i.e. who is doing the action of the sentence)?
   b. What is the main verb that goes with that subject (hint: keep reading and you will find it)?
   c. Look at the relative pronoun *who*. All relative pronouns must modify a noun (person, place or thing). What noun does this relative pronoun relate to?
   d. Part of the difficulty in this sentence is the passive verb *having been granted power*.
      - Who is the subject of that verb?
      - Try changing the passive voice verb to an active voice to make it easier to understand.
   e. What about the verb (past particle) *instructed*. Who instructed whom in this sentence?
   f. You should see that the principal is the actor of both verbs: the principal granted power [to the agent] to make a general indorsement of the check and instructed [the agent] to deposit the money from the checks into a specific bank account.
2. Now re-write the sentence into your own words. You might want to divide the sentence into two shorter sentences. You can also write the sentence as an "if-then" statement.

Your rewrite_____

_____

_____

_____

_____

Greene v. Hellman,
412 N.E.2d 1301 (N.Y. 1980).

Vocabulary and Legal Terminology

Wrongful deprivation of brokerage commissions: To deprive someone of something means to deny someone the use or enjoyment of something. This claim means that the broker, Greene, alleges that he deserved to be paid commissions for finding a buyer for the shopping center property, but that he was not paid.

To be the procuring cause of something: To procure means to obtain, especially with cure or effort. If you are the procuring cause of something, you are the reason that something or someone was found.

Bare: Empty.

In a nutshell: In a few words; concise.

Barren: (here) Without.

Fait accompli: (French) A completed fact; something already done.

Inchoate: Something that has just started to develop; incomplete.

To go over something with a fine-tooth comb: To examine something carefully and thoroughly.

Wellspring: The source of something.

Pre-Reading Questions

Before you begin reading, skim the caption and the first paragraph. Answer the following questions:
1. Is the case in federal or state court?
2. At which level of the court system was this case decided (i.e. at the trial court, court of appeals, supreme court)?
3. Who are the parties to the case?
4. Who brought the claim and on what grounds?
5. What happened procedurally at the trial court?
a. Was there a trial?
b. Who won? Plaintiff or defendant?
6. What happened procedurally at the appellate court?
7. What did the court of appeals (i.e. the highest court) decide and on what grounds?

Greene v. Hellman, 412 N.E.2d 1301 (N.Y. 1980)

Comprehension Questions

With a general idea of the case in your mind, you can now read the case. As you are reading and after you finish reading, answer the following questions:

1. What is the issue in this case?
2. Summarize the facts that led to the dispute. _____
   _____
   _____
   _____
   _____
   _____
3. What was the job of the plaintiff, Greene? _____
4. Identify the parties in this case and indicate what their role in the dispute is:
   a. Principal: _____
   _____
   b. Agent: _____
   _____
   c. Third party: _____
   _____
5. Greene is alleging that Hellman led him to believe what (this is important because it is the basis for his claim of apparent authority)? _____
6. What arguments did the defendant make to claim that it wasn't liable for paying Greene his commissions?
7. What facts does the court use to show that apparent authority did not exist?
8. According to the dissent, what mistake has the majority made in reaching its decision?
9. What facts does the dissent use to show that apparent authority did exist?
10. What policy argument does the dissent use in its decision to support its holding that apparent authority exists?
11. Which opinion do you agree with, the majority or the dissent? Why?
12. Is this case useful for our fact pattern?
    a. Why or why not?
    b. Is it more useful for SDA or Canopy? Why?

Language Focus — Idiomatic Expressions

The majority decision in the Greene v. Hellman case is characterized by the use of idiomatic expressions that add a rather informal tone to the decision, despite the fact that court decisions are formal documents with technical vocabulary and often precedential value. Nevertheless, judges often try to add character and personality to their writing, and can do so by the use of idiomatic expressions.

An idiom is an informal expression whose meaning is not apparent from the literal sense of the words. Therefore, an idiomatic expression has a figurative meaning. Some idiomatic expressions are characteristic of certain parts of the country, while others are used throughout the United States. Some idiomatic expressions are commonly used among particular groups or industries such as music or art.[23]

Here are two idiomatic expressions used in the majority decision in Greene:

> ***In a nutshell***, Hellman's defense, aside from its general denial of the conspiracy claim, was that Driscoll had lacked authority, actual or apparent, to contract with Greene.

> In sum, ***a fine-tooth-combing*** of the record discloses no proof that Hellman delegated power to choose Greene or any other broker to negotiate the sale of his property.

The definitions of "in a nutshell" and "to go over something with a fine-tooth comb" are included in the Vocabulary and Legal Terminology section and should be clear.

Can you find a non-idiomatic expression to express the same ideas? Write them below:
_____
_____
_____

Different languages sometimes have the same idiomatic expressions, while more often than not, a different expression is used to express the same concept. For example, in English we say that we "kill two birds with one stone" when we accomplish two things with one action. Italians say instead that you "catch two pigeons with one fava bean" (*prendere due piccioni con una fava*). Same idea, but a lot less violent!

Does your mother tongue have similar idiomatic expressions to express "in a nutshell" and "a fine-tooth-combing" or "to go over with a fine-tooth comb?" If you do, write them below. If you don't, what expressions or verbs would you use to say them in your mother tongue?
_____
_____
_____
_____

Here are two other sentences from the Greene majority decision, both of which use idiomatic expressions (in italics). How can you define and explain what these expressions mean? Rephrase them into "regular" English (i.e. no idioms).

> As with implied actual authority, apparent authority is dependent on verbal or other acts by a principal which reasonably give an appearance of authority to conduct the transaction, except that, in the case of implied actual authority, *these must be brought home to the agent* while, in the apparent authority situation, it is the third party who must be aware of them.

Your rewrite _____
_____
_____

---

[23] *Idiom,* THE NEW OXFORD AMERICAN DICTIONARY (2001).

Greene v. Hellman, 412 N.E.2d 1301 (N.Y. 1980)

Therefore, had the third cause of action not been dismissed by the trial court solely because it had decided to award damages on the first one, as to Hellman the third *would have had to go by the board* because no prima facie case had been made out.

Your rewrite

Regency Oaks Corp. v. Norman-Spencer McKernan, Inc.,
12 N.Y.S.3d 398 (N.Y. App. Div. 2015).

Vocabulary and Legal Terminology

<u>Professional employer organization (PEO)</u>: A company or firm that an employer contracts with to provide employee services such as payroll, hiring, worker's compensation and training that are normally offered by the employer itself. The PEO hires the employees and thus becomes the employees' employer for tax and insurance purposes.

<u>Worker's compensation insurance</u>: Insurance that employers in all states are required to have and that is used to pay an employee injured during the course of employment for his or her wages and medical costs in exchange for a waiver of the right to sue the employer for negligence.

<u>Purportedly</u>: Allegedly.

<u>To embezzle</u>: To steal money from one's employer.

<u>Axiomatic</u>: Self-evident.

Pre-Reading Questions

Before you begin reading, skim the caption and the synopsis and holdings paragraphs. Answer the following questions:

1. Is the case in federal or state court?
2. At which level of the court system was this case decided (i.e. at the trial court, court of appeals, supreme court)?
3. Who are the parties to the case?
4. What claim did the plaintiff bring?
5. What happened procedurally at the trial court?
    a. What motion was filed? By whom and was it granted?
    b. How was the case concluded?
6. What did the appellate division decide and on what grounds?

Regency Oaks Corp. v. Norman-SpencerMcKernan, Inc., 12 N.Y.S.3d 398 (N.Y. App. Div. 2015)

Comprehension Questions

With a general idea of the case in your mind, you can now read the case. As you are reading and after you finish reading, answer the following questions:

1. Summarize the facts that led to the dispute.
2. In the paragraph on the second page of the case that begins "It is axiomatic that..." identify first how many rules of apparent authority are included in that paragraph: _____
3. Rephrase them into your own words:
   a. _____
   b. _____
   c. _____
   d. _____
   e. _____
   f. _____
4. Summarize the elements of apparent authority: _____
5. Which of the above elements is in dispute in this case? _____
6. What facts does the court use to show that the reliance that the plaintiff made was reasonable?
7. What specific point do the dissenting judges disagree with? Why?
8. Do you agree with the dissent or the majority opinion? Why?
9. Is this case useful for our fact pattern? Why or why not?
10. What facts could you use in our fact pattern to show that Gina and Harvey McBride reasonably relied on the appearance of apparent authority in the agent, Charlene Thomas? Or that their reliance was unreasonable?

Language Focus — Adjectives, Verbs and Prepositions

Learning a foreign language is difficult for many reasons – pronunciation, unfamiliar grammar and vocabulary, and the sheer randomness of some words and phrases. For example, why do we say "I get in the car" but "I get on the bus?" No logical reason; we simply do. Oftentimes, you just have to memorize new words to perfect your knowledge of English.

Prepositions (*at, by, on*) and prepositional phrases (*in the car* and *on the bus*) are some of the most difficult to learn. How many of these phrases can you complete with the correct preposition without looking at a dictionary?[24]

To be liable _____ something
To rely _____ something or someone
To inquire _____ something or someone
To be accustomed _____ something
To dream _____ someone or something
To get married _____ someone
To fall in love _____ someone
To be concerned _____ someone or something
To arrive _____ a destination
To compare _____ someone or something
To disagree _____ someone or something

---

[24] While any dictionary can help you when you are unsure of the correct preposition, learner's dictionaries are often the better choice since they are written specifically for English language learners. All of the major publishing houses of dictionaries such as Oxford, Merriam-Webster, Cambridge and Macmillan have advanced learner's dictionaries.

Unit 3: Contract Formation and Promissory Estoppel

Contract Formation

Cleveland Wrecking Co. v. Hercules Construction Corp., 23 F. Supp. 2d 287 (E.D.N.Y. 1998).

Vocabulary and Legal Terminology

Letter of Intent (LOI): A document outlining an agreement that parties plan to enter into before the agreement is finalized.

Scintilla of evidence: *Scintilla* is a Latin word that means spark, and scintilla of evidence is an expression used to indicate a very small amount of evidence, such as that in support of a party's claims or defenses.

Non-movant: When we discuss a motion filed with a court, the party who files the motion is called the *movant*, while the party opposing the motion is called the *non-movant*. Also called the moving and non-moving party. Note that the movant and non-movant do not always correspond to plaintiff and defendant.

As a matter of law: In a dispute, an issue that involves a decision of the applicable law and is for the judge to decide, as opposed to a matter of fact, which is for the jury to decide.[25]

Be loath to: To be unwilling or reluctant to do something.

Weight of the evidence: The balance or preponderance of evidence; the weight of the evidence is that which is more believable and is superior to the evidence submitted by the other side in a case. "Weight" does not refer to quantity, but rather to how convincing is each side's evidence.[26]

Axiomatic: Self-evident.

Extrinsic: Facts outside the body of a document, such as oral statements. Extrinsic evidence is normally inadmissible for the purpose of defining the boundaries of an instrument.[27]

---

[25] *Matter of Law*, GILBERT'S POCKET SIZE LAW DICTIONARY (3rd ed. 2014).
[26] *Weight of the Evidence*, GILBERT'S POCKET SIZE LAW DICTIONARY (3rd ed. 2014).
[27] *Extrinsic*, GILBERT'S POCKET SIZE LAW DICTIONARY (3rd ed. 2014).

Pre-Reading Questions

Before you begin reading, skim the caption and the first paragraph and answer the following questions:
1. Is the case in federal or state court?
2. What was the motion before the court?
3. What did the district court decide?
4. What damages did the plaintiff seek?
5. What do we know about the nature of the contract?
   a. What is the relationship between the parties?
   b. What kind of agreement did they enter into?
   c. Why did the defendant fail to carry out the agreement?

Comprehension Questions

With a general idea of the case in your mind, you can now read the case. As you are reading and after you finish reading, answer the following questions:

1. During their contract negotiations, how could the parties have addressed the risk of the permit being denied?
2. What is the standard of granting or denying a motion for summary judgment?
   a. What sources did the court cite regarding the standards governing a motion for summary judgment? _____
   b. Who bears the burden of proof? _____
   c. Which jurisdictions did the court cite to? _____
   d. What is the standard for granting motion for summary judgment on a contractual dispute? _____
3. What are the essential terms of a construction contract?
   a. Are these elements important for the Stray Dog Advertising case?
   b. Why or why not?
4. Why does New York apply an objective test in determining whether a contract was formed?
5. What policy arguments support the objective test for contract formation? _____
6. What is the court's attitude towards denying enforcement on indefiniteness grounds? _____
7. What facts did the court take into account in determining whether a contract was formed? Does it help you identify the relevant facts in the Stray Dog Advertising case?
8. Write out why the established price was not subsequently binding _____
9. Apply the analysis used in this case to the Stray Dog Advertising case.

10. What is the extrinsic standard to determine the price in absence of an agreement? Is there another way to determine price?
11. Do you think the court decided the case correctly? Why or why not?
12. Is this case useful for our fact pattern?
    a. Why or why not?
    b. Is it more useful for SDA or for ALBC? Why?

Language Focus — Use of Will

When you first began studying English, you probably learned that to express the future tense in English, you use *will*. Actually, this isn't quite the case. While we use *will* to express the future,[28] we use *will* to express many other things, not all of which deal with the future.

Look at this sentence from the Cleveland Wrecking case and examine the use of *will*. Does it express a future tense? If it does not, what does *will* express?

> The substantive law governing the case *will* identify those facts that are material and only disputes over facts that might affect the outcome of the suit under the governing law *will* properly preclude the entry of summary judgment. Factual disputes that are irrelevant or unnecessary *will* not be counted.

Based on this sentence, you learn that *will* can be used to express something that is happening in the future, and want to emphasize that it *must* happen, like a sense of duty. Contractual obligations can be expressed with *will* in this sense:

> The employer *will* notify employees with a minimum of ten days' notice when the employer will conduct drug and alcohol testing.[29]

Below are other uses of *will*. Note that only the first two deal with the future.

Future Tense

> I will be there tomorrow.
> If it rains tomorrow, I will drive rather than walk to work.
> When the judge arrives, I will tell him that my client has decided to dismiss the claim.

---

[28] We also express the future using the present simple, present continuous and the verbal form *going to*. When we use one tense rather than another is not a matter of personal preference, and there are rules regarding when one tense is used rather than another. This Language Focus doesn't explore the future tense beyond *will* and for additional information, many online and hard-copy English grammar resources are available.

[29] In A Dictionary of Modern Legal Usage, legal writing expert Bryan Garner first advises that *will* should bear a consistent meaning if used within a document such as a contract. Bryan Garner, A Dictionary of Modern Legal Usage 941 (1995). Garner further explains that in legal writing, *will* can express one's own client's obligations in an adhesion contract such as a residential lease agreement, or both parties' obligations when the relationship is a "delicate" one, such as a corporate joint venture. Id. Finally, Garner instructs that *will* can be used to express future contingency. Id. at 942.

Uncertain Future and Predictions of the Future

I think I'll take the bar in February rather than July.
I don't think it will rain tonight.
I think it will rain. Look how dark the clouds are.

Promises

I won't forget.
I'll call him immediately.
He'll take care of it.

Requests, Orders, Invitations, Offers and Threats

Will you give me a hand?
Will you join me this evening at the theater?
I'll help you.
I'll get you if you ever tell anyone the truth.
Will you have some cookies with your tea?
I'll help you wash your car so that we can go to the movies together.

A Decision Made in That Moment

The phone's ringing. I'll get it!
I hear someone knocking at the door. I'll answer it.
I think I'll have the fried chicken with mashed potatoes. (at a restaurant)

Habit

He will always take a nap in the afternoons on the weekends.
My dogs will always bark when someone rings the doorbell.

Deduction

That will be John at the door. He said he'd come by around this time. (note: we can also express the same deduction with *must*: That must be John at the door.)

He will be happy that we are continuing to work on the project without him.

International Business Machines Corp. v. Johnson,
629 F. Supp. 2d 321 (S.D.N.Y. 2005).

Vocabulary and Legal Terminology

<u>Non-competition agreement</u>: An agreement that prohibits an ex-employee or ex-business owner from working for or opening a competing business within a certain geographic area and for a certain period of time after the end of the employment relationship or after the sale of a business.

<u>Misappropriation</u>: Wrongful or unauthorized use of property or funds (e.g., using trust funds other than for the beneficiary of the trust).[30]

<u>Preliminary (or temporary) injunction</u>: An injunction is a court order prohibiting a party from doing something or ordering a party to do something. A preliminary injunction is issued during litigation to maintain the status quo, and once the case is concluded, the court will determine whether to issue a permanent injunction.

<u>Expedited discovery</u>: Expedited means something that is done more quickly than normal, so expedited discovery means discovery completed within a period of time shorter than what is normal in litigation.

<u>Affidavit</u>: A written statement sworn to or affirmed before a person with authority to witness the oath.[31]

<u>In lieu of</u>: In place of.

<u>To tip (in someone's favor)</u>: To move the balance of power or influence in one person's favor.

Pre-Reading Questions

Before you begin reading, skim the caption and the first paragraph and answer the following questions:

1. Is the case in federal or state court?
2. What was the motion before the court?
3. What did the district court decide?
4. What relief did the plaintiff seek?
5. What do we know about the nature of the contract?
    a. What is the relationship between the parties?
    b. What kind of agreement did they enter into?
    c. Why did the defendant fail to carry out the agreement?

---

[30] *Misappropriation*, Gilbert's Pocket Size Law Dictionary (3rd ed. 2014).
[31] *Affidavit*, Gilbert's Pocket Size Law Dictionary (3rd ed. 2014).

Comprehension Questions

With a general idea of the case in your mind, you can now read the case. As you are reading and after you finish reading, answer the following questions:

1. What did the court find in terms of the parties' credibility?
2. What facts did the court take into account in determining whether a contract was formed? Does it help you identify the relevant facts in the Stray Dog Advertising case?
3. When did the court cite to the original words of the parties? What language from the Stray Dog Advertising case would you quote?
4. What does the court mean by saying a preliminary injunction is "one of the most drastic tools in the arsenal of judicial remedies?"
5. What is the standard of granting a preliminary injunction?
   a. Who bears the burden of proof?
   b. Which jurisdictions did the court cite to?
6. Write out a) the elements of contract formation; and b) the requirement of acceptance
   a. _____
   b. _____
7. What is the rule governing ambiguous acceptance?
   a. _____
   b. What did the court find in terms of IBM's interpretation?
   c. How can you apply this analysis to the Stray Dog Advertising case?
8. Do you think the court decided correctly? Why or why not?
9. Is this case useful for our fact pattern?
   a. Why or why not?
   b. Is it more useful for SDA or for ALBC? Why?

Language Focus – Formality

In all languages, we change the formality of our language to match our audience and the situation we find ourselves in. Some languages have personal pronouns that denote the level of formality and change depending on the relationship between the speakers. For example, in Spanish, if I am speaking to a friend, I use the pronoun *tu* to say *you*, but if I am speaking to a professor, I instead use the pronoun *usted* to say *you*. *Usted* is formal, while *tu* is informal. In Chinese, different pronouns exist and are used in a formal as opposed to an informal situation. ((你) and (您)).

English used to have the same distinction between the formal and informal you. *You* was formal, while *thou* and *thee* were used in an informal context such as between friends (*thou* was used as the subject of a sentence and *thee* as the object). If you read Shakespeare or earlier English writers, you will find these pronouns regularly used.

This is a passage from Romeo and Juliet. Juliet is addressing Romeo, and you can see how Shakespeare used *thou/thee* in an informal relationship between lovers. Try to paraphrase this old English into modern-day English.

> Art thou gone so, love-lord, aye husband friend?
> I must hear from thee every day in the hour,
> For in a minute there are many days.
> O by this count I shall be much in years
> Ere I again behold my Romeo.[32]

But nowadays, we don't use *thou/thee* and only use *you*, regardless of whether we are talking to a friend or to the president of the United States. We have to convey formality in other ways in English. Word choice and sentence structure are ways we do that.

To put your knowledge of formal vs. informal English to the test, rewrite the following sentences, from the International Business Machines Corp. case, in a more formal way.

> Hi Dave. Hate to be a pest, but we're still working on getting all of the non-compete agreements signed and filed and yours isn't booked since the original was signed in the wrong place. I'm asking my team to have a hard copy put in your mail today since anyone who hasn't returned theirs to Chris Gregory in North Castle by the end of Friday will receive a personal call from Randy regarding the status of their equity grant.

Your rewrite _____
_____
_____
_____

---

[32] William Shakespeare, Romeo and Juliet, Act III, v. 43-47.

Trademark Properties, Inc. v. A&E Television Networks,
422 Fed. Appx. 199 (4th Cir. 2011).

Vocabulary and Legal Terminology

To glean: To gather or collect, such as information from various sources.

Flipping: A real estate and business activity by which an investor (a "flipper") purchases a home with the purpose of reselling it for a profit. Flipping usually involves remodeling an older home, or a home that needs repair.

Rule 50(b) motion: A motion made under Rule 50(b) of the Federal Rules of Civil Procedure at the end of a trial, after both parties have presented all their evidence and rested their case. Also called a Judgment as a Matter of Law (JMOL) motion. A party making a 50(b) motion asks the court to grant judgment in its favor as a matter of law and alleges that based on the evidence presented by the opposing party, no reasonable jury could decide in his or her favor and that as a result, the judge should issue judgment as a matter of law.[33]

Rough estimate: An approximate and not very precise idea of what something will cost or how long something will take, often given before work is started on a project.

To track something: To take note of something such as expenses to later submit for reimbursement or some other purpose.

Out-of-pocket: From personal funds.

Pre-Reading Questions

Before you begin reading, skim the caption and the first paragraph and answer the following questions:
1. Is the case in federal or state court?
2. What happened at the trial court? Was there a jury trial?
3. What did the trial court decide?
4. Who appealed and on what grounds?
5. What did the court of appeals decide?
6. Did all of the appellate judges agree with the decision?
7. What damages did the plaintiff seek?
8. What do we know about the nature of the contract?
   a. What is the relationship between the parties?
   b. What kind of agreement did they enter into?
   c. Why did the defendant fail to carry out the agreement?

---

[33] Fed. R. Civ. Pro. 50.

Trademark Properties, Inc. v. A&E Television Networks, 422 Fed. Appx. 199 (4th Cir. 2011)

Comprehension Questions

With a general idea of the case in your mind, you can now read the case. As you are reading and after you finish reading, answer the following questions:

1. What facts did the court take into account in determining whether a contract was formed? Does it help identify the relevant facts in the Stray Dog Advertising case? If so, how?
2. When can an oral contract be binding?
3. What makes an effective acceptance?
4. How does a court determine if an ambiguous acceptance is accepted or rejected by the person making the offer (offeror)?
    a. _____
    _____
    _____
    b. What is the policy or the reasoning behind the rule?
    c. Apply this analysis to the Stray Dog Advertising case.
5. Why doesn't the court look at what a party subjectively meant or intended and instead look at what an objective, third party would interpret?
6. Why did the defendant allege that a contract was never formed?
7. How did the court interpret "Okay, okay, I get it."? What did the court find in terms of the Plaintiff's interpretation?
8. Do you think the court decided correctly? Why or why not?
9. Is this case useful for our fact pattern?
    a. Why or why not?
    b. Is it more useful for SDA or for ALBC? Why?

Grammar Review — Definite and Indefinite Pronouns

English has two types of pronouns: definite and indefinite. A definite pronoun – words like *he, she, it, they* and *you* – is a word that takes the place of a noun that has already been mentioned. Because the pronoun takes the place of a specific noun, it is called a definite pronoun. In contrast, an indefinite pronoun refers to an unidentified and unspecific noun that hasn't been mentioned. Indefinite pronouns include words such as *anyone, someone,* and *everyone*.

English speakers often use pronouns, both definite and indefinite, incorrectly due to certain peculiarities of the language. Look at this sentence from the International Business Machines Corp. case and identify the common mistake:

> If anyone from [D & Y] needs any additional information on this e-mail please have them call me directly.

A cardinal rule of pronouns is that they must agree with the noun that they refer to:

> I talked with the new attorneys, and they are all very nice.
> - Here, both the noun – *attorneys* – and the pronoun that replaces the noun – *they* – are plural.

The mistake that you should have identified in the above sentence from the International Business Machines Corp. case is that the indefinite pronoun *anyone*, (indefinite because it doesn't refer to a specific person already mentioned) is singular (If anyone needs...), yet the writer of the email says to have *them* call, using a plural pronoun. You probably have heard this a lot, and it is a very common usage in English:

- Someone left their books in the classroom.
- Does anyone need a voucher to pay for their parking?
- During today's arraignment hearings, no one told the judge that they were guilty of the crime they were charged with.

In each of these sentences, the indefinite pronoun (*someone, anyone* and *no one*) is singular, but the pronoun or possessive adjective that replaces it is always plural (they, their or them). Why?

Here is another sentence from International Business Machines case. Identify the common mistake and correct it:

> I'm asking my team to have a hard copy put in your mail today since anyone who hasn't returned theirs to Chris Gregory in North Castle by the end of Friday will receive a personal call from Randy regarding the status of their equity grant.

Finally, these sentences are from the Trademark Properties case. Pay particular attention to the use of *it* and *they*. What common mistakes of pronoun usage can you identify? After identifying the mistakes, articulate why they are mistakes and correct them.

> **Q.** Did you reach agreement concerning the real estate, the risk associated with acquiring and refurbishing real estate?
>
> **A.** Absolutely. It was very firm from him that I was 100 percent on my own on that, that A & E would not have any of the risk, any liability. It wouldn't be on deeds. It had nothing to do with that. It was clearly, totally separate, and they did not want any of the liability, any financial obligation of the risk with that.

Kowalchuk v. Stroup,
61 A.D.3d 118 (N.Y. App. Div. 2009).

Vocabulary and Legal Terminology

Equal monthly installments: A fixed amount that is paid each month by the lender to the borrower when a loan is taken out.

Outstanding amounts: The amount of money still owed and yet to be paid on a loan.

To waive confidentiality: To refrain from enforcing a right of confidentiality. If a client voluntarily discusses with a third party communications that he/she discussed with his/her attorney, the client has waived his/her confidentiality and can no longer claim that the information or communication is privileged and cannot be revealed to a third party.

Executed copies: Signed copies of an agreement or other document. To execute means to sign (in addition to meaning to carry out or put into effect, such as a plan or course of action, and to carry out a death sentence on an individual sentenced to death for a crime).

In default: Failure to perform the terms or provisions of an agreement.

Cure the default: To perform the obligations under a contract or loan for which the party is in default. For example, if you stop making payments on a loan you take out, you are in default. If you then pay the amount owed, you cure the default.

Explicit reservation: A clearly stated and defined act of withholding something. If a party clearly states that it is withholding its acceptance of an offer, the party makes an explicit reservation of the right to enter into an agreement.

Pre-Reading Questions

Before you begin reading, skim the caption and the first paragraph and answer the following questions:
1. Is the case in federal or state court?
2. What happened at the trial court? Was there a jury trial?
3. What did the trial court decide?
4. Who appealed and on what grounds?
5. What did the appellate division decide?

Comprehension Questions

With a general idea of the case in your mind, you can now read the case. As you are reading and after you finish reading, answer the following questions:
1. What do we know about the nature of the contract?
    a. What is the relationship between the parties?
    b. What kind of agreement did they enter into?
    c. Why did the defendant fail to carry out the agreement?

2. What is the defendant's argument denying a contract was formed?
3. What facts did the court take into account in determining whether a contract was formed? Does it help identify the relevant facts in the Stray Dog Advertising case?
4. Write out the elements of contract formation:
   a. _____

   b. What sources did the court cite?
   c. Apply this analysis to the Stray Dog Advertising case.
5. Write out the requirements of an effective acceptance:
   a. _____

   b. Apply this analysis to the Stray Dog Advertising case.
6. What are the factors that the court considered in determining whether the parties intended not to be bound except by a fully executed document?
   a. _____

   b. Which cases did the court draw analogies from and which cases did the court distinguish?
   c. How can you apply this analysis to the Stray Dog Advertising case?
7. Do you think the court decided correctly? Why or why not?
8. Is this case useful for our fact pattern?
   a. Why or why not?
   b. Is it more useful for SDA or ALBC? Why?

Language Focus — Sentence Structure

Legal English is characterized by long sentences and technical vocabulary, making it challenging for many people, including lawyers and law students, to read and understand. You no doubt have read cases for your LL.M. program that included lengthy, complex sentences and have likely struggled to decipher those sentences and their meaning.

One way to help understand long and complex sentences is to try to rephrase and rewrite them into two, three or even four shorter sentences (depending on how long the original sentence is). When you revise and rewrite, be sure that you don't change the meaning of the original, but only simplify it. If you try to rephrase and rewrite but find yourself unable to do so, you likely don't understand well enough the original text. Thus, rephrasing and rewriting are excellent ways to monitor your understanding of what you read.

Paraphrasing, or rewriting into your own words someone else's words and ideas, is also an important skill to develop in legal writing. Plagiarism is a serious offense in the United States, and to avoid it, you must learn to paraphrase. In U.S. legal writing, if you don't want to include direct quotations in your written document, you must paraphrase what you read in other sources and then include a citation. No paper, brief or memo should include only direct quotations.

Analyze the structure of the following rather complex sentences from the Kowalchuk case. Rewrite the sentences into shorter, simpler sentences. Note that in the second exercise, the text here has been slightly changed from the original.

> That the written formulation of the agreement had not yet been signed by plaintiffs at the time defendant sought to repudiate it did not in any way refute its existence or terms.

Your rewrite: _____

_____

_____

_____

The inclusion, in the formal document intended to encompass the terms of an agreement, of the language that the Agreement is complete and binding upon its execution by all signatories is simply insufficient to be treated as an explicit reservation that the parties should not be bound by the terms of their agreement until the written agreement is fully executed since there is no indication that at any time in the course of arriving at the terms of the agreement was it proposed that the parties not be bound until a written agreement was fully executed.

Your rewrite: _____

_____

_____

_____

Bazak International Corp. v. Tarrant Apparel Group,
378 F. Supp. 2d 377 (S.D.N.Y. 2005).

Vocabulary and Legal Terminology

Diversity jurisdiction: One of the reasons for which a federal court can exercise jurisdiction over a case: when all parties are citizens of different states and the amount of money in dispute (in controversy) is more than the amount established by statute (currently $75,000).

Unjust enrichment: A civil claim brought when a defendant has obtained the benefits of the plaintiff's efforts or work, but without paying any compensation for such work or efforts. The plaintiff brings the claim to recover the gains that the defendant unjustly earned.

Pro forma: A standard form, document or financial statement.

Closeout: Sale to get rid of old inventory, usually a very low prices.

Perjury: The criminal offense of making a false statement under oath in a legal proceeding with no sincere belief in its truth, when it is relevant to a material issue in the proceeding.[34]

Merits (decision on the merits): Decision by a court based on an analysis of the factual issues presented in a case rather than on some technical issue.[35]

Bright line (rule): A rule applied by courts to resolve issues in a clear and predictable way rather than examining the facts of each case. A bright-line rule saves time and promotes certainty but is sometimes less fair and equitable than deciding an issue on a case-by-case basis.

Pre-Reading Questions

Before you begin reading, skim the caption and the first paragraph and answer the following questions:

1. Is the case in federal or state court?
2. What was the motion before the court?
3. What did the district court decide?
4. What damages did the plaintiff seek?
5. What do we know about the nature of the agreement?
   a. What is the relationship between the parties?
   b. What kind of agreement did they enter into?
   c. Why did the defendant fail to carry out their agreement?

---

[34] *Perjury*, Gilbert's Pocket Size Law Dictionary (3rd ed. 2014).
[35] *Judgment on the Merits*, Gilbert's Pocket Size Law Dictionary (3rd ed. 2014).

Bazak International Corp. v. Tarrant Apparel Group, 378 F. Supp. 2d 377 (S.D.N.Y. 2005)   47

Comprehension Questions

With a general idea of the case in your mind, you can now read the case. As you are reading and after you finish reading, answer the following questions:

1. Identify the statute that governs this contractual dispute.
2. What source of authority did the court use in determining whether email can satisfy the writing requirement?
   a. What approach did the other courts use?
   b. Are these cases binding on this court?
3. Write out the court's reasoning FOR email to satisfy the writing requirement.
   a. _____
   _____
   _____
   _____
   b. Write out the arguments AGAINST email to satisfy the writing requirement.
   _____
   _____
   _____
   _____
   c. How did the court apply this reasoning to this case?
   d. How can you apply this reasoning to the Stray Dog Advertising case?
4. What facts did the court take into account in determining whether a contract was formed? Does it help you identify the relevant facts in the Stray Dog Advertising case? How?
5. Do you think the court decided correctly? Why or why not?
6. Is this case useful for our fact pattern?
   a. Why or why not?
   b. Is it more useful for SDA or ALBC? Why?

Legal Focus — How to Draw Analogies and Distinguish Cases

When carrying out legal reasoning in the U.S. system, we use case law to support our arguments. We use cases that are similar to ours to show that if a court decided a case with similar facts or a similar legal issue in a particular way in the past, the court deciding the case at hand should decide in the same way. In this way, we analogize cases, or we show analogies between our case and case law.

We also use cases that are different, either for facts or for the legal issue, and show the court how the case law is different from the case at hand. In this case, we say that we distinguish our case from case law or from precedent. We also say that the case law is distinguishable from our case.

When you read carefully through the cases included in this Unit, or in a casebook for your other classes in the LL.M. program, you will see how courts analogize and distinguish other cases in their analysis and reasoning.

These sentences from the Bazak case provide you examples of language that the court uses to analogize and distinguish.

Analogy

Just as messages sent using these accepted methods can be rendered tangible, thereby falling within the UCC definition, ***so too can*** e-mails.

Consequently, there appears to be little distinction between e-mails and other forms of communication regularly recognized under the Statute as adequate "writings."

Distinguish

Although e-mails are intangible messages during their transmission, ***this fact alone does not prove*** fatal to their qualifying as writings under the UCC.

The reference citation ***implies that they were insufficient due to*** these substantive flaws ***as opposed to a bright line rejection by the court*** of the e-mails as writings simply because of their format as e-mails.

As you are reading different cases for your LL.M. classes, be sure to take note of when the court is using case law and analogizing or distinguishing from the case at hand. Paying particular attention to how judges carry out this important part of legal analysis will help you when you write your own analysis.

Promissory Estoppel

Goff-Hamel v. Obstetricians & Gynecologists, P.C., 588 N.W.2d 798 (Neb. 1999).

Vocabulary and Legal Terminology

To jump ship: To quit something.

Anomalous: Unusual, not expected.

Pre-Reading Questions

Before reading the case, read the caption and the first paragraph and answer the following questions:
1. Is the case in federal or state court?
2. What court issued this decision?
3. What claims did the plaintiff bring against the defendant?
4. What did the district court decide?
5. Who appealed?
6. What did the supreme court decide?
7. Why was the case remanded to the district court?

Comprehension Questions

With a general idea of the case in your mind, you can now read the case. As you are reading and after you finish reading, answer the following questions:

1. Summarize in your own words the facts of the case that led to the dispute.

2. Articulate in your own words the policy arguments for:
    a. Employment at-will
    b. Promissory estoppel
    c. Denying a claim for promissory estoppel in employment at-will
    d. Allowing a claim for promissory estoppel in employment at-will

3. In a successful claim of promissory estoppel, what type of damages can a plaintiff recover?
    a. Punitive damages
    b. Non-economic compensatory damages (i.e. pain and suffering, embarrassment)
    c. Reliance damages
    d. Expectation damages
    e. Consequential damages

f. Specific performance
　　　g. Nominal damages
　　　h. Liquidated damages
4. What facts show that the plaintiff relied on the promise that she would be employed by Obstetricians & Gynecologists?
5. What damages did Goff-Hamel suffer?
6. Based on the rules in <u>Goff-Hamel</u>, what damages could SDA recover if it were successful in bringing a claim of promissory estoppel against ALBC?
7. Is this case useful for the analysis of our case? How?
8. Is it more useful for SDA or ALBC? Why?

Language Focus — Synonyms

When you are learning a foreign language and encounter a new word, the first thing you do is look up the meaning in the dictionary so you understand what it means. However, in addition to learning the meaning of a new word, you also need to learn its *register*, or in other words, its level of formality and the context in which we use it.

We use some words in a very formal context, while others are more suited to a more informal, everyday use. If you don't learn the register, you risk misusing the word, leading to misunderstanding, offense or awkwardness.

Look at this sentence from the <u>Goff-Hamel</u> case:

> Goff-Hamel asserts that the trial court **erred** in sustaining Obstetricians' motion for summary judgment and in overruling her motion for summary judgment.

To err means to make a mistake, and the two words are synonyms, words that have the same or nearly the same meaning in a language. But the fact that the two words are synonyms does not mean that they are interchangeable. The following verbs are all synonyms for *to err* and are listed in decreasing levels of formality.

> To err
> To be in error
> To make a mistake
> To make a mess of something
> To mess up
> To screw up

When writing a formal document such as a brief submitted to the court, we say *The court erred in dismissing the plaintiff's claims*, as *to err* is more formal and more suited to written English. We would not write in a written brief or other formal document *The court screwed up when it dismissed the plaintiff's claims* as that verb is too informal and has the wrong register for the situation.

When talking with colleagues, we might say that the court screwed up, but we would not use this verb with a client. Instead, with a client, we would say *The court made a mistake when it dismissed the plaintiff's claims*.

Note also that in the sentences, the construction "in sustaining" or "in dismissing" gives the sentences a more formal tone, but in spoken English, we would more likely use a construction like in the second example above (when the court dismissed…).

Maxell, Inc. v. Kenney Deans, Inc.,
No. A-98-930, 1999 WL 731846 (Neb. Ct. App. Sept. 21, 1999).

Vocabulary and Legal Terminology

<u>Sui generis</u>: (Latin) Unique.

<u>Action at law</u>: Claim for which monetary damages may be awarded.

<u>Action in equity</u>: Claim for which non-monetary damages, such as a declaratory judgment, specific performance, injunctive relief, may be awarded.

<u>Illusory</u>: Not true, imaginary.

Pre-Reading Questions

Before you begin reading, skim the caption and the introduction paragraph of the case and answer the following questions:

1. Is the case in federal or state court?
2. What claim did the plaintiff bring against the defendant at the trial court?
3. Was there a trial?
4. What decision did the trial court reach?
5. Who appealed and on what grounds?
6. What disposition did the court of appeals reach?

Comprehension Questions

With a general idea of the case in your mind, you can now read the case. As you are reading and after you finish reading, answer and complete the following questions:

1. Summarize in your own words the facts of the case that led to the dispute.
2. In this case, why did the court conclude that the option contract was not definite to give rise to a legally enforceable contract? _____
_____
3. List the elements of promissory estoppel:
   a. _____
   b. _____
   c. _____
4. What do Nebraska (and thus, Jefferson) courts require of a promise for it to give rise to a claim of promissory estoppel? _____
5. When is a promise "illusory?" _____

6. Why did the court in the Maxell case find that no promise had been made and that it was illusory? _____

7. In the SDA/ALBC case, was a promise made or was it illusory? If a promise was made, what was the promise for? _____

8. If you decided in question #7 that a promise was made in our case, what language did Ricky Saucedo use that indicates he/ALBC made a promise? _____

9. If instead you think that the promise in our case is illusory, explain why.

10. How does the case apply to the Stray Dog Advertising case?

11. Do you think that the court decided correctly? Why or why not?

12. Is this case useful for our fact pattern? Why or why not?

Language Focus – Phrasal Verbs

Phrasal verbs, which are verbs composed of a short verb and one, two or even three prepositions, are very common in English. *To get up* is a very common and relatively simple phrasal verb that everyone knows from their beginning English course, while other phrasal verbs like *to make up* are much more difficult to learn as this one verb has at least twelve different meanings![36]

Here is a phrasal verb from the Maxell, Inc. v. Kenney Deans, Inc. case.

> The record uncontrovertedly shows a pattern of conduct by the parties under which they would enter into tentative agreements and subsequently ***flesh out*** the details at a later date.

Do you know the meanings of the phrasal verb *to flesh out*? If you do, write it down. If you don't, look it up and write down the meaning. _____

Many phrasal verbs are used in legal writing and in a legal context. Find the meaning of the following phrasal verbs.

To wind down = _____
To write up = _____
To write off = _____

---

[36] Those meanings are:
1. To put together; construct: *the team was made up of outstanding athletes.*
2. To constitute; form: *twelve months make up a year.*
3. To change one's appearance for a theater role, such as with a costume.
4. To apply cosmetics.
5. To invent a falsehood: *my son always made up an excuse for why he was late.*
6. To eliminate a deficit: *can you make up the difference of what we owe?*
7. To compensate: *we made up for lost time by talking all night long.*
8. To make peace and end a fight: *we made up after a bitter dispute.*
9. To flatter, often excessively: *she made up to her professor to try to get a good grade.*
10. To take an exam or course again or at a later date because of an absence or failure.
11. To set in order: *I make up my bed every day so my room looks tidy.*
12. In printing, to arrange material: *three articles made up the front page.*
To Make Up, THE FREE DICTIONARY BY FARLEX, (last visited April 30, 2016).

To strike out = _____
To put off = _____

Note too that phrasal verbs are separable or non-separable, and the category of verb dictates whether you can put an object (noun, pronoun) between the verb and the particle(s). Some verbs are always non-separable, while others can be either separable or non-separable. It is important that you learn whether a phrasal verb is separable or not and how to compose sentences with these verbs.

To enter into is a non-separable phrasal verb. I cannot separate enter and into.
    We entered into an agreement. We entered into it.
    NOT: We entered an agreement into.

In contrast, *to draw up* is either separable or non-separable:
    We drew up an agreement.
    We drew an agreement up.
    NOTE: When the object of a separable phrasal verb is a pronoun, the verb must be separated from the preposition or particle.
        We drew it up.
        NOT: We drew up it.

For each of the verbs, identify whether they are separable or non-separable. Once you have found the meaning of the verbs and determined whether they are separable or non-separable, write a sentence using each of them.

To wind down
_____
_____

To write up
_____
_____

To write off
_____
_____

To strike out
_____
_____

To put off
_____
_____

deNourie & Yost Homes, LLC v. Frost,
854 N.W.2d 298 (Neb. 2014).

Vocabulary and Legal Terminology

Recitals section: Specific statements in a document, deed, or statute, listing the reasons or basis for enacting the document, usually beginning with the word "whereas."[37]

Lien: A claim on another's property asserted in order to secure payment upon a debt.[38]

Foreclosure: Cutting off or termination of a right to property. "Foreclosure" describes both the process and the result and is usually done by the person who holds the mortgage. In addition to taking the property away from the mortgagor and ending his rights in it, the property is usually sold publicly to the highest bidder to pay off the mortgage debt.[39]

Draw: To take money from or against an account.

Pre-Reading Questions

Before you begin reading, skim the caption, synopsis and holdings and answer the following questions:
1. Is the case in federal or state court?
2. What is the relationship between the parties?
3. Who was the plaintiff in the district court?
4. Who was the defendant?
5. Why did the plaintiff sue the defendant?
6. What happened at the trial court level?
7. Who appealed and on what grounds?
8. What did the supreme court decide?

Comprehension Questions

With a general idea of the case in your mind, you can now read the case. As you are reading and after you finish reading, answer and complete the following questions:
1. What happened between the parties that led to the dispute?

---

[37] *Recital*, Gilbert's Pocket Size Law Dictionary (3rd ed. 2014).
[38] *Lien*, Gilbert's Pocket Size Law Dictionary (3rd ed. 2014).
[39] *Foreclosure*, Gilbert's Pocket Size Law Dictionary (3rd ed. 2014).

2. What two claims[40] did the plaintiff bring against the defendant?
   a. _____
   b. _____
3. What did the court decide with regard to the claims? _____
4. What does a plaintiff have to show in Nebraska (and thus in Jefferson) to recover on a claim of promissory estoppel? _____
5. What arguments did the plaintiff make as to why it was entitled to recover against the defendants on the claim of promissory estoppel? _____
6. According to the general contractor/plaintiff, what promises did the bank make regarding the financing? Identify in the case those facts that show, according to the plaintiff, that a promise was made.
7. Why did the trial court decide that no promises were made? _____
8. Why did the trial court decide that it was unreasonable for the general contractor to rely on the "promises" that the bank made? _____
9. What facts, if any, in our case show that the parties (both SDA and ALBC) acted in good or bad faith?
10. Do you think that the court reached the correct decision? Why or why not?
11. How does the case apply to the Stray Dog Advertising case?
12. Is this case useful for our fact pattern? Why or why not?

Grammar Review — Should Have, Could Have and Would Have

Since the legal issue of promissory estoppel involves an assessment of what a "reasonable person" would do or would have done, we often find these rather complex verb tenses when reading these cases: *should have*, *could have* and *would have*.

Should have

Look at this sentence from the DeNourie case, paying particular to the verb in italics:

> The absence of the relevant material terms *should have put* Kenney Deans on notice that the parties needed to negotiate before finalizing an agreement.

We use the verb *should* + *have* + past participle to express an action that didn't happen in the past, but that it would have been best, or appropriate if it had.

---
[40] The claims that are discussed here do not include all of the claims that were actually brought. If you are curious about which other claims the plaintiff brought, you can read the unedited case online.

I should have filed the complaint before leaving for the evening but forgot to.

I should have applied for that clerkship position that was open at the district court.

I should have studied more in law school!

We also use *should have* to express regret over past actions.

I should have spent more time with my grandmother before she died.

I should have exercised more this past year as my doctor just diagnosed me with high blood pressure.

I should have studied more in law school but spent too much time playing soccer! If I had studied more, I would have had a higher class rank.

NOTE: We often use a contraction in place of *should have*.

We should've gone to the movies instead of studying in the library.

BUT when we are writing legal documents such as a brief, memo or correspondence, it is more correct to use the complete verb and not the contraction.

Would have

The conditional past tense — *would have* — also describes an event that didn't take place in the past, a hypothetical past event that the speaker or writer is describing.

Like *should have*, *would have* is formed with *would* + *have* + past participle, as indicated in this sentence from the DeNourie case:

DeNourie and Yost *would have been* reluctant to contract for the work without some explanation for why the first builder stopped its work – even if they generally believed Frost ran a successful business.

Don't confuse the conditional past tense with the use of *would* + the verb stem to describe a past habit:

When I was young, I would always go to baseball games with my dad.

Before personal computers, most lawyers would dictate their letters to their secretaries, who would then type them up.

Could have

Instead, *could have* is used to describe a past action that was possible, or that someone was able to do, but did not. Like the other two verbs, it is formed with *could* + *have* + past participle. This sample sentence is from the Goff-Hamel case:

Recognizing that both the prospective new employer and the prior employer *could have fired* the employee without cause at any time, they have concluded that the employee would have continued to work in his or her prior employment if it were not for the offer by the prospective employer.

In this sentence, the court is explaining that the employer had the possibility of firing the employee at any time, but did not. For that reason, we often use *could have* in past hypotheticals or conditional sentences:

The jury could have reached a decision today if the one juror hadn't left early due to a family emergency.

He could have gotten an A on the exam if he had just studied more.

168th and Dodge LP v. Rave Reviews Cinemas, LLC,
501 F.3d 945 (8th Cir. 2007).

Vocabulary and Legal Terminology

Plat: A plot of land.

Comprehensive zoning ordinance: A general plan to regulate the commercial and residential development in a city or town.

Pre-Reading Questions

Before you begin reading, skim the caption, the synopsis and the holding and answer the following questions:

1. Is the case in federal or state court?
2. What is the relationship between the parties?
3. Why do you think that the plaintiffs filed the promissory estoppel claim against the defendants?
4. Why did the defendant fail to carry out the agreement?
5. What claims did the plaintiffs bring against the defendant?
6. Summarize the complete procedural history.

Comprehension Questions

With a general idea of the case in your mind, you can now read the case. As you are reading and after you finish reading, answer the following questions:

1. State in your own words the facts that led to the dispute.
2. According to the plaintiff, what is the promise that the defendant made?
3. Why did the court find that the promise was only "illusory" and thus insufficient to support a claim of promissory estoppel?
4. Write the two most important principles of a claim of promissory estoppel:
   a. _____
   b. _____
5. Even if the court had found that a promise had been made, why was it unreasonable for the plaintiff to rely on it? _____
6. As for our case, what arguments can be made that SDA's reliance on the promise that ALBC made to sell it the ad spot was reasonable? _____

7. As for our case, what arguments can be made that SDA's reliance on the promise that ALBC made to sell it the ad spot was unreasonable? _____

8. Do you think that the court decided correctly? Why or why not?

9. How does this case apply to the Stray Dog Advertising case?

10. Is this case useful for our fact pattern? Why or why not?

Language Focus — "Fixed Phrases" in Business Communication

In the 168th and Dodge case, the COO of Rave, Painter, sent a letter to RED stating:

> *I look forward to* moving on to the completion of the lease documentation, which we can then take to our Board for final discussion and approvals—which, as you know from Jefferson Pointe, is our final step in the approval process.

The use of the italicized phrase — *I look forward to* — followed by a gerund is very common in business correspondence in the United States. It is what we can call a "fixed phrase," a phrase or expression that is commonly used in emails and letters. When used in this context, the expression shows a certain level of formality that is expected in professional business correspondence.

While *to look forward to* is often used outside of a business correspondence context — I am really looking forward to going on vacation – we often use it in the following ways to conclude a formal letter or email:

- I look forward to hearing from you soon.
- I look forward to meeting you next Friday to discuss your new business venture.
- I look forward to seeing you in court this Thursday.

Another "fixed phrase" that you might have seen is used when beginning an email:

> Dear James,
>
> I hope this email finds you well. I was wondering if you could help me with an important project that I am working on. The deadline is next Monday. If it isn't a bother, would you be willing to proofread my final paper?
>
> Thanks in advance,
> Melinda

We often start emails with a phrase like *I hope this emails finds you well*, or *I hope you are well*, or *I hope you are enjoying this lovely weather*. Such an introductory phrase blunts the message of the email and provides a pleasant and polite introduction to the topic. We are more likely to use such an expression when we are asking the recipient to do something for us, or when sharing bad news.

Moreover, there are other ways that we express formality and politeness in business correspondence.

Past continuous tense[41]

In the above email example, you also note that the writer used the past continuous tense to ask the question about whether James could help: *I was wondering if you could help me with an important project that I am working on.*

This is much more polite than asking *Dear James, could you help me with an important project?*

Even with the conditional tense "could," the sentence is much too direct for most Americans, at least in a business context. The phrase *I was wondering if* softens the request. Other examples of using the past continuous tense to soften what the writer is saying include:

- I was hoping that we could meet on Thursday to discuss the problems that the department has been facing.
- I was thinking that it would be smart to purchase a new photocopier.

Use of "would"

Here is another sentence from the 168th and Dodge case:

> Early after the first of the new year, I *would want* to get Terry Parish together with your construction people for a visit to the site.

Like with the past continuous, the use of *would* softens the request. The verb *want* on its own seems very forward and almost too bold. Using *would* makes the request more polite. We can also use *would like* instead of *would want*.

Qualifiers

If you have to tell someone some bad news, or provide criticism for something, using qualifiers like *a little, some, a bit, a few* can help to make the news less harsh:

- I noticed that you were having a few problems with your understanding of this case.
- My boss told me that my legal analysis was a bit confusing.

---

[41] Jeremy Bentley, *Polite Expressions in English: Words, Questions and Phrases to be Kind*, MY ENGLISH TEACHER http://www.myenglishteacher.eu/blog/polite-expressions-in-english-words-phrases-and-questions-to-be-kind/ (last visited April 30, 2016).

Unit 4 — Trespass and Nuisance

Trespass

Public Service Co. of Colorado v. Van Wyck,
27 P.3d 377 (Colo. 2001).

Vocabulary and Legal Terminology

Adjacent: Next to something else.

Motion to dismiss for failure to state a claim: A motion filed by a defendant pursuant to Rule 12(b)(6) of the Federal Rules of Civil Procedure or the comparable state rules of civil procedure that alleges that the plaintiff's complaint should be dismissed because the plaintiff cannot prove the case that she alleges in the complaint.[42]

Certiorari: An order or writ of a higher court, such as the Supreme Court, that states that it will review a lower court's decision.

To encroach: To advance onto something, such as someone else's property, without right or permission.

Quasi-judicial: Quasi is a Latin word that means "almost." Quasi-judicial thus means that a decision is partially judicial in character, such as the decision reached by an administrative agency that has the force and effect of a judicial decision, but was not issued by a judge.

Dispositive: Something that brings about the conclusion or the settlement of a legal dispute or case.[43]

To adjudicate: To make judgment about a dispute.

To bar: To stop or prevent something.

Strict liability: Legal doctrine that holds a manufacturer or a seller liable for all the defects and injuries caused by his products regardless of the degree of care that it exercised.[44]

Averment: In pleadings, a positive statement alleging facts; an allegation.[45]

Mass litigiousness: A large amount of litigation.

---

[42] See generally Rule 12 of the Federal Rules of Civil Procedure for the various grounds upon which a complaint can be dismissed and the procedure for doing so.
[43] *Dispositive*, Gilbert's Pocket Size Law Dictionary (3rd ed. 2014).
[44] *Liability*, Gilbert's Pocket Size Law Dictionary (3rd ed. 2014).
[45] *Averment*, Gilbert's Pocket Size Law Dictionary (3rd ed. 2014).

Pre-Reading Questions

Before you begin reading, skim the caption and the first paragraph. Answer the following questions:

1. Is the case in federal or state court?
2. Who are the parties to the case and what is the relationship between them?
3. What claim did the plaintiff bring and what facts supported that claim?
4. What happened procedurally at the trial court?
    a. What motion was filed and by whom?
    b. Was it granted?
5. What did the court of appeals decide and do with the case?
6. What did the supreme court hold and what was the disposition?

Comprehension Questions

With a general idea of the case in your mind, you can now read the case. As you are reading and after you finish reading, answer the following questions:

1. Summarize the issue that was before the Colorado Supreme Court.
2. Summarize in your own words the facts of the dispute.
3. In their complaint, why did the plaintiffs allege that the defendant had trespassed on their property? _____
4. Why did the district court dismiss the plaintiffs' complaint? _____
5. On what grounds did the appellate court reverse the trial court's decision? _____
6. According to the supreme court, when can an intangible object constitute trespass? _____
7. What policy reasons support limiting when a plaintiff can recover for trespass when the object is intangible, as in this case? _____
8. How does this case apply to the Stray Dog Advertising/Happy Tails Rescue dispute?
9. Is the case good or bad for Stray Dog Advertising? Why?
10. Do you agree with the supreme court's holding? Why or why not?

Language Focus — Latin vs. Germanic words in English

Look at this sentence from the Van Wyck case:

> We agree with the court of appeals that **quasi-judicial** PUC determinations do not preclude trespass claims as a result of the effects of upgrades previously approved by PUC.

Quasi is one of the many Latin words and phrases that we use in legal English. You are probably familiar with many others such as *stare decisis, quid pro quo, pro tempore, de facto* and *de jure*.

Did you know that 60% of English words are derived from Latin (i.e. have Latin roots)?[46] Some of these words have entered English through Latin directly, while others have entered through other Romance languages such as Italian, Portuguese and especially French.[47] This high percentage of Latin-based words in English is unusual given that English is a Germanic language whose grammar and basic structure share more in common with German than with Latin or French. In fact, English coalesced from the different language dialects that were spoken by the various Germanic tribes (Saxons, Angles, Jutes) that migrated to England from the mid-5th century to the 7th century.[48] About 25% of the words in the English language come from Germanic languages.[49]

As a result of this unique blend of Latin-based words with a Germanic-based language and words, as well as a remarkable ability to borrow words from other languages and "make" them English, English has a rich and vast vocabulary.

As a language learner, you are no doubt aware of this. English often has more than one word to express the same idea, action or thing. Here are a few examples:

To ask	To interrogate
To begin	To commence
To chew	To masticate
To free	To liberate or to emancipate
To get	To receive or to obtain
To flood	To inundate
To go	To depart

Examine the words pairs in each row in the table above. What do you notice about the words? Despite being synonyms, what differences can you note in the sound and feeling of the words in the left-hand column when compared with those in the right-hand column?

What you might have noticed is that the list in the left-hand column includes Germanic-based words. They are shorter, more "everyday" and more concrete. In contrast, the words on the right are all Latin-

---

[46] R. Malatesha Joshi et al., *How Words Cast Their Spell: Spelling is an Integral Part of Learning the language, Not a Matter of Memorization*, AMERICAN EDUCATOR, Winter 2008-2009, at 10.
[47] Approximately 50% of the Latin-based words in English have entered directly through Latin, while another 10% are from Latin through French. Id.
[48] JOHN ALGEO & CARMEN ACEVEDO BUTCHER, THE ORIGINS AND DEVELOPMENT OF THE ENGLISH LANGUAGE 86 (7th ed. 2014).
[49] Joshi, *supra* n.46 at 10.

based words and have a more intellectual and elevated feel to them. Choosing a Germanic-based word or a Latin-based word, when the two words have more or less the same meaning, greatly influences the sound and feel of your writing or speech.

Germanic Words	Latin Words
Short, often monosyllabic	Longer, almost always polysyllabic
More concrete sounding	Abstract sounding
Give writing and speech a more every-day and informal sound	Give writing and speech a more intellectual, formal and elevated feel
"feeling" words[70]	"thinking" words

To really get a feel for the difference between Latin-based and Germanic-based words, look at the differences between these sentences, paying particular attention to the boldfaced words:[51]

> While I was lying **on my back** on the beach, I heard this guy **talking** with his friends. He was **really loud**. He said, "You are **so pretty**! I'd love **to take a walk** with you and show you off to my friends!" But he seemed **really full of himself** so I told him to **leave**.

> While I was **supine** on the beach, I heard this guy **conversing** with his friends. He was really **vociferous**. He said, "You are **pulchritudinous**! I'd love to **ambulate** with you and show you off to my friends!" But he seemed very **supercilious** so I told him to **depart**.

How can you describe the different feeling in these sentences and the differences between the sentences with the Germanic words and those with the Latin-based words?

What you should note is that the highlighted words in the first paragraph are all short and mostly monosyllabic. They are Germanic words, and they give the sentences a very everyday feel and sound. There is nothing sophisticated or elevated about the language. On the other hand, the second paragraph includes Latin-based words. They are longer — most multi-syllabic and none monosyllabic — and give the sentences a very different feel and sound: more sophisticated and academic. Most people don't talk this way in everyday life as it sounds overly formal. What can you conclude therefore about the use of Germanic-based words as opposed to Latin-based words in our writing and speech? Do you think it is preferable to use Latin-based words in your writing or Germanic-based words? Why?

Another way that we see the presence of both Germanic and Latin-based words in modern English is the use of legal doublets, standardized phrases of two or three words that have essentially the same meaning:

True and correct	Last will and testament
Power and authority	Due care and attention
To perform and discharge	Terms and conditions
Promise, agree and covenant	Indemnify and hold harmless

---

[50] Corrine Jackson, *Tuesday Writing Tips: Anglo-Saxon vs. Latinate Diction*, CORRINE JACKSON, http://corrinejackson.com/wordpress/2013/04/23/tuesday-writing-tips-anglo-saxon-vs-latinate-diction/ (last visited May 1, 2016).

[51] Id.

Of these pairs or doublets, you will notice that there is a Latin-based word, often longer and with more syllables (attention, conditions, indemnify, testament, covenant and promise) and a Germanic-based word (agree, will, due care, terms, hold). Both are used together in the same phrase.

Interestingly enough, there is a historical explanation for what seems to be just excessive wordiness on the part of modern-day attorneys. When the Normans conquered England in 1066, the ruling class and gentry spoke a dialect of French (Norman French), which became the administrative language, used in courts, on documents and in government business. In contrast, Old English with its Germanic roots remained the language of the lower classes and peasantry. To ensure that a document was understood by all — those who spoke both Old English and Norman French — these legal doublets began to be used.

This same historical reasoning explains the difference between these word pairs:

cow	beef
sheep	mutton
calf	veal
deer	venison
pig	pork

When the animal is still alive, we use the Germanic-based words, those in the left-hand column. When the Normans invaded and conquered England, the lower classes and farmers were those who raised and bred the animals, hence these words that we now use in English to refer to the live animal are the Germanic-based ones.

In contrast, the words on the right are from French and are the words of the animals once slaughtered and ready to be cooked and eaten. The Normans, as the ruling class, were not farming and raising animals. The words that entered English reflected what the French Normans did with the animal — ate it once it was cooked and prepared. Even today, those differences remain in the words we use. At the grocery store, we buy beef, veal or pork, not cow, calf or pig.

Hoery v. United States,
64 P.3d 214 (Colo. 2003).

Vocabulary and Legal Terminology

<u>Federal Tort Claims Act</u>: A federal statute that allows individuals to bring a civil claim against the United States government for torts committed by individuals on behalf of the government.

<u>Migration</u>: Movement of something from one place to another; often used to refer to the seasonal movement of animals.

<u>To certify a question</u>: The certification of questions is regulated by court rules and is done upon motion. A court will certify a question to a court in another jurisdiction when the pending litigation involves a question to be decided under the law of that other jurisdiction or when the answer to that question is not provided by a controlling appellate decision in the jurisdiction that it presents the motion for the certified question.[52]

<u>To abate</u>: To cause or make something less intense, to cause to diminish.

<u>Well</u>: An underground hole or reservoir where water is kept and from which it is retrieved.

<u>Plume</u>: An emission of smoke that rises in the air in the shape of a feather.

<u>Unabated</u>: Without becoming weaker in strength.

<u>To accrue</u>: To become a legally enforceable claim.[53]

<u>To date back</u>: To be made to begin at a particular time in the past, here with regard to the statute of limitations.

Pre-Reading Questions

Before you begin reading, skim the caption and the first paragraph. Answer the following questions:
1. Is the case in federal or state court?
2. Who are the parties to the case?
3. What claim did the plaintiff bring, and what facts supported that claim?
4. What happened procedurally at the trial court?
5. Why do you think the federal appellate court certifies questions to the Colorado Supreme Court, a state court?
6. What did the Colorado Supreme Court hold?
7. What do you think happened in this case after the Colorado Supreme Court certified these questions?

---

[52] See, e.g., MINN. STAT. ANN. §480.065 (West 2016); SUP. CT. RULES, RULE 19; ILL. SUP. CT. RULES, RULE 308.
[53] *Accrue*, MERIAM-WEBSTER ONLINE DICTIONARY, http://www.merriam-webster.com/dictionary/accrue (last visited May 2, 2016).

Comprehension Questions

With a general idea of the case in your mind, you can now read the case. As you are reading and after you finish reading, answer the following questions:

1. Summarize in your own words the facts of the dispute, or in other words, what happened that led the plaintiffs to bring a claim against the United States Government.
2. Summarize in your own words the trial court's reasoning as to why it granted the defendant's motion to dismiss.
3. The paragraph beginning "The plaintiff, Robert Hoery" answers the question of why the federal appellate court certified the questions to the Colorado Supreme Court. Was your answer to question #5 above in the pre-reading questions correct?
4. Summarize in your own words the difference between a permanent and a continuing trespass.
5. Why does it matter whether a trespass or another tort is permanent or continuing?
6. This case is the first time that the Colorado Supreme Court is deciding what issue?
7. What phrase tells you that a court is deciding an issue for the first time?
8. In our case, is there a permanent or a continuing trespass? What difference might that make?
9. How is this case useful for the Stray Dog Advertising/Happy Tails case?

Language Focus — Active vs. Passive Vocabulary

In a second language and even in our mother or native tongue, we have both an active and passive vocabulary. Our active vocabulary includes those words that we understand and use when speaking and writing and that are readily accessible in our memory. Our passive vocabulary, in contrast, includes those words that we understand when used by others or when we read them, but that we don't actively and voluntarily use. Everyone's passive vocabulary is larger than their active vocabulary; we all recognize and understand words that we would likely never think of using on our own. You've no doubt noticed this during your LL.M. program. You read cases and understand many of the words in them and in your professors' lectures, but when asked to describe the procedure, or the facts, or the holding of the same case, the words just don't come to your mind.

Expanding your active vocabulary, therefore, is fundamental to improving your English. To help you move more words from your passive to your active vocabulary, complete the following sentences from the Hoery case, of all which have key legal and non-legal words deleted. How well do you do at completing these sentences with the correct words? You can check your answers with the text of the case.

1. The plaintiff, Robert Hoery, brought _____ the Federal Tort Claims Act against the Defendant, the United States, asserting _____ for, among other things, continuing trespass and nuisance.
2. The District Court _____ the United State's motion to dismiss all of Hoery's claims for lack of subject matter jurisdiction [holding that] the claims were time-barred.
3. In Wright, we held that harmful noises and stenches _____ from the slaughterhouse to the plaintiff's property constituted a continuing nuisance.
4. The alleged tortious conduct of the United States includes its failure to _____ and to remove the toxic chemicals it placed _____ the property.

Now let's try something different. Below are other sentences from the Hoery case, and you are given three options of a word to fill in the blank. Choose the correct word from the three choices. After you make your selection, compare your answer with the sentence from the case.

1. _____ *Moreover/Besides/In addition to* the ruling construing federal statutes, the District Court further held that its ruling was _____ *consistent /in agreement /in compliance* with Colorado law.

2. The Court _____ *argued/reasoned/stated* that the only wrongful act alleged by Hoery was the _____ *real/true/actual* release of toxic chemicals by the United States, and that no continuing tort _____ *was alleged/had been alleged/was being alleged* because this act had ended in September 1994 when the United States stopped operating Lowry.

3. For example, in Middelkamp, the defendant built an irrigation ditch in loose, porous _____ *soil/dirt/land*. As a result, water seeped through the bottom and sides of the ditch, causing flooding damage to the plaintiff's _____ *next door/ close /adjacent* properties.

4. Colorado courts have _____ *embraced/hugged/included* the concepts of permanent trespass and nuisance to _____ *differentiate/ distinguish/ make a distinction* those unique factual situations – primarily in the _____ *area/context/situation* of irrigation ditches and railway lines – where the trespass or nuisance would and should continue _____ *forever/indefinitely/without stop*.

Cook v. Rockwell International Corp.,
273 F. Supp. 2d 1175 (Colo. 2003).

Vocabulary and Legal Terminology

<u>Class action</u>: A lawsuit brought on behalf of a plaintiff and an ascertainable group of persons the plaintiff represents.[54]

<u>Exemplary damages</u>: Damages awarded in excess of actual damages (i.e., more than is required to compensate plaintiff for injuries sustained). Such damages are awarded to punish defendant, to discourage him and others from committing acts similar to the one for which he is being punished, and to provide some solace to plaintiff for mental anguish and shame. Same as "punitive damages" and "vindictive damages."[55]

<u>De minimis</u>: (Latin) Small, minimal.

<u>Trespassory</u>: Constituting a trespass.

<u>Nominal damages</u>: A small and insignificant sum awarded the plaintiff as recognition of a legal injury where damages are nonexistent, or where the plaintiff has not established a recoverable loss.[56]

<u>To push the envelope</u>: Idiomatic expression meaning to go beyond the accepted boundaries or limits.

<u>Impalpable</u>: Incapable of being touched; intangible.

<u>Contaminants</u>: Particles that pollute or contaminate something and make it unsuitable for use.

<u>Perceptible</u>: Able to be perceived.

Pre-Reading Questions

Before you begin reading, skim the caption and the first paragraph. Answer the following questions:

1. Is the case in federal or state court? Trial court or appellate court level?
2. Who are the parties to the case and what is the relationship between them?
3. Who are the plaintiffs?
4. What happened to lead the plaintiffs to bring a claim against the defendants?
5. What did the court rule?

Comprehension Questions

With a general idea of the case in your mind, you can now read the case. As you are reading and after you finish reading, answer the following questions:

---

[54] *Class Action*, Gilbert's Pocket Size Law Dictionary (3rd ed. 2014).
[55] *Examplary Damages*, Gilbert's Pocket Size Law Dictionary (3rd ed. 2014).
[56] *Nominal Damages*, Gilbert's Pocket Size Law Dictionary (3rd ed. 2014).

1. What are the defendants' arguments as to why no trespass occurred?
2. What policy has traditionally supported the claim of trespass?
3. How has the claim evolved over the years?
4. This case distinguishes between three types of things that can intrude on a plaintiff's property and give rise to a claim of trespass. Those three things are:
    a. _____
    b. _____
    c. _____
5. To recover under trespass, does a plaintiff need to prove that the substance or thing that has intruded upon her property can be seen? Why or why not?
6. How does the court distinguish between intangible substances like electromagnetic fields and something like a contaminant, which still cannot be seen by human eyes?
7. Why is this distinction important?
8. How is this case useful for our fact pattern?

Language Focus – Prepositions

The New Oxford American Dictionary defines a preposition as "a word governing, and usually preceding, a noun or pronoun and expressing a relation to another word or element in the clause, as in 'the man *on* the platform,' 'she arrived *after* dinner' 'what did you do it *for?*'"[57] Prepositions are often the hardest words to master in a second language for several reasons. First, if you use the wrong preposition, the person with whom you are speaking will still understand, so there may be less incentive to memorize and master prepositions than other words that simply matter more. Second, prepositions have no logic, making them harder to remember. Why do we get married *to* someone, rather than get married *with* someone when we fall in love *with* someone, not *to* someone? And finally, prepositions vary from language to language,[58] and it is all too easy to translate literally and use the same preposition in your mother tongue when you speak in English. Sometimes that works, but not always.

The following sentences are taken from the Cook v. Rockwell International Corp. case. Complete them with the correct missing preposition, preferably without looking at the case.

1. This action arises _____ operations at the Rocky Flats Nuclear Weapons Plant, a former nuclear weapon manufacturing facility owned _____ the United States and once operated _____ Defendants Dow Chemical Company and Rockwell International Corporation _____ government contract.
2. The elements of the tort of trespass _____ Colorado law are a physical intrusion _____ the property _____ another _____ the proper permission _____ the person legally entitled _____ possession of the property.
3. _____ the law of nuisance there are countless ways _____ which a defendant can substantially interfere _____ a plaintiff's use and enjoyment _____ lands, including the threat _____ future injury that is a present menace and interference _____ enjoyment.
4. Defendants also complain that Plaintiffs _____ this case impermissibly seek recovery _____ nuisance based _____ the mere proximity of their properties _____ Rocky Flats.

---

[57] *Preposition*, THE NEW OXFORD AMERICAN DICTIONARY (2001).
[58] For example, in Italian you say to fall in love *of* or *about* someone, rather than with someone, as in English. And you wait something or look something, rather than wait *for* something or look *for* something.

Miller v. Carnation Co.,
516 P.2d 661 (Colo. Ct. App. 1973).

Vocabulary and Legal Terminology

Thrust: The main point of something.

Triable: A case that can be tried and decided in a court of law, either by a judge or jury.

Manure: Waste, especially of animals such as horses or cows.

Obnoxious: Very unpleasant.

Insecticide: A substance used for killing insects.

Encroachment: Intrusion on another person's property or rights.

Incident: Resulting from.

Specific performance: A remedy that a party can seek in a complaint, asking the court to order the other party to perform such as the obligations of a contract.

To pray: (here) To request relief in a complaint or cause of action; prayers for relief.

At bar: (here) The case at hand; the present case.

Pre-Reading Questions

Before you begin reading, skim the caption and the first paragraph. Answer the following questions:
1. Is the case in federal or state court?
2. Who are the parties to the case and what is the relationship between them?
3. What claim did the plaintiff bring, and what facts supported that claim?
4. What happened procedurally at the trial court?
5. What did the court of appeals decide and what was the disposition of the case?

Comprehension Questions

With a general idea of the case in your mind, you can now read the case. As you are reading and after you finish reading, answer the following questions:
1. Summarize in your own words the facts of the dispute, or in other words, what happened that led the plaintiffs to bring a claim against the Carnation Company.
2. What facts are there in this case that are similar to our SDA/HTRO case, and what facts are different? How might these facts be useful for your analysis of the client matter?

3. What is the main issue before the court of appeals?
4. Summarize in your own words the distinctions between legal claims and equitable claims.
5. Why is this distinction important?
6. What impact, if any, might this distinction and the different types of claims have upon our case?
7. Find the rule for when a plaintiff can recover exemplary or punitive damages. How can that rule and the facts specifically mentioned by the court with regard to this rule be applied to our case?
8. How is this case useful for our fact pattern?
9. If you represent Happy Tails, how might you use the facts of this case to distinguish it from our facts?

Language Focus — Thereto, Herein, Hereby, Etc.

Legal English is replete with words that are a combination of *here*, *there* or *where* with a preposition: *hereby*, *hereinafter*, *whereby*, *thereof*, *herein*, *wherefore* and *therein*. If you check the meanings of these words in a dictionary, the entry of the word will likely state that it is formal or even obsolete. Today, most legal writing experts urge writers to eliminate these words from their writing or to use more concise and specific words or phrases in their place. Bryan Garner, in the Dictionary of Modern Legal English, calls these words flotsam,[59] or useless or unimportant.

Although you should eliminate these words from your own writing, you will encounter them on a routine basis when reading legal writing, whether contracts, memos or cases. Therefore, you need to be able to understand quickly and easily what the words mean.

In words that begin with *here* such as herein, hereinafter and hereby, the *here* refers to the agreement or document.

> *I hereby grant my house to my sister.* = By means of this document, I grant my house to my sister.

Oftentimes, the word adds no real meaning to the sentence and can be eliminated without subtracting anything from the sentence. Let's take the above example. If this sentence is in my will, it is clear that the granting is *by means of* the will. If I write *I grant my house to my sister*, the meaning is exactly the same, the sentence is more concise, and the legalese *hereby* is eliminated.

Below you will find three examples of sentences from the Miller case, as well as three sentences from other cases, with words such as *thereby*, *hereby*, *whereon*, etc. highlighted. Your job is to rewrite the sentence by eliminating that word and thus improve the sentence. Before you start rewriting, be sure that you understand the purpose that the word serves in the sentence and its meaning.

1. In applying the general rule of law, the court concluded that the primary purpose of the suit was injunctive relief, with damages as a mere incident ***thereto***.

---

[59] BRYAN A. GARNER, DICTIONARY OF MODERN LEGAL ENGLISH 402 (2nd ed. 1995).

2. The cause is remanded with directions to the trial court to enter judgment on the award for annoyance and discomfort, together with interest **thereon** at the rate of six per cent per annum from the date of the filing of the original complaint in this action to the date of the entry of judgment pursuant to this remand.

3. Restatement (Second) of Torts s 158 states the rule that: 'One is subject to liability to another for trespass, irrespective of whether he **thereby** causes harm to any legally protected interest of the other, if he intentionally enters land in the possession of the other, or causes a thing or a third person to do so.

4. It is the intent and purpose of this Agreement to assure sound and mutually beneficial working and economic relationships between the parties **hereto**. Maywood Police Officers Ass'n v. City of Maywood, 2016 WL 399780, at *5 (Cal. Ct. App. Feb. 2, 2016).

5. Now, having duly deliberated upon the motion, the opposition, the reply, the supporting affirmations, exhibits and all of the papers filed **hereinbefore**, the Court finds and determines the application as follows. Halley v. Servedio, No. CV-11-3884, 2016 WL 783126, at *1 (N.Y. City Ct. Feb. 26, 2016).

6. Officer Meehl searched Appellant and recovered from his pants pocket a bottle containing pills identical to those supplied by Mr. Curry in the exchange with Officer Hamski; in a statement to Officer Meehl, Mr. Curry explained he made a deal with Appellant **whereby** Mr. Curry would receive $50.00 for arranging the drug sale and Appellant would keep the remaining $175.00 Commonwealth v. Langley, 2016 BL 67463, 6 (Pa. Super. Ct. Mar. 04, 2016).

Cobai v. Young,
679 P.2d 121 (Colo. Ct. App. 1984).

Vocabulary and Legal Terminology

To slide: To move smoothly over a surface.

To adjoin: To be next to.

Outrageous: Beyond or outside the accepted boundaries of conduct or speech.

To propel: To move forward, often by force.

Non-conforming: To not comply with something such as a rule or ordinance.

Set-back: The distance one building must be placed from another building, from a property line or from the street.

Eave: The part of a roof that hangs over the wall of a house or other building.

To jar: To hit something forcefully.

To propagate: To make something such as an idea widely known.

Contention: Argument.

Pre-Reading Questions

Before you begin reading, skim the caption and the first paragraph. Answer the following questions:
1. Is the case in federal or state court?
2. Who are the parties to the case, and what is the relationship between them?
3. What claim did the plaintiff bring, and what facts supported that claim?
4. What happened procedurally at the trial court?
5. What did the court of appeals hold with regard to the grounds of appeal?
6. What was the disposition of the case?

Comprehension Questions

With a general idea of the case in your mind, you can now read the case. As you are reading and after you finish reading, answer the following questions:
1. Summarize in your own words the facts of the dispute, or in other words, what happened that led the plaintiffs to bring a claim against their neighbors.
2. Summarize in your own words the defendants' arguments on appeal as to why they should not be liable for trespass.

3. Summarize in your own words the court's ruling as to each of the grounds for appeal.
4. How is this case useful for our fact pattern?
5. Does it support more the arguments that SDA would make as to why HTRO would be liable for trespass, or the arguments that HTRO would make that it was not liable for trespass? Why?
6. If an injunction were issued in a case that SDA were to bring against HTRO and based on the language of the injunction included in the Cobai case, how might a court draft an injunction against HTRO?

Language Focus – Hyphens, En-Dash and Em-Dash: What's the Difference?

A hyphen is the short line or "sign (-) used to join words to indicate that they have a combined meaning or that they are linked in the grammar of a sentence (as in *pick-me-up, rock-forming*), to indicate the division or a word at the end of a line, or to indicate a missing or implied term."[60] Look at the following paragraph from the Cobai case. Hyphens are used in three separate occasions.

> The roof of the Cobais' **one-story** house slopes toward defendants' house, and the roof of defendants' two-story house similarly slopes toward the Cobais' house. While defendants' house complies with minimum **set-back** requirements of 7.5 feet, the eaves of the two houses are separated by a horizontal distance of only 7 feet, 7.5 inches. Snow accumulates on defendants' roof and then slides off, occasionally striking the roof and west side of the Cobais' house. The sliding snow creates a thunderous noise, jars the Cobais' house, and has caused some **non-structural** damage. Should the snow continue to slide into the Cobais' house, it will likely cause structural damage in the future.

Which of the highlighted hyphenated words is a compound word?

Examine the other two words: one-story and non-structural. What parts of speech (verb, noun, adjective, adverb) make up these word phrases?

Based on your analysis of these two words, what rule can you construct about when we use hyphens in English?

With these rules in mind, choose the correct word or phrase in the following sentences:

1. The circuit court began a _____ (two day/two-day) bench trial on the plaintiffs' complaint on April 15, 2009.
2. The trial lasted _____ (two days/two-days).
3. The plaintiffs and the defendants all live on a _____ (dead-end/dead end) road.
4. During _____ (cross-examination/cross examination/ crossexamination), the witness admitted he had lied during his deposition.
5. The court found that the defendants were not _____ (well-suited/well suited) to be parents.

---

[60] *Hyphen*, The New Oxford American Dictionary (2001).

6. In New York, it is _____ (well established/well-established) that to be successful in bringing a claim of trespass, a plaintiff must show an intentional invasion of her property.

An en dash is another punctuation mark that you will frequently encounter. It is also a short line, like a hyphen, but slightly longer. A hyphen looks like this (-) while an en dash looks like this (–). Although the two are similar, they are used in different situations.

An en dash is used to indicate a span or range of related numbers, dates or time. No space is inserted between the en dash and the adjacent words or numbers.[61]

> For the U.S. Supreme Court, the 2015–2016 term was marked by tragedy when Justice Antonin Scalia died unexpectedly on February 13, 2016.

> For tomorrow's class, please read chapters 2–4.

We also use the en dash to report scores:

> The bill passed the House with a vote of 400–35 but was defeated in the Senate, losing by a vote of 45–55.

> The New York Yankees beat the Boston Red Soxs by a score of 7–3.

Finally, we use the en dash to indicate conflict, connection or direction.[62]

> I traveled overnight on the Rome–Paris train.

> The main north–south thoroughfare through the city is Interstate 45.

> The first Republican–Democratic debate of the presidential election season is almost always interesting.

If using Word, you can insert the en dash with the command Ctrl + - (on the number keyboard). Instead if you are a Mac user, you insert the en dash using Option + the dash (-) key.

The last punctuation similar to both a hyphen and an en dash is the em dash. The em dash is longer than both the hyphen and the en dash. The em dash takes the place of other punctuation in a sentence — commas, parentheses, or colons.[63] The punctuation mark in that last sentence is an em dash — it separates the word *sentence* from the last phrase, commas, parentheses or colons. This sentence could also be written with a colon. *The em dash takes the place of other punctuation in a sentence: commas, parentheses, or colons.*

An em dash is often used for emphasis or to show a change in the writer's thoughts.[64]

---

[61] *En Dash,* THE PUNCTUATION GUIDE, http://www.thepunctuationguide.com/en-dash.html (last visited May 4, 2016).
[62] Id.
[63] *Em Dash,* THE PUNCTUATION GUIDE, http://www.thepunctuationguide.com/em-dash.html (last visited May 4, 2016).
[64] Id.

We use the em dash:

To replace commas:

> Senator Harry Severs, the luckiest man alive, was reelected by a margin of only fifteen votes.

> Senator Harry Severs — the luckiest man alive — was reelected by a margin of only fifteen votes.

To replace parentheses:

> When addressing the jurors (all twelve of them), the attorney was very informal and used their first names.

> When addressing the jurors — all twelve of them — the attorney was very informal and used their first names.

To replace a colon:

> During their first year of law school, all students take the same core classes: torts, property, contracts, civil procedure, and legal writing.

> During their first year of law school, all students take the same core classes — torts, property, contracts, civil procedure, and legal writing.

If using Word, you can insert the em dash using Ctrl + Alt + - (on the number keyboard). Instead, if you are a Mac user, you insert the em dash using Option + Shift + the dash (-) key.

Nuisance

Wernke v. Halas,
600 N.E.2d 117 (Ind. Ct. App. 1992).

Vocabulary and Legal Terminology

Lamentably: Unfortunately.

To abut: To touch along a border.

Astride: Extending across.

Vinyl strip: Long pieces of a type of plastic fabric.

Vandal: An individual who deliberately destroys or damages property; from the name of the Germanic people who sacked Europe and Rome.

Accoutrement: Equipment needed for a particular activity.

Tenet: General principle or belief.

Dispositive: Something that brings about the conclusion or the settlement of a legal dispute or case.

Aesthetic: Of or relating to appearance or beauty.

Myriad: A large number of things.

Mores: /more – ays/ The main customs or moral principles of a community or society.

Inexorable: Something or someone that cannot be stopped.

Trifle: A small, insignificant thing without value.

Obdurate: Stubborn.

Pre-Reading Questions

Before you begin reading, skim the caption and the first paragraph and answer the following questions:

1. Is the case in federal or state court?
2. What is the relationship between the parties?
3. What happened procedurally at the district court level?
4. What motion was filed and by whom?
5. Did the trial court grant it?
6. What happened at the appellate court?

Comprehension Questions

With a general idea of the case in your mind, you can now read the case. As you are reading and after you finish reading, answer the following questions:

1. Restate in your own words the facts of the case that led to the dispute.
2. This is a case between next-door neighbors. Most of the time, when neighbors have a dispute, they don't end up in court.
   a. What is your opinion about a case in which a neighbor sues a neighbor?
   b. Why do you think someone would go to the extreme of going to court for a dispute with their neighbor?
   c. How would a dispute like this be handled in your home country? In the courts? In another way?
   d. What does the fact that the neighbors did end up in court (and up to the court of appeals!) tell you about Americans and American culture?
3. Write in your own words the definitions of two important terms presented in the case:
   a. Private nuisance: _____
   b. Public nuisance: _____
4. If Happy Tails Rescue Organization were deemed a nuisance, would it be private or public? ____
   _____
5. Give examples of each type to show that you understand the difference between the two types of nuisance (public and private).
   a. _____
   b. _____
6. The case recites an important rule for determining whether something is a nuisance *per accidens*. Find the rule and write it here:_____
   _____
   _____
7. Summarize in your own words the court's reasoning as to why:
   a. The fence was not a nuisance: _____
   b. The toilet was not a nuisance: _____
   c. The graffiti was not a nuisance: _____
8. Do you agree with the court's reasoning? Why or why not?

9. If this case were decided in your country, how would a court decide?

10. How is this case useful for our fact pattern?

11. How can you analogize or distinguish the case from our facts?

Language Focus — Transition Words[65]

Transition words are words or phrases that help connect one idea to another idea. They help the reader follow the writer's arguments and the points that he or she is trying to make and understand how the writer's arguments are connected to each other. Transition words also add to the style and readability of your written work.

Depending on the point you are trying to make, there are different transition words that you might use. Look at these sentences from the Wernke case for some examples of transition words, which are in bold, italicized font.

> Wernke ***also*** appeals the trial court's subsequent award of compensatory damages, punitive damages, and attorney fees.

> ***Prior to*** Wernke's erection of the fence, the Peacocks nailed a toilet seat to a tree facing Wernke's yard.

> He ***therefore*** ordered the orange fencing and the vinyl strips removed, and Wernke complied.

> ***Thus***, for example, a house of prostitution and an obstruction that encroaches on the right-of-way of a public highway are nuisances *per se*.

> ***Moreover***, freedom of expression is at issue here, and although the language is offensive and vulgar, it is a "bedrock principle underlying the First Amendment that the government may not prohibit the expression of an idea simply because society finds the idea itself offensive or disagreeable."

Conflict

The transition words *however, on the other hand* and *contrary to* are used to denote conflict, contradiction or concession. Here are words that we use to signify a difference or a conflict of some sort between two arguments or two facts.

But	However	In contrast
On the other hand	(And) yet	While
Whereas	Conversely	Though

---

[65] Numerous resources are available online to help with your writing, and you can find online other resources about transition words, as well as other writing topics. The Purdue University Online Writing Lab (OWL) is one excellent resource, https://owl.english.purdue.edu, and the Student Writing Support at The Center for Writing at the University of Minnesota is another. http://writing.umn.edu/sws/
Follow this link for a PDF table of other transition words: http://writing.umn.edu/sws/quickhelp/style/transitions.html

Effect

Summation transition words are used to demonstrate effect.

Therefore	Thus	Consequently
Hence	Accordingly	As a result

Addition

Here, you will find the most common transition words that we use to indicate to the reader that we are including more facts, arguments or information.

Furthermore	In addition	Also	Moreover
Too	Again	Even more	Further
Last, lastly	Finally	Besides	And
First	Second, secondly, etc.	In the first (second) place	Next

Note that these words are almost always separated from the rest of the sentence with commas, whether they are the first word in the sentence or in the middle of the sentence.

Owens v. Phillips,
73 Ind. 284 (Ind. 1881).

Vocabulary and Legal Terminology

To pray: (here, in a legal context) To request (a prayer or request for relief).

Abatement: Something reduced.

Dwelling house: Residence.

Flouring mill: Building where flour is ground.

Cistern: A tank for storing water.

Writ of injunction: Order issued by the court telling a party to stop doing something or ordering the party to do something.

Imperious: Arrogant.

Incommoded: Inconvenienced.

Abode: Home.

Pre-Reading Questions

Before you begin reading, skim the caption and the first paragraph and answer the following questions:
1. Is the case in federal or state court?
2. Which party is which:
    a. Who were the appellants — the plaintiffs or the defendants at the trial court?
    b. Who were the appellees at the trial court?
3. What claim was brought at the trial court?
4. What happened procedurally at the trial court level?
5. Why did the case go from the trial court directly to the supreme court?
6. Who appealed and why?
7. Skip ahead to the last sentence of the case to see how the supreme court decided.

Comprehension Questions

With a general idea of the case in your mind, you can now read the case. As you are reading and after you finish reading, answer the following questions:

Owens v. Phillips, 73 Ind. 284 (Ind. 1881)

1. Restate in your own words the facts of the case that led to the dispute.

2. What facts did the plaintiffs cite to support their claims that the defendant's business was a nuisance? _____
   _____
   _____
   _____

3. This case cites this rule: "*A lawful and useful business is not to be destroyed by injunction unless the necessity for doing so be strong, clear and urgent.*" What policy arguments support this rule? _____
   _____
   _____
   _____

4. What must a plaintiff show to establish that the necessity to "destroy" a business is strong, clear and urgent? (hint: look on page 291 of the case) _____
   _____
   _____
   _____

5. A case of this nature, in which the plaintiff seeks an injunction to stop a business from operating, involves the court carefully balancing the interests of both parties.
   a. What competing policy interests are there that a court must consider when deciding whether to issue an injunction and order a business to stop operating?
   b. Are the competing interests different when one of the parties is a business, as in this case, as opposed to when they are both individuals, like in the Wernke case? Why or why not?
   c. Are any of these interests more important than others? Why or why not?

6. An injunction is not the appropriate remedy for all cases involving a nuisance. When will a court award a plaintiff damages but not issue an injunction? _____
   _____
   _____

7. The court states that "*[n]o man has a right to take away from another the enjoyment of what are regarded by the community the reasonable and essential comforts of life.*"
   a. How does the court know and determine what are the "reasonable and essential" comforts of a particular community?
   b. Will these essential comforts vary from community to community? How?
   c. Could there be cultural differences in what comforts are considered essential? Why or why not?
   d. What would you consider the "reasonable and essential" comforts of your community?

8. Do you agree with the court's reasoning? Why or why not?

9. If this case were decided in your country, how would a court decide?

10. How is this case useful for our fact pattern?

11. How can you analogize or distinguish the case from our facts?

Language Focus — Reading Old Cases

In the classes you take during your LL.M. program, you will most likely encounter old cases, like the Owens one, which was issued in 1881. Some classes, especially torts and property, seem to have their fair share of older cases. Reading and understanding them present particular challenges.

Before reading a case, it is always recommended that you read first the caption to get a general idea of the case — the parties, the court (state or federal), and the year the decision was issued. The pre-reading questions provided with each case in this ESL Workbook aim precisely at this. When you see that a decision was issued nearly 140 years ago, you should mentally prepare yourself for a more challenging reading task. That begs the question, then, of why are older cases so difficult to read?

Language Choices

First, judges in the past used different language, sentence structure and vocabulary than we do today. Language is living and constantly changes. Slang changes from year to year, so you can imagine how much language will change over the course of more than a century.

Here are two sentences from the Owens case, both written in an English that we most likely would not use today in the 21st century. Rewrite the sentences below to make them easier to understand and more modern sounding.

> Issue was joined upon the complaint of appellants, wherein they charged appellees with maintaining a nuisance, and ***prayed*** for an injunction against its continuance and for an order of ***abatement***.
>
> The necessity which will authorize the granting of the writ of injunction, to restrain the carrying on of a business lawful in itself, must be a strong and imperious one.

Your rewrite: _____
_____
_____
_____
_____

Formatting

Judges writing in the 1880s didn't have personal computers, and the length of their decisions reflects that. Today's judicial decisions are much longer on average than even the decisions written thirty years ago, before personal computers became commonplace. A 2007 Supreme Court decision, Parents Involved v. Seattle, has more than 47,000 words. Compare that with the landmark case of Brown v. Board of Education of Topeka, which desegregated the public school system in fewer than 4,000 words![66]

Aside from being shorter than today's decisions, older ones like Owens also lack the formatting that

---

[66] Adam Liptak, *The Roberts Court: Justice are Long on Words but Short on Guidance*, N.Y. TIMES, Nov. 17, 2010, at A1.

we are accustomed to. You don't see the headings and boldface that you do in recent cases, and those formatting choices help the modern reader to navigate the decision. Older cases seem to be just one block of text. To our eyes, used to shorter newspaper and magazine articles and to reading online, that solid text with less white space and formatting can be daunting. We look for something that tells us we are moving on to the next issue in a decision, and the older decisions don't provide us that. Thus reading them requires a readjusting of our eyes and of our expectations of what will help us move through a decision.

Direct vs. less direct style of writing

Finally, older decisions seem to be less direct than the decisions issued by today's courts, which don't hide what the issue is. Here are two sentences, the first from another nuisance case in this Unit (issued in 2009), and the second from one of the trespass cases (issued in 2001). You see that the court specifically tells the reader what the issue is.

> The issue here is the off-site impact of infringements from a new business inserted into the neighborhood and whether that impact would offend persons of ordinary sensibilities. Bonewitz v. Parker.

> This case presents the issue of whether the Colorado Public Utilities Commission's (PUC) approval of electrical line upgrades by the Public Service Company of Colorado (PSCo) precluded claims by adjacent property owners for . . . trespass . . . against PSCo based on those upgrades. This case also presents the issue of whether the class-action complaint, filed by Mark and Erica Van Wyk and all others similarly situated (collectively the Van Wyks), stated claims sufficient for relief against PSCo. Public Service Co. of Colorado v. Van Wyck.

In contrast, while reading the Owens case, you note that the court never explicitly states what the issue is (you can check the full, unedited version online too). You have to infer what it is, and you oftentimes find the rules hidden in the middle of a paragraph, rather than explicitly stated like you find in today's cases. Reading older cases, therefore, requires a more careful attention so that you don't miss important rules or parts of the analysis.

Even though reading older cases may be more challenging, and our initial reaction might be to ignore them while doing research, thinking that they are "too old" or no longer relevant because of their age, that isn't always the case. Older cases can provide us with the origin of a legal rule, or the initial stages of the evolution of a rule, and provide needed insight into the issue that we are grappling with in our client matter or fact pattern.

Bonewitz v. Parker,
912 N.E.2d 378 (Ind. 2009).

Vocabulary and Legal Terminology

Furnace: An appliance that produces heat for heating a home or other building.

Unabated: Not reduced or lessened.

Smokestack: A tall chimney on a factory.

Variance: Permission from the city or local government to deviate from code or ordinances for a building or construction.

Stench: A very bad odor.

To dump: To leave or get rid of something carelessly.

Evidentiary hearing: Hearing in both the criminal and civil system at which the parties present evidence rather than legal argument.[67]

Sua sponte: (Latin "of one's own accord;" voluntarily) To take a course of action without the suggestion of another (e.g., a court may raise an issue sua sponte, that is, on its own).[68]

To envelop: To wrap or cover completely.

To permeate: To spread through something.

Pre-Reading Questions

Before you begin reading, skim the caption, the synopsis and the holdings and answer the following questions:

1. Is the case in federal or state court?
2. What is the relationship between the parties?
3. What happened procedurally at the district court level?
4. What motion was filed and by whom?
5. Why did the trial court refuse to grant a permanent injunction against the defendant's business?
6. Who appealed and on what grounds?
7. What did the court of appeals decide?

---

[67] *Hearing*, BLACK'S LAW DICTIONARY (10th ed. 2014).
[68] *Sua Sponte*, GILBERT'S POCKET SIZE LAW DICTIONARY (3rd ed. 2014).

Comprehension Questions

With a general idea of the case in your mind, you can now read the case. As you are reading and after you finish reading, answer the following questions:

1. Restate in your own words the facts of the case that led to the dispute.
2. Summarize in your own words the facts that support the plaintiffs' argument that the defendant's business was a nuisance. _____
_____
3. What arguments did the defendant make in response to the claims that his business was a nuisance? _____
_____
4. The decision discusses the "reasonable use" of one's property and includes three important rules about "reasonable use." Write the rules here:
   a. _____
   b. _____
   c. _____
5. Like in the <u>Owens</u> case, the court here discusses the competing interest of landowners. What are those competing interests in this case? In the SDA/Happy Tails case? _____
_____
6. The defendant makes the argument that his activity is an agricultural activity. Why do you think he makes this argument? _____
_____
7. Like in the SDA/Happy Tails case, the defendant is operating his business in conformity with local ordinances. Does that matter? Why or why not?
8. The case here was remanded to the district court. What did the district court have to do with the case upon remand? _____
_____
9. The issuance of a permanent injunction would destroy the defendant's livelihood and leave him without a way to earn a living. Does that seem fair? Why or why not?
10. Do you agree with the court's reasoning? Why or why not?
11. If this case were decided in your country, how would a court decide?
12. How is this case useful for our fact pattern?
13. How can you analogize or distinguish the case from our facts?

Language Review — Proverbs

The defendant in this case claims that the plaintiffs were trying to "*make a mountain out of the proverbial molehill.*" This expression is a proverb that means that the plaintiffs are trying to exaggerate the importance of what they claimed was a nuisance. A proverb is a "short pithy saying in general use, stating a general truth or piece of advice."[69] Sometimes, proverbs are the same from

---
[69] *Proverb*, THE NEW OXFORD AMERICAN DICTIONARY (2001).

language to language and culture to culture, but other times can be completely different. The idea or belief might be the same, as many are universal, but how the idea is expressed can vary greatly. It can be amusing to see how different languages express that same belief.

Below are five common proverbs in American English. Write their meaning on the space provided. If you are unsure, search the meaning online. After you have written or found the meanings of the proverbs, find the same proverb in your own language. How differently are the same ideas expressed?

1. Too many cooks spoil the broth. _____
2. It's no use crying over spilt (or spilled) milk.[70] _____
3. Don't count your chickens before they're hatched. _____
4. A stitch in time saves nine. _____
5. Look before you leap. _____

---

[70] "Spilt" is British English, while most Americans use the regular past participle "spilled." For more examples of differences between U.S. and U.K. English, see the Language Focus exercise with the case Herlihy v. The Metropolitan Museum of Art (Section II, Unit 2) on page 130.

Davoust v. Mitchell,
257 N.E.2d 332 (Ind. Ct. App. 1970).

Vocabulary and Legal Terminology

Dog pen: An outdoor space, enclosed by a fence where a dog stays.

Seepage: Small quantity of liquid that escapes through small holes.

Concrete slab: A large piece of concrete.

Saga: A long, involved story.

In heat: When a female animal is in the period of her sexual cycle during which she can become pregnant.

Dog stool: Excrement or feces.

In derogation of the rights: Ignoring of rights.

Untenable: Not able to be defended, such as an argument.

Lap dog: A dog that enjoys sitting on someone's lap.

To harbor: To keep.

Pre-Reading Questions

Before you begin reading, skim the caption and the first paragraph and answer the following questions:
1. Is the case in federal or state court?
2. What is the relationship between the parties?
3. What happened procedurally at the district court level?
4. Who appealed and on what grounds?
5. What did the court of appeals decide?

Comprehension Questions

With a general idea of the case in your mind, you can now read the case. As you are reading and after you finish reading, answer the following questions:
1. Restate in your own words the facts of the case that led to the dispute.
2. Like the Wernke case, this case is also one between neighbors. Do the parties in this case seem more reasonable than those in Wernke? Less reasonable? Why?
3. State in your own words the plaintiff's arguments as to why the defendant's dog and dog pen were a nuisance. _____

4. Upon what grounds did the defendant appeal the trial court's issuance of the injunction and the award of damages? _____

5. This case includes a citation from the Meeks v. Wood case, which discusses the right of a landowner to do what he wants with his property, the duty not to injure others, and the qualifications of that duty. What are those "qualifications?" _____

6. What facts did the court use to rule that the defendant's dog pen was a nuisance? _____

7. On page 542, the court says that it would be "offensive" for someone of the appellee's "social level" to look out their living room window and see dog feces (stool), a dirty dog pen and a dog left in the rain. The court also mentions that "employees" in the plaintiff's home saw the dog stool.
   a. Based on these facts, it seems as though the plaintiffs are rather wealthy. Why do you think that the court mentions the plaintiff's "social level?" Should it matter? Why or why not?
   b. If the plaintiffs lived in a very poor part of town, do you think the court would reach the same conclusion? Should that matter?

8. Why did the trial court err in awarding damages?

9. How is this case useful for our fact pattern?

10. How can you analogize or distinguish the case from our facts?

Grammar Review — Capital (or Uppercase) Letters

Look at the use of capital letters in this sentence from the Davoust v. Mitchell case:

> Appellants answered each of the paragraphs of the complaint under **Rule** 1-3 and the case was submitted to trial by the court without a jury. The court entered judgment and ordered that appellees recover upon **Paragraph** I of their complaint

When do we use capital letters in English? Below are the Bluebook rules of when we capitalize in English.[71] Once you have reviewed the rules, determine whether the capitalization in the above sentences is correct.

When you are reading the rules below, also compare them to the rules of capitalization in your mother tongue. Are they similar to the rules in English? Different? Pay particular attention to the rules that are different, as those are the rules that you are more likely to make a mistake with.

1. Headings and titles: The rule in writing is that we capitalize words in a heading or title, such as for a book or a newspaper article, and a word that follows a colon. We do not capitalize articles, conjunctions or prepositions that have fewer than four letters. An exception is when the preposition is the first word in a title or heading, or when it follows a colon.

   Examples: *All Quiet on the Western Front*, BUT *On Crime and Punishment*.
   The World is Flat: A Brief History of the Twenty-First Century

---

[71] THE BLUEBOOK: A UNIFORM SYSTEM OF CITATION R8 at 91-93 (Columbia Law Review Ann's et al. eds., 20th ed. 2015). In this exercise, the headings are those of the Bluebook, and quotation marks in the explanations and examples note the text when taken directly from the Bluebook.

2. <u>Internet main page titles and URLs</u>: URLs and titles of Internet pages are capitalized in accordance with the original site.
3. <u>Text</u>: The following rules are to be followed when capitalizing everything but headings, titles, and Internet URLs and page titles. When in doubt about capitalization and if the following rule does not provide an answer, consult a style guide such as the Chicago Manual of Style.
    a. According to the Bluebook, "nouns that identify specific persons, officials, groups, government officers or government bodies"[72] should be capitalized as shown in the following examples:

    > Last week, the Administrator of the Department of Labor issued an interpretation of the Fair Labor Standards Act and the rules regarding overtime.

    > The Department of Homeland Security was created following the terrorist attacks in September 2001.

    > The Agency announced that it will issue new regulations regarding renewable energy.

    > In the United States, Congress is made up of the Senate and the House of Representatives.

    > Under the Constitution, the President is elected for a four-year term.

    But when *congressional* and *presidential* are used as adjectives, we do not capitalize.

    > Under the Constitution, congressional term limits are two years for members of the House of Representatives and six years for senators.

    > The presidential powers are vast although not unlimited.

    b. The following words should always be capitalized:
        (1) <u>Act</u>: When referring to a specific legislative act, capitalize it.

            1. The Immigration and Nationality Act was signed into law in 1952 by President Dwight D. Eisenhower.
            2. The legislative history of the Act shows that there was little debate over some of the more popular provisions.

        (2) <u>Circuit</u>: When writing the name of one of the federal appellate circuits, write the name with a capital letter.

            1. States in the Seventh Circuit include Illinois, Indiana and Wisconsin.

        (3) <u>Code</u>: We capitalize when we refer to a specific code.

            1. Title 18 of the United States Code deals with federal crimes and criminal procedure.

---

[72] The Bluebook: A Uniform System of Citation R8 at 91-93 (Columbia Law Review Ann's et al. eds., 20th ed. 2015).

(4) <u>Commonwealth and State</u>: Capitalize the name of a state or commonwealth if part of the full title, if it modifies a word that is capitalized, or when it is a party to litigation.

1. The Commonwealth of Massachusetts has 6.7 million residents.

2. The State of South Dakota brought a claim against a company engaged in fraud.

(5) <u>Constitution</u>: When we refer to the U.S. Constitution and to state constitutions (with the name), we always capitalize. When referring to parts of the constitution in a sentence, use capital letters to refer to those parts, but use small case letters in a citation. See Rule 11 of the Bluebook for how you format citations to the Constitution.

1. Under the California Constitution, the right to privacy is enumerated, while in the U.S. Constitution it is not.

2. The First Amendment grants people freedom of speech.

NOTE that like the adjectives *congressional* and *presidential*, the adjective *constitutional* is not capitalized.

In your opinion, which constitutional rights are the most important?

(6) <u>Court</u>: "Capitalize when naming any court in full or when referring to the U.S. Supreme Court."[73] If you are not naming a court in full, do not use capital letters.

1. The U.S. Supreme Court usually issues its most controversial and important decisions in June, at the end of the term.

2. The Wisconsin Supreme Court found the state's right-to-work law unconstitutional.

3. The supreme court reviews all first degree homicide convictions.

4. There is a circuit split between the Second and Ninth Circuits on this important issue.

5. After the district court issued its decision, the plaintiff immediately filed an appeal with the court of appeals.

(7) <u>Federal</u>: The adjective "federal" acts differently than the other adjectives discussed in this section. We capitalize federal when it refers to a noun that is capitalized, but don't capitalize it when it refers to a noun that is not capitalized.

1. The Federal Constitution was first ratified by New Hampshire in 1788.

2. The federal government has very vast powers, although they are limited.

---

[73] <u>Id.</u>

(8) <u>Judge, Justice</u>: When we refer to a specific judge, we capitalize the word. We also capitalize when we refer to a Justice of the Supreme Court.

1. My youngest sister has always wanted to be a judge.

2. My case is being heard by Judge Jones.

3. During the 2015-2016 term, Justice Antonin Scalia unexpectedly died.

4. The Arizona Supreme Court has five justices.

(9) <u>Party designations</u>: We capitalize the names of the parties of a lawsuit (e.g. plaintiff, defendant) only when referring to the parties of the lawsuit we are referencing or dealing with.

1. In this case, the Defendant has wrongfully used Plaintiff's confidential trade secrets.

2. In the case <u>State v. Wilson</u>, the court held that the defendant had not been advised of his Miranda rights.

(10) <u>Court documents</u>: The rule for capitalizing court documents is similar to the rule of party designations. Use capital letters when referencing a document filed in the litigation that is the subject of your document and you are referencing the document's actual title or a shortened form of the document's title (see Bluepages Table 1 (BT1) of the Bluebook for suggested abbreviations of court documents).

1. The Plaintiffs argue in their Memorandum of Law in Opposition to Defendant's Motion for Summary Judgment that there are facts in dispute that a jury should decide.

2. We have until next Friday to file and serve the memorandum of law in the Stray Dog Advertising matter.

3. When is the answer due?

Hendricks v. Tubbs,
92 N.E.2d 561 (Ind. 1950).

Vocabulary and Legal Terminology

Rubbish: Trash or garbage.

Filth: Extreme dirt.

Decomposed: Broken down or rotted, often into dirt.

Noxious: Harmful or dangerous.

Pre-Reading Questions

Before you begin reading, skim the caption and the first paragraph and answer the following questions:

1. Is the case in federal or state court?
2. What is the relationship between the parties?
3. What happened procedurally at the district court level?
4. Who appealed and on what grounds?
5. What did the court of appeals decide?

Comprehension Questions

With a general idea of the case in your mind, you can now read the case. As you are reading and after you finish reading, answer the following questions:

1. Restate in your own words the facts of the case that led to the dispute.
2. What arguments did the defendants make as to why the trial court erred in issuing the injunction? _____
_____
3. The facts in this case are quite extreme (the defendants have for three years (!) deposited garbage, rubbish and trash across the street from the plaintiffs). Do you think that a case need be so extreme to constitute a nuisance? Why or why not? _____
_____
4. As noted in the case, the real issue in all of these nuisance cases is "what is the discomfort that the law will protect." How can a court quantify that discomfort and inconvenience? _____
_____

5. Why does this court, as well as the courts in the other cases you have read, consider so carefully whether a remedy at law is adequate? _____
_____
_____

6. How is this case useful for our fact pattern?

7. How can you analogize or distinguish the case from our facts?

Language Review — Same Words, Different Meanings

Law students, both native speakers and second-language learners, often complain about the new vocabulary that they must learn. Legal vocabulary can be very precise, and becoming a member of the legal community means understanding and fluently using that vocabulary, much like learning a foreign language. To become a fluent speaker of legal English (or legal Spanish, or Russian, or Chinese, or any language), you must learn the precise words that are used to express a certain thing or action. Having the command of such precise vocabulary demonstrates a speaker's expertise.

Here are a few examples of precise legal terminology that we use:
- Instead of a sworn statement, we say an <u>affidavit</u>.
- A witness isn't requested to testify at a hearing, but is <u>subpoenaed</u>.
- The police don't ask a suspect questions, but rather <u>interrogate</u> her.
- A civil discovery tool isn't an interview of a witness, but rather a <u>deposition</u>.

But on the other hand, there is also a lot of vocabulary used in legal writing that we use not just in a legal context but also in an everyday context, and the words often have very different meanings depending on that context. To become an expert in not just legal English but English in general means knowing the different meanings of words and how they can greatly change from context to context.

The following sentences are taken from the <u>Hendricks</u> case, and one or more words in each sentence is underlined. For each underlined word, do the following:

1. Define how the word is used in that sentence
2. Determine what another commonly used meaning of the same word is
3. Use the word in another sentence that demonstrates its second meaning

The first word in the first sentence has been done for you as an example.

1. Whether a <u>complaining</u> party has a legal remedy which will <u>afford</u> complete justice must be determined under all the circumstances of the case, and in view of the conduct of the <u>parties</u>.
    a. <u>Complaining</u>: <u>here, it means someone who has filed a complaint with the court and seeks relief. It can also mean someone who expresses their annoyance or unhappiness: The woman was complaining because she had to wait more than an hour for her dinner.</u>
    b. <u>Afford</u>: _____
    _____
    _____
    c. <u>Party</u>: _____
    _____
    _____

2. Where there is a legal remedy, equity will frequently grant injunctive relief to prevent a multiplicity of suits.

   a. Grant: _____
   _____

   b. Suit: _____
   _____

3. Finally, appellants say that there was a failure of proof that appellees have no adequate remedy at law, and that they have an adequate remedy in an action for damages.

   a. Remedy: _____
   _____

   b. Action: _____
   _____

SECTION II

Unit 1: Negligence/Duty to Warn

Lundgren v. Fultz,
354 N.W.2d 25 (Minn. 1984).

Vocabulary and Legal Terminology

<u>To rehospitalize</u>: To hospitalize (admit to a hospital) again, after being discharged.

<u>To brandish</u>: To wave something, especially a weapon, as a threat.

<u>Delusion</u>: A belief based on false ideas, generally removed from reality.

<u>Omnipotence</u>: Having unlimited powers.

<u>To strike</u>: To hit forcefully.

<u>Pool cue</u>: A rod used when playing billiards or pool to hit the pool balls.

<u>Paranoid schizophrenic</u>: A person suffering from the mental illness of paranoid schizophrenia.

<u>Remission</u>: The decrease or disappearance of the symptoms of a disease.

<u>To confiscate</u>: To seize.

<u>To seethe</u>: (of a person) To be intensely angry.

<u>Cacophony</u>: Unpleasant loud sound.

<u>Lay person</u>: A person who is not a member of a particular profession.

<u>Guise</u>: A disguise, assumed with the intent to deceive.

Pre-Reading Questions

Before you begin reading, skim the caption and the first paragraph and answer the following questions:

1. Is the case in federal or state court?
2. What cause of action did the plaintiff bring?
3. What was the relationship between the parties?
4. What did the defendants do that led to the lawsuit?

5. Who did the plaintiff name as defendants?
6. What happened procedurally at the trial court?
7. What did the supreme court decide?

Comprehension Questions

With a general idea of the case in your mind, you can now read the case. As you are reading and after you finish reading, answer the following questions:

1. Summarize in your own words the "troubling" facts of the case.
2. What does the plaintiff allege that the defendant should have done? _____
   _____
   _____
3. Did the defendant Cline really have an "ability to control" Fultz? Why or why not? _____
   _____
   _____
4. Do you think that the court decided correctly? Why or why not? _____
   _____
   _____
5. This case dealt with very tragic facts that can elicit a personal reaction. Someone whose life has been affected by gun violence might view the case and the court's decision differently than someone who is a psychiatrist or a psychologist and who deals with mentally ill patients on a regular basis.
   a. How can a reader's personal history or experiences affect his or her opinion of a case?
      _____
   b. Did you have any personal reaction to the case? _____
      _____
   c. If so, did that reaction in any way color whether you viewed the court's decision as correct or not? How? _____
      _____
6. Policy is very important in this case, as noted in the comments.
   a. Identify all of the policy considerations that the court states. _____
      _____
   b. Which ones are the most important? _____
      _____
   c. How does the court balance these considerations? _____
      _____
   d. Is policy so important in court decisions in your country? Why or why not? _____
      _____
7. Is this case useful for our fact pattern?
   a. Why or why not? _____
      _____
   b. Is it more useful for the plaintiff or the defendant? Why? _____
      _____

Legal Focus

Should Who You Are Affect How You Reason as a Lawyer or as a Judge?

The Lundgren v. Fultz case deals with difficult facts and issues, as does our fact pattern: a shooting, the violent death of an individual at the hands of another person, and the potential liability of a third person (SDA and Cline, the therapist, and the University of Minnesota) for that person's actions, over which they arguably had no control. One person, when reading the Lundgren case or dealing with a client in a similar situation (as either plaintiff or defendant), might have a more extreme reaction to the facts than someone else due to personal experiences, opinions, and beliefs. A judge whose husband or wife was lost due to gun violence might react differently to the case than a judge who has never experienced such loss, or someone who is a strong defender of the Second Amendment.[74]

This poses thought-provoking questions: Should we let our life experiences, our personal opinions and beliefs — the essence of who we are — influence our professional actions, reactions and decisions? Should the personal self be separated from the professional? Is that even possible?

Before her nomination to the U.S. Supreme Court in 2009, Justice Sonia Sotomayor spoke about her Latina identity (her parents immigrated from Puerto Rico to New York, where she was born and raised) and about the importance of diversity among judges. She also stated that a judge's gender and national origin will influence the decisions that a judge makes from the bench. Below are excerpts from a 2001 lecture that she gave entitled "A Latina Judge's Voice."

Read the short passage and reflect upon the questions that follow.

> Whether born from experience or inherent physiological or cultural differences . . . our gender and national origins may and will make a difference in our judging . . . I would hope that a wise Latina woman with the richness of her experiences would more often than not reach a better conclusion than a white male who hasn't lived that life . . . [O]ne must accept the proposition that a difference there will be by the presence of women and people of color on the bench. Personal experiences affect the facts that judges choose to see . . . I simply do not know exactly what that difference [from my personal experiences] will be in my judging. But I accept there will be some based on my gender and my Latina heritage.[75]

1. Do you agree with Justice Sotomayor that a judge's gender and national origin (or race) will affect that person's judging? Why or why not?
2. Would it be more accurate to say only *may affect*, or *could affect*? If so, why?
3. Why do you think that Justice Sotomayor asserted that a Latina woman, because of her personal experiences, would reach a *better* conclusion than a white male? Or just a different one? Do you agree? Why or why not?
4. Justice Sotomayor was speaking about how a person's experiences affect his or her decisions as a judge. How might a person's personal experiences affect the work that he or she does a lawyer?
5. Many people believe that lawyers and judges should simply apply the law and not let their personal experiences affect their decisions. Is this possible? Why or why not?

---

[74] The Second Amendment of the Constitution provides people the right to bear arms and states: "A well regulated Militia, being necessary to the security of a free State, the right of the people to keep and bear Arms, shall not be infringed." U.S. Const. amend. II. Those who believe that few regulations should be in place on the right to own guns are known as defenders or supporters of the Second Amendment.

[75] Lecture: "A Latina Judge's Voice," N.Y. Times, May 14, 2009, *available at* http://www.nytimes.com/2009/05/15/us/politics/15judge.text.html. The text of the lecture was printed in the spring 2002 issue of the Berkley La Raza Law Journal. Sonia Sotomayor, *A Latina Judge's Voice*, 13 Berkeley La Raza L.J. 87 (2002).

Bjerke v. Johnson,
742 N.W.2d 660 (Minn. 2007).

Vocabulary and Legal Terminology

Invitee: One who is invited onto the property of another, either expressly or impliedly, to conduct business for their mutual benefit or for the benefit of the occupier, or to engage in an activity which the occupier permits to be conducted on his property (e.g., a customer who enters a store is an invitee regardless of whether he makes a purchase).[76]

Chores: Tasks around the house, often those that children do to help their parents, such as washing dishes, setting the table, or making their bed.

To mind your manners: To be polite and courteous to others.

Vulgarity: Rude or offensive qualities or behavior.

To disparage: To say unpleasant things about someone, often with the intent of harming that person's reputation.

Person of ordinary prudence: Another way of saying "reasonable person."

Overtones: A hidden or implicit meaning to something.

To rub: To move firmly something (your hand, a piece of fabric) against another surface.

Flirtation: Behavior that shows that you are sexually interested in or attracted to another person.

Pre-Reading Questions

Before you begin reading, skim the caption, the synopsis paragraph and the holdings and answer the following questions:

1. Is the case in federal or state court?
2. What was the motion before the trial court?
3. Who filed the motion?
4. Did the trial court grant it?
5. What happened at the appellate court? At the supreme court?
6. What do we know about the facts that led to the dispute?
7. Why is the plaintiff claiming that the defendant, Johnson, was negligent?

---

[76] *Invitee*, Gilbert's Pocket Size Law Dictionary (3rd ed. 2014).

Comprehension Questions

With a general idea of the case in your mind, you can now read the case. As you are reading and after you finish reading, answer the following questions:

1. Summarize the facts of the case.
2. What are the three different scenarios that can give rise to a special relationship?
    a. _____
    b. _____
    c. _____
3. Which one is (or could be) present in the Bjerke case?
4. Which one is present in our case?
5. Identify the facts that the court used in determining that a special relationship existed between the parties: _____
6. Are the facts that you identified in #5 "legally relevant" to the case? Why or why not?
7. Identify and write the rule (with the proper citation) of foreseeability: _____
8. Why is foreseeability so important when determining whether someone is liable for failure to warn or failure to protect?
9. Identify the facts that the court used in determining that the harm that Bjerke suffered (the sexual abuse) was foreseeable: _____
10. Are the facts that you identified in #9 "legally relevant?" Why or why not?
11. This case was quite controversial and generated concurring and dissenting opinions. Identify some of the policy considerations that came into play in the court's decision. _____
12. In the United States, many battles like this over liability — who should bear the responsibility for harmful actions, the balance of interests — are fought out and decided in the courts. How does your home country resolve such disputes?
13. Do you think that the court decided correctly? Why or why not?
14. Is this case useful for our fact pattern?
    a. Why or why not?
    b. Is it more useful for the plaintiff or the defendant? Why?

Language Focus — Synonyms

A *synonym* is a word or a phrase that has the exact or nearly exact meaning as another word in the same language. *Simple* is a synonym of *easy*, while *hard* is a synonym of *difficult*. These are just two of the many examples of synonyms in English.

Learning synonyms of words that you are familiar with can be an excellent way to expand your vocabulary and improve your English. A dictionary of synonyms is a *thesaurus*. You use a thesaurus like a dictionary: you look up a word but instead of finding its definition, you will find a list of words with the same or a similar meaning. You find *antonyms* (words with the opposite meaning) too.

However, just because words are synonyms doesn't mean that they can be used interchangeably. Oftentimes, one word will have slightly different nuances than another word, or be suited for a particular context (such as more formal speaking or writing) than another word. Learning the subtle differences in meaning is important in mastering new vocabulary.

In the Bjerke case, we saw the verb *to rub*, which can have many meanings. In the case, it is used in the meaning of moving one's hand repeatedly back and forth on the surface of something (here another person) with firm pressure.

If you look up *to rub* in a thesaurus, you will find listed as synonyms the verbs listed below. But none of them has exactly the same meaning of *to rub*.

Find these verbs in a dictionary to learn the slight differences in meaning from *to rub*. If the dictionary doesn't provide you with enough information, doing an online search to see how the verb is used can often help to better understand when and how we use the verb. After you have found the definition, write a sentence that demonstrates the nuance of the verb.

To knead _____
_____

To stroke _____
_____

To massage _____
_____

To pet _____
_____

To brush _____
_____

Patzwald v. Krey,
390 N.W.2d 920 (Minn. 1986).

Vocabulary and Legal Terminology

Wedding reception: The dinner or celebration held after a wedding.

Indiscriminately: Randomly; haphazardly.

Erratic: Unpredictable.

To break off: To end, especially for an engagement.

To honk (the horn): To make a car's horn sound.

To "get" someone: (here) To kill, attack or punish someone.

State a claim upon relief can be granted: Rule 12(b)(6) of the Federal Rules of Civil Procedure allows a defendant to file a motion to dismiss if the allegations in the complaint show that the plaintiff is not entitled to relief because he has failed to state a claim upon which relief can be granted.[77]

Judgment on the pleadings: When a judge issues a judgment based only on what is stated and alleged in the complaint and answer.

Propensities: Tendencies or inclinations.

Pre-Reading Questions

Before you begin reading, skim the caption, first paragraph and the syllabus and answer the following questions:

1. Is the case in federal or state court?
2. What do we know about the parties and their relationship?
3. What was the motion before the district court?
4. What did the district court decide?
5. Who appealed and on what grounds?
6. What did the court of appeals decide and what was the reason for its decision?

---

[77] Fed. R. Civ. Pro. 12(b)(6).

Patzwald v. Krey, 390 N.W.2d 920 (Minn. 1986)

Comprehension Questions

With a general idea of the case in your mind, you can now read the case. As you are reading and after you finish reading, answer the following questions:

1. According to the plaintiff, what should the defendant have warned the guests about?

2. Summarize the plaintiffs' arguments as to why the defendant should be liable for the injuries they suffered: _____

3. Summarize the defendant's arguments as to why she should not be held liable: _____

4. A "special relationship" must exist between a defendant in a negligence/duty to warn case and what other person in order for liability to be imposed (provided the harm suffered was foreseeable):
    a. _____
    b. _____

5. List the facts that the court used in reaching the conclusion that the harm that the guests suffered was not foreseeable: _____

6. Why does the court cite the <u>Larson</u> case in its analysis? _____

7. Why does the court cite the <u>Cairl</u> case in its analysis? _____

8. What is your "gut feeling" about this case. Did the court decide correctly or do you agree with the dissent? Why? _____

9. Here is another policy question: should someone always be held legally liable when something bad (even very bad or tragic happens)? Why or why not? _____

10. How would this case be decided in your legal system? _____

11. Is this case useful for our fact pattern?
    a. Why or why not?
    b. Is it more useful for the plaintiff or the defendant? Why?

Language Focus — To Get

This case introduces you to perhaps a new use of the verb *to get*: Krey told Patzwald, his ex-girlfriend, that he would *get her*. In the Larson case, the defendant police officer was told that "his house was going to '*get it*.'"

You learned in the Vocabulary and Legal Terminology section that in this context, *to get* means to kill, attack or punish someone. When a person says that a house will *get it*, he means that the house will somehow be damaged or destroyed, whether by an explosion like in the Larson case or an intentionally-set fire.

We use *to get* to express many other actions in English, and *to get* is the most frequently used verb in English, especially everyday spoken English.[78] But that doesn't mean that you should use *to get* in your legal or academic writing, as it lends an informality that is ill suited for that type of writing. Instead, you want to ask yourself what the true meaning of *to get* is in a particular sentence and replace it. Give it a shot[79] here:

1. Tom was very surprised when he <u>got</u> a new computer for his birthday.

   Your Rewrite: _____

2. I can't believe that I <u>got</u> the flu over the holidays! What a bummer!

   Your Rewrite: _____

3. Over the last decade, it <u>has gotten</u> warmer across the entire world, evidence scientists say of global warming.

   Your Rewrite: _____

4. Shelly was shocked and disappointed that she <u>got</u> a C on her contract exam because she studied weeks for it and thought she had done better.

   Your Rewrite: _____

5. When did you <u>get</u> home?

   Your Rewrite: _____

---

[78] See Oxford Dictionaries for a complete list of the most common words in English. *Get* is the 47th most common word, and the most commonly used verb. OXFORD DICTIONARIES, *What Can the Oxford English Corpus Tell Us About the English Language?*, http://www.oxforddictionaries.com/words/the-oec-facts-about-the-language (last visited May 2, 2016).

[79] Make an attempt; try.

6. After receiving a large inheritance, Frank immediately went to a car dealership and <u>got</u> a new car.

   Your Rewrite: _____

7. We <u>got</u> to the top of the mountain after six long and tough hours of hiking and climbing.

   Your Rewrite: _____

8. When I took a quiz in my torts class last week, I <u>got</u> only 75% of the questions correct.

   Your Rewrite: _____

Udofot v. Seven Eights Liquor,
No. A10-431, 2010 WL 5071313 (Minn. Ct. App. March 15, 2011).

Vocabulary and Legal Terminology

Racial epithet: A word or phrase that is offensive and insults an individual's race.

To elicit: To get information from someone.

Groin area: The part of the body between the lower abdomen and the upper thigh.

Business invitee: In tort law, a person who enters the premises (such as a business) of another person.

Pre-Reading Questions

Before you begin reading, skim the caption and the first paragraph and answer the following questions:

1. Is the case in federal or state court?
2. Who are the parties to the lawsuit?
3. What is the relationship between the parties?
4. Why is the plaintiff claiming that the defendant is liable?
5. What was the motion before the trial court?
6. Who filed the motion?
7. Did the trial court grant it?
8. What happened at the appellate court? Why?

Comprehension Questions

With a general idea of the case in your mind, you can now read the case. As you are reading and after you finish reading, answer the following questions:

1. This case is helpful for one specific rule that is included. Identify that rule and write it here: ____
   _____
   _____
   _____

2. Provide a citation for the rule.

3. Is this case useful for our fact pattern?
   a. Why or why not?
   b. Is it more useful for the plaintiff or the defendant? Why?

Legal Focus — Use of Cases

As you have no doubt learned during your LL.M. program, the U.S. legal system, being a common-law system, is based on cases and case law. Cases provide the rules of law for areas of law like torts, contracts and property. Even for areas of law that are codified, like criminal law and many other areas, cases are essential to understand the legal issue and the law, and to carry out legal analysis.

When researching a client matter, you will read many cases and find that they are useful for different reasons. Some cases might provide you parts of the rule that you will use in your rule statement. Other cases might be useful as they demonstrate how the rule has been applied and interpreted in prior cases. You analogize or distinguish those cases from your client matter to show how the court should or will likely decide.

The Udofot case is one that will serve a limited purpose. Why? First, it is unpublished, as you see in the caption of the case, and unpublished court of appeals cases don't involve significant legal issues, or don't establish a new rule of law. The court of appeals itself decides whether cases will be published (with precedential value) or not. Simply put, unpublished cases are not very important cases as they simply restate a well-established rule or deal with a settled legal issue. Since all parties have the right to appeal, the appellate courts handle all types of cases, including those that aren't very important, at least from a precedential sense.

But these cases can still be useful to you as you research. First, they can provide you with additional cases to read and research. Let's say that you hadn't read the Bjerke v. Johnson case before reading the Udofot case. But while reading Udofot, you would see the citations to Bjerke, see that it was a state supreme court decision and know that it was important and worth reading.

The Udofot case also provides a clarification of an important rule for our fact pattern: the special relationship. The Bjerke case tells you that a special relationship exists between "parents and children, masters and servants, possessors of land and licensees, [and] common carriers and their customers."

But what if you aren't sure what a "master-servant" relationship is? Or if you think that master-servant means more like a relationship of a lord or a member of royalty, a wealthy property owner with servants waiting on him? You might not understand that "master-servant" can also mean "employer-employee."

The Udofot case provides some clarification for you of that important master-servant rule: "It is undisputed that the employer-employee relationship between Seven Eights and Clark created a special relationship." By reading this one sentence in the Udofot case, you instantly understand that "master-servant" means "employer-employee." That is an important point to understand for the Stray Dog Advertising case.

Sometimes, a case might provide just one useful or important piece of information, or part of a rule, or clarification. You might use other cases extensively in both your rule statement and your analysis. But understanding how you can use cases will help you read them more strategically and help you identify what those useful and important parts of the cases are.

H.B. ex rel. v. Whittemore,
552 N.W.2d 705 (Minn. 1996).

Vocabulary and Legal Terminology

<u>Trailer park</u>: An area where mobile or manufactured homes are secured and where residents live. Residents often own the home and thus rent the lot (the land upon which the trailer stays) from the trailer park owner.

<u>To perpetrate</u>: To commit an illegal act or a crime.

<u>Unruly</u>: Difficult or impossible to control.

<u>Lascivious</u>: Filled with or showing sexual desire.

<u>Treats</u>: A special gift given to yourself or to another person, often food.

<u>To retaliate against someone</u>: To do something bad against someone who has treated you badly; to get revenge.

Pre-Reading Questions

Before you begin reading, skim the caption, first paragraph and the syllabus and answer the following questions:

1. Is the case in federal or state court?
2. What are the basic facts of the case as we know them so far?
3. What is the relationship between the parties?
4. Why is the plaintiff claiming that the defendant is liable?
5. What was the motion before the trial court?
6. Who filed the motion?
7. Did the trial court grant it?
8. What happened at the appellate court?
9. At the supreme court?

Comprehension Questions

With a general idea of the case in your mind, you can now read the case. As you are reading and after you finish reading, answer the following questions:

1. Summarize the facts of the case: _____
_____
_____

2. Why did the district court grant the motion for summary judgment? _____
_____
_____

3. Why did the appellate court reverse? _____
_____
_____

4. Examine how the court uses the Erickson case as a distinguishing case to argue that no special relationship was formed here. The Erickson case seems to be a "special circumstance" for the imposition of a duty. What is unique about a parking ramp that would necessitate the imposition of a duty upon the ramp owner? _____
_____
_____

5. Examine how the court uses the Andrade case as a distinguishing case to argue that no special relationship was formed here. That case also involves children, but imposed a duty upon the day care owner to protect the children. How is that case distinguishable from the Whittemore case?
_____

6. Examine how the court uses the Harper case as an analogous case to argue that no special relationship was formed here. Why is the Harper case analogous to the Whittemore case? _____
_____
_____

7. Finally, examine how the court uses the Donaldson case as an analogous case to argue that no special relationship was formed here. Why is the Donaldson case analogous to the Whittemore case? _____
_____
_____

8. Summarize the court's arguments as to why Whittemore owed no duty to the children who told her about the abuse that they were suffering at the hands of a park resident: _____
_____
_____

9. Summarize the dissent's opinion in the case: _____
_____

10. Who do you agree with? The majority or the dissent? Why? _____
_____
_____

11. Like many of the cases that you have read for this Unit, the facts of this case are troubling and tragic. As the dissent states, child sexual abuse is an emergency that should be addressed. Strong policy arguments exist for taking all steps against child sexual abuse. Should these be reasons enough to impose a duty to act and to protect upon an individual like in this case? Support your answer. _____
_____
_____

12. Is this case useful for our fact pattern?
    c. Why or why not?
    d. Is it more useful for the plaintiff or the defendant? Why?

Language Focus — Punctuation (Period, Commas, Semicolons and Colons)

"With educated people, I suppose, punctuation is a matter of rule; with me it is a matter of feeling. But I must say I have a great respect for the semi-colon; it's a useful little chap." — Abraham Lincoln

Punctuation marks are used to create clarity, comprehension, and emphasis in written language.[80] In English, there are sixteen punctuation marks: period (called a full stop in British English), question mark, exclamation point, comma, semicolon, colon, dash (including the en dash and the em dash), hyphen, parentheses, brackets, braces, apostrophe, quotation marks and ellipses. This Language Focus will examine four of those punctuation marks: periods, commas, semicolons and colons.[81]

Of your concerns when writing, punctuation may seem to be the least important. After all, aren't verb tenses, correct vocabulary and sentence structure more important? Not really, and to show you how important punctuation is, take a look at these sentences. What is the difference in meaning between them?

> Let's eat Grandma.
> Let's eat, Grandma.
>
> My sister likes to eat chocolate hot dogs and broccoli.
> My sister likes to eat chocolate, hot dogs and broccoli.[82]

These two pairs of sentences should underscore the importance of learning correct punctuation! Not only can the meaning of a sentence change drastically due to punctuation, but incorrect punctuation detracts from the quality and credibility of your work, just as spelling and grammatical mistakes do. How we use punctuation in English is likely different than in your mother tongue, making it even more important that you learn or review the rules.

Period:

The period is one of the three ways that we can end a sentence (the other two being with an exclamation point or a question mark). However, that is not the only use of periods in English.

We also use periods to indicate when a word or words have been omitted from a quotation. These periods are called an ellipsis, three periods separated by spaces and set off by a space before the first period and after the last period.[83] The following sentence is from the Whittemore case, and while the edits and omissions are not noted in the Commented Cases and Legal Authorities book, the sentence below shows

---

[80] *Punctuation*, EDUFIND.COM, http://www.edufind.com/english-grammar/punctuation/ (last visited May 8, 2016).

[81] The Language Focus in the Cobai v. Young case (Section I, Unit 4) examines hyphens, as well as en dashes and em dashes. Refer to this exercise for additional information on those three types of punctuation marks. Online resources also provide additional information on the other types of punctuation not covered in this ESL Workbook.

[82] Example from *Punctuation Marks in English*, REALLY-LEARN-ENGLISH.COM, http://www.really-learn-english.com/punctuation-marks.html (last visited May 8, 2016).

[83] See Rule 5.3 of the Bluebook for additional information and examples of how to use the ellipsis and indicate omitted words from a quotation. Rule 5.3, THE BLUEBOOK: A UNIFORM SYSTEM OF CITATION (Columbia Law Review Ass'n et al. eds., 20th ed. 2015).

the actual edits and omissions. The ellipsis tells you that words from the original have been omitted between the words *Appeals* and *affirmed*. Note the space before and after the first and final period.

> The Court of Appeals . . . affirmed in part, reversed in part, and remanded.

We also use a period with abbreviations, including initials. The sentence is from the <u>Whittemore</u> case. Because the victims were children, the court did not use their names for privacy concerns. The initials are used instead, with periods after the initial for the first and the last name.

> The family of two of the children, N.T. and K.T., moved to Eaton in 1983.

The days of the week and the months are abbreviated as follows with a period:

> <u>Days of the week:</u>   Mon., Tues., Wed., Thurs., Fri., Sat., Sun.
>
> <u>Months:</u>   Jan., Feb., Mar., Apr., May, June, July, Aug., Sept., Oct., Nov., Dec.
>
> a.m.   p.m.   etc.

For organization and entities with commonly recognized initials, we usually omit the periods from the abbreviations.[84]

> FBI   NLRB   CIA   AARP

And finally, we use a period with sums of money to separate the whole number from the decimal (not commas as in many parts of the world).

> $81.35 $17.25 $8.50

But note that we use commas with numbers to separate all but the decimal.

> 1,800,356   1,560 $1,450.25 (note the comma and the period)

Commas:

Commas are the most common punctuation mark that we use, and we use them in many various situations.

First, we use commas to set apart an introductory clause, introductory phrase, or introductory word.[85] In this sentence from the <u>Whittemore</u> case, the introductory word *generally* is set apart by a comma. An introductory word adds continuity and flow between sentences, as do other words such as *however, furthermore, in addition,* etc.[86]

> Generally, a special relationship giving rise to a duty to warn is only found on the part of common carriers, innkeepers, possessors of land who hold it open to the public, and persons

---

[84] Rule 6.1, THE BLUEBOOK: A UNIFORM SYSTEM OF CITATION (Columbia Law Review Ass'n et al. eds., 20th ed. 2015).
[85] *Commas After Introductions*, ONLINE WRITING LAB OF PURDUE UNIVERSITY, https://owl.english.purdue.edu/owl/resource/607/03/ (last visited May 8, 2016).
[86] <u>Id.</u>

who have custody of another person under circumstances in which that other person is deprived of normal opportunities of self-protection.

Under this rule, a special relationship could be found to exist between the parties only if Herman had custody of Harper under circumstances in which Harper was deprived of normal opportunities to protect himself.

Note that some introductory phrases, if moved to a different position in a sentence, no longer require a comma.

Because the children believed that they should seek help from Arndt and expected her to act to protect them in some way, the court concluded that they entrusted themselves to her.

The court concluded that the children entrusted themselves to Arndt because they believed that they should seek help from her and expected her to act to protect them in some way.

We also use commas to separate words and word groups in a series of three or more items.

I spent the past week studying for my exams, packing for my trip, and getting ready for graduation.

I went to the store and bought bread, coffee, milk, and peanut butter.

I would like to see Frozen, Finding Nemo, Cinderella, or The Lion King.

The last comma in the above three lists (before *and* and *or*) is known as the Oxford or serial comma. Style guides differ as to whether you should include it, and you will likely see many writers choose not to (I went to the store and bought bread, coffee, milk and peanut butter). However, as confusion can arise if you don't include the Oxford comma and to ensure clarity, a good rule of thumb is to always include a comma before *and* or *or* and separate the last items in the list.

In addition, we use commas to separate two adjectives when the order of the adjectives is interchangeable. Not all adjectives are interchangeable, however. If you are unsure when the order of adjectives can change and when the order is pre-determined depending on the nature of the adjective, refer to the Language Focus for the State v. Rodriquez case (Section II, Unit 4) for additional information about the order of adjectives.

He is a tall, handsome man.
He is a handsome, tall man.

It is a red American sports car.
NOT: ~~It is an American red sports car~~.

We also use commas to join together two independent clauses when they are connected with a connector word such as *and* or *but*. In this situation, the comma indicates to the reader that the clauses are separate. In the sentence below, you know that the clauses are independent and the comma is necessary since you could eliminate the *and*, put a period after *granted*, and start a new sentence with *any*.

In so doing, we view the evidence in a light most favorable to the party against whom summary judgment was granted, and any doubts of the existence of a material fact are resolved in favor of the losing party.

Contrast this rule with when we don't need a comma when a sentence has two clauses, but the first one is an independent clause and the second one a dependent clause (i.e. not a sentence that can stand on its own).

The judge granted our motion for summary judgment and denied the plaintiff's motion for sanction.
> Here, the subject of both verbs, granted and denied, is the same: the judge. The clause after the *and* is not a complete sentence, so you do not need a comma.

The judge denied the defendant's motion for summary judgment since there were material facts in dispute.
> *since there were no material facts in dispute* is not an independent clause so no comma is needed after *judgment*

BUT: Since there were material facts in dispute, the judge denied the defendant's motion for summary judgment.
> Here, the phrase beginning with *since* is an introductory phrase so requires a comma.

Finally, we use commas when we include in our sentence a non-restrictive relative clause, which is a relative clause that provides additional, non-essential information to the reader.[87]

The judge, who is originally from Florida, was nominated to the bench in 1999.

The table, which is made from oak, was handmade in 1955.

Semicolon:

Think of a semicolon as a happy compromise between a period and a colon; a semicolon indicates a pause between two sentences, longer than a comma but shorter than a full stop. We use semicolons to indicate that two independent sentences are so closely linked together that they should not be separated by a period.

> Unlike Erickson, here there was no acceptance by Arndt of the children's entrustment; indeed it was specifically rejected when Arndt instructed the children to tell their parents about Whittemore's abuse.

Note that the sentences on each side of the semicolon are complete sentences that could stand on their own. But the idea in each of the two sentences — Arndt's acceptance of the care for the children — is the same and thus the sentences are closely tied together. For this reason, the judge decided to use a semicolon instead of two separate sentences separated by a period.

Note that to use a semicolon to connect together two sentences, each must be a complete sentence and be able to stand on its own.

---

[87] See the Language Focus for the Atkinson v. McLaughlin case (Section III, Unit 2) for additional information about non-restrictive and restrictive relative clauses.

> NOT: ~~Although the weather was very nice; we decided to stay inside~~.
> NOT: ~~Unlike Erickson, here there was no acceptance by Arndt of the children's entrustment; because she had specifically rejected it when she told the children to talk to their parents about the abuse~~.

We also use semicolons to separate units of a series, when one or more of the units has a comma. The semicolon indicates to the reader which items go together and avoids confusion.[88]

> Last year, we traveled to Franklin, Tennessee; Atlanta, Georgia; Raleigh, North Carolina; and Austin, Texas.

> NOT: ~~Last year, we traveled to Franklin, Tennessee, Atlanta, Georgia, Raleigh, North Carolina, and Austin, Texas~~.
> > ➢ With only commas separating the items in the list, the reader doesn't know that "Franklin, Tennessee" go together and the list seems to be one long list of only cities or states.

Colon:

Colons are used when we list a series of items.

> The judge visited three countries during her vacation: Colombia, Brazil and Argentina.

But don't use a colon immediately following a verb, even if you are listing a series of items.

> NOT: ~~At the grocery store, please buy: bread, coffee, and apples~~.
> I need three items: bread, coffee, and apples.

> NOT: ~~First year law school classes include: property, torts, contracts, civil procedure and legal writing~~.
> During their first year of law school, all students take the same classes: property, torts, contracts, civil procedure and legal writing.

We also use a colon between two independent clauses when the second sentence explains, illustrates, paraphrases or expands on the first sentence.[89] The first example is from the <u>Whittemore</u> case.

> Under the "Miscellaneous" section, the rules provide for the processing of tenant complaints: "Any complaint you have about the park or other residents must be submitted to the park in writing and signed by you."

> In this case, the plaintiff has established a prima facie case of contract formation: she made an offer, the defendant accepted it, and there was consideration.

---

[88] Jane Straus, Semic*olons*, Grammar Book.Com, http://www.grammarbook.com/punctuation/semicolons.asp (last visited May 9, 2016).
[89] Jane Straus, *Colons*, Grammar Book.Com, http://www.grammarbook.com/punctuation/colons.asp (last visited May 9, 2016).

Finally, we use colons to provide emphasis to what follows the colon.

> After listening to the attorney make her compelling arguments, the judge issued his decision right then and there: motion denied.

> After waiting months for the response, George received a response from the Admissions Office at Harvard Law School: accepted.

Putting It All Together:

Examine these three sentences. The first two are from the <u>Whittemore</u> case, while the third sentence is from the next case, <u>Wood on Behalf of Doe v. Astleford</u>. Note that the sentences include all of the punctuation marks that have been analyzed in this Language Focus: commas, semicolons, colons and periods. For each of the punctuation marks in the sentence, examine its use. Then articulate the rule as to why each punctuation mark is used.

> Here, the court of appeals depended on *Erickson* and cited three factors in reaching its conclusion that Arndt owed the children a duty: first, that Faelon had held Arndt out as the local authority who would enforce the rules in the park and evict problem residents; second, that the children reported the abuse to Arndt because of her perceived position of authority; and third, that Arndt had prior knowledge of Whittemore's history of criminal sexual conduct.

> Generally, a special relationship giving rise to a duty to warn is only found on the part of common carriers, innkeepers, possessors of land who hold it open to the public, and persons who have custody of another person under circumstances in which that other person is deprived of normal opportunities of self-protection.

> This appeal is from an entry of summary judgment in favor of respondents. B.S., T.S. and their mother brought an action against Dale Astleford's wife, Lola Mae Astleford; his employer, Astleford Equipment Company, Inc.; and Sandra Dawson, president and director of Astleford Equipment from November 1979 through January 16, 1982.

Wood on Behalf of Doe v. Astleford,
412 N.W.2d 753 (Minn. Ct. App. 1987).

Vocabulary and Legal Terminology

Pedophiliac: An individual who is sexually attracted to children.

Proclivity: Tendency.

Darkroom: A room with no light, used to develop photographs.

Sexually explicit: Very clearly sexual in nature.

Outlying building: A building far away from the main home or building on the property.

Foster son (or child): A child who is placed in the care of another family, either temporarily or for a long period of time.

To impute: To attribute.

Innuendo: An indirect comment that suggests or implies something improper or unpleasant.

Aberrant behavior: Unusual or abnormal behavior.

To level (threats) against someone: To make or state threats.

Pre-Reading Questions

Before you begin reading, skim the caption, first paragraph and the syllabus and answer the following questions:
1. Is the case in federal or state court?
2. Who are the parties and what is their relationship?
3. Why is the plaintiff claiming that the defendant is liable?
4. What was the motion before the trial court?
5. Who filed the motion?
6. Did the trial court grant it?
7. What happened at the appellate court?
8. Why did the appellate court decide as it did?

Comprehension Questions

With a general idea of the case in your mind, you can now read the case. As you are reading and after you finish reading, answer the following questions:

1. Summarize the facts of the case.
2. Dale Astleford abused the plaintiffs and thus is the defendant. Who are the other parties in the case?
   a. Lola Mae Astleford: _____
   b. Astleford Equipment Company, Inc. _____
   c. Sandra Dawson: _____
   d. B.S. and T.S. _____
3. The court tells us that the abuse "took place almost exclusively at the Astleford residence, although some took place at the Astleford Equipment Company in an out-lying building during non-office hours." What arguments did the plaintiff make as to why the Company should be held liable for Dale Astleford's actions? _____
_____
_____
4. How does the court respond to those arguments? _____
_____
_____
5. The Cairl case held that the duty to warn must be to specific targeted victims, rather than to the population at large. Plaintiffs argue that Lundgren reverses that rule and held that a duty to warn can exist to the population at large. The Astleford court disagrees. How does it reason to eliminate this apparent contradiction between the cases? _____
_____
_____
6. Why did the court rule that the harm that the plaintiffs suffered was unforeseeable to Dale Astleford's wife? _____
_____
_____
7. Is this case useful for our fact pattern?
   a. Why or why not?
   b. Is it more useful for the plaintiff or the defendant? Why?

Language Focus — Compound Words and Pronunciation

In the Astleford case, you learned that the police conducted a search of Dale Astleford's home and found pornographic materials in a **darkroom** in his basement.

What is the difference in meaning and pronunciation between a darkroom, as in the Astleford case, and a dark room?

First, **darkroom** is a compound noun. Compound nouns are very common in English and can be written as one word, as one hyphenated word, or sometimes as two separate words. You should check a dictionary if you are unsure which is the preferred way to spell the word. Instead **dark room** is two separate words, an adjective and a noun; the adjective describes the noun that follows. A darkroom (compound word), as explained in the Vocabulary and Legal Terminology section, is a room with no light that is used to develop photographs. In contrast, a dark room is a room (any room) that is dark, but not because it is used to develop photographs but because the lights are turned off, or the windows are closed, or because it is nighttime.

While it might seem to you that the compound word *darkroom* and the two words *dark room* would be pronounced the same way, they are not. The pronunciation changes depending on which word you use and the sense of what you are saying. If you pronounce the word incorrectly, the meaning of the word and the sentence change, and you risk confusing your listener.

In the compound word, both syllables are stressed, but the first part of the word (dark) receives the primary stress:

> ➤ I developed my pictures from our vacation in a DARKroom in my father's house.

In the adjective + noun pair, the pronunciation changes. The noun, or the second word, takes the primary stress:

> ➤ I am a light sleeper so I close all the blinds and drapes and make sure I am in a dark ROOM before I go to sleep.

Below is another example of word pairs that seem identical in meaning and in pronunciation but are not. What is the difference in meaning between these two sentences, the first of which has a compound noun and the primary stress on the first syllable, and the second of which is an adjective + noun pair, with the primary stressed syllable on the noun or the second word?

> *He lives in a GREENhouse.*

> *He lives in a green HOUSE.*

The first sentence, with the primary stress on GREEN, means that the man lives in a greenhouse, a glass building that is kept warm and in which plants that need protection from the weather are grown. That would certainly be strange as not many people live in greenhouses!

In the second sentence, with the primary stress on HOUSE, the man lives not in a white, or blue, or brown house, but in a green house. The difference in meaning changes significantly just because the stress of the word changes from the first syllable to the second.

Here are some other examples to show you how it works. What is the difference between the pronunciation and the meaning of these pairs of words? While saying the words, pay particular attention to where the primary stressed syllable goes. Note that not all of the pairs include a compound word.[90]

---

[90] See generally, *Stress in Compound Words*, Useful English, http://usefulenglish.ru/phonetics/stress-in-compound-words (last visited May 27, 2016) for additional information about the different pronunciations of the compound word compared to the noun + adjective.

BLACKboard	black BOARD
EVEning dress	evening SKY
SINGing lesson	singing GIRL
MOBile phone	mobile PERson
STONE Age	stone BUILDing
HOT dog	hot TEA
PAPer knife	paper BAG
SUMmertime	summer CLOTHES
NIGHT school	night HOURS
SOFTware	soft PILLOW
HARDware	hard ROCK

Unit 2 Defamation

Herlihy v. The Metropolitan Museum of Art,
633 N.Y.S.2d 106 (N.Y. App. Div. 1995).

Vocabulary and Legal Terminology

Actionable: An act or occurrence that provides grounds for a lawsuit.[91]

To aver: To allege or claim.

Whore: A vulgar term for a prostitute.

To assert: To allege or claim.

Rosh Hashanah: An important Jewish holiday that marks the Jewish New Year.

Reprimand: A strong warning.

Purportedly: Allegedly.

To get to be: To become.

To interpose: To bring (a claim).

Untenable: Unable to be defended.

To bolster: To strengthen.

Widespread: Spread or distributed over a large area or region.

To cloak: To cover.

To shelter: To provide protection.

Denunciation: A formal accusation made against someone.

Vituperative: Very strong criticism; a verbal or written attack.

Cross: Angry, annoyed.

Brazen: Shameless.

---

[91] *Actionable*, Gilbert's Pocket Size Law Dictionary (3rd ed. 2014).

Herlihy v. The Metropolitan Museum of Art, 633 N.Y.S.2d 106 (N.Y. App. Div. 1995)

Pre-Reading Questions

Before you begin reading, skim the caption and first paragraph and answer the following questions:

1. Is the case in federal or state court?
2. Who are the parties in the case and what is their relationship?
3. What claim did the plaintiff bring against the defendants?
4. Who filed a motion in the district court?
5. What did the district court decide?
6. Who appealed?
7. What did the appellate court decide?

Comprehension Questions

With a general idea of the case in your mind, you can now read the case. As you are reading and after you finish reading, answer the following questions:

1. Summarize in your own words the issue in this case.
2. Summarize in your own words the facts of this case that led to the dispute.
3. What are the two types of privilege?
   a. _____
   b. _____
4. Write the rule stated by the court regarding absolute privilege: _____
   _____
5. What is qualified privilege? _____
   _____
6. What public policy supports cloaking some statements, which would otherwise be defamatory, with a privilege? _____
7. Can absolute privilege be lost? If yes, how? _____
   _____
8. Can qualified privilege be lost? If yes, how? _____
   _____
9. Which type of privilege is more common and why? _____
   _____
10. What are examples of when a communication may be protected by a qualified privilege?
11. What is malice in the context of a defamation case?
12. How does a plaintiff prove that a statement was made with malice?

13. In the Herlihy case, why did the court conclude that the statements made by the volunteer defendants were not protected by privilege?

14. Why did the court conclude that the statements were defamatory *per se*?

15. How does this case apply to ours?

16. Is this case useful for the plaintiff, Fran Beaumont, or the defendant, Pamela Park? Why?

17. If Park were to use the privilege defense in the claim Beaumont brought against her, which privilege would she raise: absolute or qualified? Why? _____
_____
_____

18. Would Park be successful in raising this privilege? Why or why not? _____
_____

Language Focus — U.S. vs. U.K. English

In the Herlihy case, the court cites an early New York case (1810), Yates v. Lansing, to explain the origins of the doctrine of absolute privilege and how the defense to defamation claims is rooted in English law and forms an important part of English and American common law.

> Absolute privilege is an ancient doctrine. Long recognized by English law as a means to protect freedom of speech and deliberation in Parliament, it was later embodied in American Constitution so that our legislators would enjoy an uninhibited range of freedom to propose, oppose, debate, adopt or reject ideas as precursors to legislative action. By a parallel development in the judicial sphere it has served to bolster our Judges' freedom to act without fear or ***favor*** in the furtherance of a "vigorous and independent administration of justice.

Note in the last sentence the italicized word, *favor*. Even though the Herlihy and the Yates courts were discussing this originally English doctrine of absolute privilege, you see that the court used the American spelling, ***favor*** instead of ***favour***, which is the spelling used in the U.K.

This spelling difference — words that end is -*or* in American English are spelled with -*our* in U.K. English — is one of the differences between British and American English.

American English	British English
Favor	Favour
Color	Colour
Neighbor	Neighbour
Behavior	Behaviour

What other differences are there between U.S. and U.K. English? In terms of spelling, words that end in –*er* in American English end in –*re* in British English.[92]

---

[92] Other regional varieties of English such as Canadian, Indian, Australian, or Irish English tend to follow British English in terms of spelling.

American English	British English
Theater	Theatre
Center	Centre
Liter	Litre
Caliber	Calibre

Second, words that end in *–ize* or *–ization* in American English end in *–ise* or *–isation* in British English:

American English	British English
Organize/organization	Organise/organisation
Realize/realization	Realise/realisation
Recognize	Recognise

Third, some words that end in *–se* in American English end in *–ce* in British English:

American English	British English
Defense	Defence
Pretense	Pretence
Offense	Offence

But, for words that change between the noun and verb based on whether the word ends in *–ce* or *–se*, American and British English are the same: advice (noun) – advise (verb) and device (noun) – devise (verb).

Next, British English has kept the irregular past for some verbs for which American English has changed to a regular past:

American English	British English
Burned	Burnt
Learned	Learnt
Dreamed	Dreamt
Spelled	Spelt
Spoiled	Spoilt
Spilled	Spilt

British English uses double consonants in many situations in which American English uses only a single consonant:

American English	British English
Jewelry	Jewellry
Traveler/traveled	Traveller/travelled
Canceled	Cancelled
Counselor	Counsellor
Modeled	Modelled

Finally,[93] there are a few other spelling differences worth noting:

American English	British English
Gray	Grey
Draft	Draught
Plow	Plough
Program	Programme
Pajamas	Pyjamas

What about grammar? Here, we can find some grammatical differences between British and American English:

Plural vs. Singular Verbs:

Speakers of British English use a plural verb when discussing a collective noun, while American speakers use the singular:

British: The government are trying to pass legislation to raise the minimum wage.[94]
American: The government is trying to pass legislation to raise the minimum wage.[95]

British: Many say that the Real Madrid soccer team are the best in the world.
American: Many say that the Real Madrid soccer team is the best in the world.

Definite Article "The:"

There are a few expressions in which British English does not use the definite article *the*, while American English does:

British: My father was admitted to hospital yesterday afternoon.
American: My father was admitted to the hospital yesterday afternoon.

---

[93] Finally at least for our purposes here. There are many other words that are spelled differently that aren't included here for space reasons. Many online sources provide full lists of words, and you are encouraged to go online to learn more about the differences between the two varieties of English.

[94] *See, e.g.*, Sisters Uncut, *The Government are Quietly Asking Women Refuges to Close*, Politics.co.uk., http://www.politics.co.uk/comment-analysis/2016/03/31/the-government-are-quietly-forcing-women-s-refuges-to-close (last visited May 2, 2016).

[95] *See, e.g.*, Margaret Chadbourn, *Why the Government is Redesigning the $10 Bill*, ABC News, http://abcnews.go.com/News/government-redesigning-10-bill/story?id=38028973 (last visited May 2, 2016).

British: How long have you been at university?
American: How long have you been at the university?

Use of shall:

With the exceptions of contracts, statutes and regulations, Americans use *shall* much less often than British speakers do. When used in the U.S., it sounds affected and formal.

British: I shall call you tomorrow.
American: I will call you tomorrow.

British: Shall we go?
American: Do you want to go?

Present Perfect vs. Past Simple:

British English tends to use the present perfect tense more often than American English, and in place of the present perfect, American speakers will use the past simple. Americans replace the present perfect with the past simple in particular in two situations:

1. When the past action has an effect on the present.

British: I've *lost* my keys. *Have* you *seen* them anywhere?
American: I *lost* my keys. *Did* you *see* them anywhere?

British: Look at the huge puddles outside! I can't believe how much it *has rained*!
American: Look at the huge puddles outside! I can't believe how much it *rained*!

2. When we use the words *just, already* or *yet*.

British: *Have* you already *done* your homework?
American: *Did* you already *do* your homework?

British: I'd love to go to dinner with you, but I've just *eaten*. I'll take a rain check!
American: I'd love to go to dinner with you, but I just *ate*. I'll take a rain check!

British: *Have* you *seen* the new Star Wars movie yet?
American: *Did* you *see* the new Star Wars movie yet?

Have Got vs. Have

When asking a question with the verb *to have*, British and American speakers often phrase the question differently, with British speakers more likely to use *have got*, while American speakers tend to use *do/does* instead:

British: *Have* you *got* $10 that I can borrow? Yes, I have.
American: *Do* you *have* $10 that I can borrow? Yes, I do.

Got vs. Gotten

Brits use *got* as the past participle of to get, while Americans (or Yankees, as some say!) tend to use *gotten*:

British: A famous cricket player has got married, and the news was all over social media![96]
American: Did you see that no celebrities have gotten married recently?

Prepositions:

There are often differences in the prepositions that are used in British and American English:

British: What are you doing *at* the weekend?
American: What are you doing *on* the weekend? OR What are you doing this weekend?

British: They live *in* Main Street.
American: They live *on* Main Street.

British: *At* Christmas, many families stay at home in the morning to open presents.
American: *On* Christmas, many families stay at home in the morning to open presents.

British: Law schools in the United States are different *to/from* law schools in my country.
American: Law schools in the United States are different *than/from* law schools in my country.

In sum, the differences between the English spoken on both sides of the Atlantic are minor in terms of spelling and grammar, while the differences in terms of vocabulary and accent are more significant. As an ESL student, how do you know whether you should follow and use American or British English? As many answers in the law, it depends. Neither American nor British English (or any version for that matter) is better, and using one version of English instead of another is not wrong or less correct.

If you are making a personal decision, choose the version that you like best, or the version of the country where you will study and work. Americans use American spellings and usages while in the United States, and Brits use British English spelling, usages and vocabulary while in their home country. As an ESL student, you should adapt to the country in which you live and be consistent. Don't use a mix of both American and British spellings in the same document. As for grammar, the differences are so slight that most people don't even know the differences, with the exception of "shall," which sounds overly formal to American ears (except in the context of contracts).

If you are working for a law firm in your home country and dealing with international clients, first find out if the law firm has a policy. Some firms might require attorneys to stick to British spelling when dealing with clients from the U.K. or American spelling with a U.S. client, while other firms might not have a specific policy and it is up to you to decide and be consistent.

---

[96] Luxman, *Famous Cricketer Irfan Pathan has got married Jeddah based model Safa Baig*, 24 NEWS SPOT, http://24newsspot.com/politics/famous-cricketer-irfan-pathan-has-got-married-jeddah-based-model-safa-baig-1552/ (last visited May 2, 2016).

Baldwin v. Shell Oil Co.,
419 N.Y.S.2d 752 (N.Y. App. Div. 1979).

Vocabulary and Legal Terminology

Cross motion: When both parties file the same motion with the court, both requesting the same relief.

To supersede: To take the place of something.

Costs and disbursements: Expenses and money paid from an account or fund.

To sound in: To be based on.

To recapitulate: To restate.

To attach: (here) To protect.

To rectify: To fix or make correct.

Astonished: Very surprised.

Incensed: Very angry.

To reinstate: To return someone to his original job.

Deterioration: The process of becoming gradually worse.

Gratuity: Tip given to a waiter, taxi driver or other service provider.

Incumbent: Imposed as a duty or responsibility.

Pre-Reading Questions

Before you begin reading, skim the caption and first paragraph and answer the following questions:

1. Is the case in federal or state court?
2. Who are the parties and what is their relationship?
3. What claim did the plaintiff bring?
4. What motion was filed and who filed it?
5. What did the district court decide with regard to the motion?
6. Who appealed and what did the appellate court decide with regard to the motion?
7. Did the appeals court decide that the statements were defamatory? If not, what did the court decide?

Comprehension Questions

With a general idea of the case in your mind, you can now read the case. As you are reading and after you finish reading, answer the following questions:

1. Summarize in your own words the facts of this case.
2. Summarize the procedural history with regard to the complaint, the motions, the argument, and the appeal to the Appellate Division.
3. Why did the trial court dismiss all of the plaintiff's causes of action? (hint: look at the paragraph that begins with **754) _____
4. According to the appellate court, what factual dispute exists to justify the reversal of the granting of defendant's motion for summary judgment? _____
5. If a plaintiff is trying to prove malice, what type of facts would he or she try to find during discovery? _____
6. What facts will Fran Beaumont use to demonstrate that Park acted with malice in communicating the defamatory statements to Timothy? _____
7. What facts will Park use to rebut Beaumont's arguments as to malice? _____
8. How is this case useful for our case?
9. Is it more useful for the plaintiff or the defendant? Why?

Language Review — Direct vs. Indirect Speech

In English, when we are reporting what someone has said we use either *direct speech* or *indirect speech*.

Direct speech: When we are reporting exactly what someone else (or we) said, we use direct speech:

> In his inaugural address on January 20, 1961, President John F. Kennedy said, "Ask not what your country can do for you — ask what you can do for your country."

This is an example of direct speech because we are reporting exactly what President Kennedy said, and we use quotation marks around his words to indicate to the reader that those were his exact words.

Indirect speech: Instead, indirect speech is used when we are speaking about the past and about what someone has said. We normally change the tense of the verbs when we use indirect speech, and we don't use quotation marks. Look at these examples from the Baldwin v. Shell Oil Co. case:

> Respondent McGloin states that at the meeting [he *was asked*] whether appellant *had* ever *made* use of a concealed tape recorder [and] whether appellant *had* keys to a cabinet in McGloin's office where confidential records were kept.

McGloin states that later that same day he, not the appellant, spoke with Mr. Dorries who *informed* him that appellant *could not be dismissed* summarily.

Compare these two sentence with the two sentences below to see if you can find the grammatical pattern for how the verbs change from direct to indirect speech:

At the meeting, he was asked, "Have you ever made use of a concealed tape recorder? Have you ever had keys to a cabinet in McGloin's office where confidential records are kept?"

McGloin stated, "Baldwin cannot be dismissed summarily."

Below you will find a table with the verb changes listed for you, as well as examples of the verbs in use, in both direct and indirect speech.

Direct Speech	Example	Indirect Speech	Example
Simple present	He said, "My son *lives* in Washington D.C.."	Simple past	He said that his son *lived* in Washington D.C..
Present continuous	He told me, "I *am eating* very well these days."	Past continuous	He told me that he *was eating* very well these days.
Past simple	In his inaugural address, JFK said, "[T]he same revolutionary beliefs for which our forebears *fought are* still at issue around the globe."	Past perfect	JFK said in his inaugural address that the same revoluntiary beliefs for which our forefathers *had fought were* still at issue around the globe.
Future will (and past simple in example)	In his inaurugal address in 1933, Franklin Delano Roosevelt said, "I *will* return the courage and the devotion that *befit* the time. I *can* do no less."	Would	In his inaugural address in 1933, Franklin Delano Roosevelt said that he *would* return the courage and devotion that *befitted* the time, and that he *could* do no less.
Present perfect	Near the end of World War II, FDR told the nation in his fourth inaugural address in January 1945, "We *have learned* that we *cannot* live alone, at peace; that our own well-being *is* dependent on the well-being of other nations far away... We *have learned* to be citizens of the world, members of the human community."	Past perfect	In his fourth inaugural address in January 1945, FDR said that the nation *had learned* that we *could not* live alone, that our own well-being *was* dependent on the well-being of other nations far away and that we *had learned* how to be members of the human community.

Buckley v. Litman,
443 N.E.2d 469 (N.Y. 1982).

Vocabulary and Legal Terminology

Carbon copy: A copy of something, once made with carbon paper.

To engage: (here) To hire.

Debilitating: Something like an illness that makes someone very ill or weak.

To retain: To keep for oneself.

To utter: To speak or to say.

To warrant: To justify.

To tender proof: To offer evidence to the court in support of your claim or position.

Pre-Reading Questions

Before you begin reading, skim the caption and first paragraph and answer the following questions:
1. Is the case in federal or state court?
2. Who are the parties in the case and what is their relationship?
3. What claim did the plaintiff bring against the defendants?
4. Who filed a motion in the district court?
5. What did the district court decide?
6. Who appealed?
7. What did the state supreme court decide?

Comprehension Questions

With a general idea of the case in your mind, you can now read the case. As you are reading and after you finish reading, answer the following questions:
1. Summarize in your own words the issue in this case. _____
   _____
2. Summarize in your own words the facts of the case that led to the dispute. _____
   _____
3. According to the plaintiff, what language in the letter was defamatory? _____
   _____

4. Two letters were sent and read: one to the Licensure Board and one to Dr. Chalom. Why did the district court rule that the letter to Dr. Chalom was not privileged? _____

5. Why did the appellate court disagree? _____

6. What evidence did the plaintiff bring forward to demonstrate malice? _____

7. What is the "common interest" that the defendant shared with both the Board and Dr. Chalom? _____

8. How does this case apply to ours? _____

9. Is there a "common interest" between Park and her nephew, Timothy? Why or why not? _____

Language Focus — Latin Words and Phrases in Legal English

This sentence of the Buckley case includes a commonly used Latin phrase:

> The letter charged, *inter alia,* that plaintiff had stolen a large number of confidential clinical records without proper authorization.

The phrase *inter alia* means "among other things," and here tells you that the letter not only accused the plaintiff of stealing the confidential clinical records, but accused him of other things as well. *Inter alia* is one of the many Latin phrases and words that we use in legal writing. You have no doubt encountered others in the cases that you have read during your LL.M. program. If your native tongue is a Romance language (French, Spanish, Italian, Portuguese or Romanian), all of which derive from Latin, it is probably easier for you to understand these phrases and words, even if you don't use a dictionary. But if your native tongue is not one of these languages, or if your legal system does not routinely use Latin words and phrases, it can be difficult to understand them. However, it is important to understand these words and phrases since they are frequently used in legal English, although the trend nowadays is to use them less frequently or even to avoid them altogether.

The following table includes in the left-hand column some of the most commonly used Latin words and phrases in legal English. Complete the blank spaces in the other columns with the translation and meaning of the Latin word or phrase, as well as the area of law that it is used in.

Latin Term	Translation	Area of Law Used In	Meaning
Nolo contendere	"I do not wish to contend"	Criminal law	Plea in criminal cases, defendant does not admit guilt but subjects him/herself to punishment as if a guilty plea were entered or he/she were found guilty
Pari passu			
Per stirpes		Property law	

Latin Term	Translation	Area of Law Used In	Meaning
Pro bono	"for the public good"	All areas of law	When an attorney provides free legal services to individuals or organizations that otherwise could not afford it
Pro temp			
Sua sponte		All litigation (civil and criminal)	
Res judicata	"for a matter already adjudicated"	Civil procedure	Also called claim preclusion; when a claim has already been adjudicated (a final decision issued) and can no longer be appealed or litigated
Ultra vires			
Respondeat superior	"Let the master respond"	Agency and employment law	Doctrine under which the employer or principal is held legally liable for the actions of its employee or its agent done during the course of employment
De facto			
De iure			
Quid pro quo		Employment law (sexual harassment)	
Ad hoc	"for this"	All areas (and not only law)	Something such as a committee created for a specific use or purpose: *The ad hoc committee met to discuss the recent increase in crime on campus.*
Ad hominem			
Caveat emptor		Torts	
Inter vivos		Wills and trusts	
Locus delicti	"the place of the crime"	Criminal law	
In camera		All litigation (civil and criminal)	
In limine		All litigation (civil and criminal)	
Amicus curiae		Appeals	
Ex post facto			
Habeas corpus		Criminal law	

Byam v. Collins,
19 N.E. 75 (N.Y. 1888).

Vocabulary and Legal Terminology

Flood-gates: In a figurative sense, something that allows something else, usually negative, to happen.

Officious intermeddling: To take interest in something in which one has no interest, and in an annoyingly authoritative way.

To be apt to: To be inclined or to have a tendency to act in a certain way.

Estranged: To no longer be friendly with someone.

In pursuance of: The act of carrying out something.

Averment: Claim or allegation.

To subserve: To be useful or helpful.

Imputation: Accusation.

Door-latch: The device for holding a door closed.

Disparagement: Statement that describes another person in a negative way.

Reproach: Criticism; disapproval.

Pre-Reading Questions

Before you begin reading, skim the caption and first paragraph and answer the following questions:
1. Is the case in federal or state court?
2. What are the general facts of the case?
3. What claim did the plaintiff bring against the defendants?
4. What did the New York Court of Appeals (i.e. the New York supreme court) decide? (when you continue reading, you will learn what happened at the district court).

Comprehension Questions

With a general idea of the case in your mind, you can now read the case. As you are reading and after you finish reading, answer the following questions:
1. After reading the first four paragraphs of the case, what strikes you as unusual about the structure of this case, especially when compared to modern-day cases?

2. Summarize in your own words the facts of this case that led to the dispute.
   a. Who are the parties involved?
   b. What were their relationships?
   c. Who said what to whom, and on whose urging or request?
   d. What did that party request to be told?
   e. What damages did the plaintiff suffer from any alleged defamation?

3. Who decides whether a statement is protected by a qualified or absolute privilege? The judge or the jury? Identify in the case the sentence that tells you this. _____
   _____
   _____
   _____

4. Who decides whether the privilege was lost? The judge or the jury? Identify in the case the sentence that tells you this. _____
   _____
   _____
   _____

5. When is a statement "malicious," or defamatory? _____
   _____
   _____
   _____

6. According to the court, what is the duty that all people have towards others? Do you agree? Why or why not?

7. Do you agree with the court that "the propensity to tale-bearing and slander is so strong among mankind?" Why or why not?

8. In the case, find the case law that the court uses to analogize and distinguish from the case at hand. How does the court use these cases to bolster its reasoning that the communications at issue were privileged?

9. Do you agree with the majority decision? Why or why not? _____
   _____
   _____
   _____

10. Why did the dissenting judge disagree with the majority's decision? _____
    _____
    _____
    _____

11. In analyzing these cases regarding qualified privilege, why is it important to determine whether the communication was made to a "person of interest" or one with a "common interest?"

12. How does this case apply to ours?

13. Is it more useful for Park or for Beaumont? Why?

Language Focus — Figures of Speech and Metaphors

A figure of speech is "a rhetorical device that achieves a special effect by using words in distinctive ways."[97] Using figures of speech in your writing adds interest and effect and keeps the reader interested in what you have to say.[98] While there are hundreds of figures of speech that you can use in your writing, one of the most common is a metaphor.

The Byam case contains the following three examples of metaphors, which have been italicized. By analyzing the italicized words, what do you think a metaphor is?

> [O]rdinarily one cannot with safety, however free he may be from actual malice, as a volunteer, *pour the poison of such rumors into the ears* of one who might be affected if the rumors were true.

> Their intimacy continued after the marriage of Mrs. Collins until January before the letter was written, when *a coldness sprang up* between them.

> The rule as to privileged communications should not be so extended as to *open wide the floodgates of injurious gossip and defamation*.

A metaphor is a figure of speech in which an implied comparison is made for stylistic effect between two different things that are unrelated but share something important in common.[99]

In the first sentence, the evil effect (poison) of gossip or rumors can't really be poured into someone's ears since we can't touch, let alone pour, words. But by comparing rumors or gossip to a liquid that is poured into someone's ears when the defamatory statements are heard, the idea of spreading rumors becomes very vivid in our mind.

The creative imagery certainly makes for more interesting reading than if the judge in the Byam case had written: "*Ordinarily one cannot with safety, however free he may be from actual malice, as a volunteer, communicate defamatory statements of one who might be affected if the statements were true.*"

In the second sentence, a coldness, or a distance between two previously close friends, can't really jump. A person can jump, as can a cat or other animal. But coldness isn't even a thing, let alone an animate being that can move or jump. But by comparing the coldness that arose between Dora and Mrs. Collins to something that suddenly emerged between them, the judge creates again in the mind of the reader a vivid and creative image, much more so than if he had said "*when Mrs. Collins and Dora grew distant.*"

How can you analyze and describe the metaphor in the third sentence above?

Now that you know what metaphors are, start to look at them as you read cases for your classes[100] and other writings in English, whether newspaper articles or books. You will likely be surprised at how many you see!

---

[97] Richard Nordquist, *Top 20 Figures of Speech*, About Education, http://grammar.about.com/od/rhetoricstyle/a/20figures.htm (last visited May 2, 2016).

[98] Id.

[99] Richard Nordquist, *What is a Metaphor?*, About Education, http://grammar.about.com/od/qaaboutrhetoric/f/faqmetaphor07.htm (last visited May 2, 2016).

[100] In fact, if you are taking or have taken constitutional law, you are very likely familiar with two of the most famous metaphors in that area of law: we talk about *the wall of separation* between church and state when dealing with the First Amendment and freedom of religion, and *the penumbra of rights* when discussing the right to privacy.

Van Wyck v. Aspinwall,
17 N.E. 190 (N.Y. 1858).

Vocabulary and Legal Terminology

Trustee: An individual responsible for managing a trust for the purposes for which it was established.

Spurious: Fake or fraudulent.

Adulterated: Impure, such as by the adding of additional ingredients.

Custom house: (also customs house or customhouse) Governmental office where duties are collected for goods imported into or exported out of the country.

To aver: To claim or allege.

To demur: To object in a pleading to the sufficiency at law of the opposing party's pleading. In modern civil procedure, parties no longer file a demurrer as it has been replaced by the motion to dismiss.[101]

Commendable: Something worthy of praise.

Legal canon: An accepted principle of law.

Pre-Reading Questions

Before you begin reading, skim the caption and first paragraph and answer the following questions:
1. Is the case in federal or state court?
2. What claim did the plaintiff bring against the defendants?
3. What facts led to the dispute?
4. What did the court of appeals decide?
5. Is it unusual that the first paragraph doesn't include what happened at the trial court?
6. What do you think happened at the trial court?

Comprehension Questions

With a general idea of the case in your mind, you can now read the case. As you are reading and after you finish reading, answer the following questions:
1. After reading the first four paragraphs of the case, what strikes you as unusual about the structure of this case, especially when compared to modern-day cases?

---

[101] *Demurrer*, Gilbert's Pocket Size Law Dictionary (3rd ed. 2014).

2. Were you correct about your prediction about what happened at the trial court?

3. Now that you have read the first four paragraphs, summarize what happened at the district court. _____
_____

4. Summarize in your own words the facts of this case that led to the dispute.

5. What is the main issue before the court of appeals? _____
_____

6. Why did the court in this case decide that the statements in the report, although defamatory, were privileged and thus protected against a claim? _____
_____
_____

7. Why did the court in this case conclude that the defendants were acting "in good faith?" _____
_____

8. One reason for finding privilege was that the statements regarded a "public interest." Do all defamatory statements, to be privileged and thus protected, have to regard a "public interest?" Why or why not? _____
_____

9. The court also says that the "occasion of the publication" repels or rejects the inference of malice. What was the "occasion of publication" and why was it so important in finding that there was no malice? _____
_____

10. How do the answers to questions 7, 8 and 9 apply to our case? _____
_____

11. How does this case apply to ours?

12. Is it more useful for Park or for Beaumont? Why?

Language Focus — Placement of Prepositions

Prepositions are words like *on*, *for*, *under* and *through*. In English, prepositions usually go (or are supposed to go) before the noun that they accompany, hence the name *preposition*. *Pre* is a Latin prefix that means *before*.

> I put the book *on the table*.
> The attorneys waited for the subway *at the 95th Avenue station*.

In these sentences, the italicized words form prepositional phrases, made of a preposition (*on* and *at*) followed by a noun. True to their name, the prepositions all go before the noun.

Some languages don't even have prepositions as they place words like *on* and *in* after the noun or pronoun they refer to rather than before. So rather than prepositions, they are called postpositions (post is Latin for *after*).[102] English has one example of a postposition: I bought my first car fifteen years

---
[102] Gaston Dorren, Lingo: Around Europe in Sixty Languages 182 (2015).

ago.[103] Ago is placed after the phrase that it refers to and is thus a postposition. To express *ago*, does your native tongue use a preposition or a postposition? What about other words that are prepositions in English? In your native language, what placement do they have in a sentence?

Look at these sentences from the Van Wyck case:

> The subject matter of the publication was pertinent to the object *for which* the committee had been appointed.

> The investigation which the defendants had been directed to make, and the result of which is contained in the report, was within the purposes *for which* the College of Pharmacy had been incorporated, and involved matters of public interest.

Here, the prepositions precede the relative pronoun. However, in everyday spoken English, we rarely use prepositions as they are meant to be used, i.e. before the relative pronoun, as here.

If I were speaking, or writing something less formal than a legal document, I would write the above sentences like this:

> The subject matter of the publication was pertinent to the object *that* the committee had been appointed *for*.[104]

> The investigation that the defendants had been directed to make, and that result contained in the report, was within the purposes *that* the College of Pharmacy had been incorporated *for* and involved matters of public interest.

What you note is that the phrase *for which* is separated, with the *which* becoming *that*, and the preposition moving to the end of the sentence or phrase. You have probably seen this phenomenon in other places:

For whom are you waiting?	⟶ Who are you waiting for? (whom becomes who, and the preposition moves to the end of the sentence)
Against which defendants did you file claims?	⟶ Which defendants did you file claims against?
To which city are you moving?	⟶ What (or which) city are you moving to?
To whom did your sister get married?	⟶ Who did your sister get married to?

---

[103] Id.
[104] Actually, an even better revision of this sentence is this: The subject matter of the publication was pertinent to the purpose of the committee.

| The city to which I moved last year is very nice. | → | The city that I moved to last year is very nice. (which becomes that, and the preposition moves to the end of the relative clause (that I moved to))[138] |

In this list of examples, the second sentence, with the preposition at the end of the sentence or the relative clause, is more informal and used in everyday, spoken English. It is unusual for someone to say *to which* or *for whom* or similar phrases in everyday conversation.

But the writing that we do as lawyers is often formal, and we often use the formal structure of preposition + *whom/which/where* rather than the informal construction of moving the preposition to the end of the sentence or the end of the relative clause. Of course that is a general rule and as always in the law, it depends. If you are writing a brief or memo to submit to the court, it is recommended that you follow the more formal format of preposition + relative pronoun.

Instead, if you are writing an email to a colleague, senior partner or a client, you will likely use the more informal, everyday format and put the preposition at the end of the sentence or clause and use *who*, *what* or *that*. In correspondence, it will likely depend on who you are writing to (or to whom you are writing) and the register (level of formality, tone) that you want to give to your document. This is a choice that you make as a writer.

---

[105] When the preposition begins a relative clause, it moves only to the end of the relative clause, not to the end of the sentence: The car in which he was driving was hit by another car. The car that he was driving in was hit by another car. NOT: ~~The car that he was driving was hit by another car in.~~

Unit 3: Constitutional Right to Privacy

State v. Boland,
800 P.2d 1112 (Wash. 1990).

Vocabulary and Legal Terminology

Legend drugs: Drugs that under federal law cannot be obtained without a doctor's prescription.

Power records: The records from the companies or agencies that distribute electricity, gas or other utilities and that show where someone lives (by showing where he/she has an account for such utilities).

Motion to suppress evidence: A motion filed in a criminal case by which the moving party asks the court to not include (suppress) certain pieces of evidence for reasons such as the evidence being seized without a warrant or in some other unlawful way.

"Fruit of the warrantless search:" Criminal procedure doctrine under which all evidence that was the result (the fruit) of a search done illegally (such as without a warrant) should be excluded or suppressed.

Pen register: A device that records all numbers dialed or received from a certain phone.

Scavengers: People who search for lost treasure or other items.

Snoops: People who secretly investigate another person, looking for private information or items.

To sift through: To go through something very carefully while looking for something of value.

Rummage through: To search thoroughly a space while looking for something, often by moving other items.

Telltale refuse: Garbage that reveals or indicates something (in the case, evidence of drugs).

Inculpatory: (here, evidence) Evidence that shows or indicates someone's guilt or involvement in a crime.

Indeterminative: Something undefined or indefinite.

State v. Boland, 800 P.2d 1112 (Wash. 1990) **143**

Pre-Reading Questions

Before you begin reading, skim the caption and first paragraph and answer the following questions:

1. Is the case in federal or state court?
2. What motion was filed at the district court? Who filed it?
3. What did the district court decide with regard to the motion, and what effect did that ruling have on the case?
4. Who appealed?
5. What did the court of appeals decide?
6. Who appealed to the state supreme court?
7. What did the state supreme court decide? Why?
8. Did the supreme court base its decision on state or federal grounds? Why might this matter?
9. Put into your own words what you know about the case so far, both for the facts of the case and the legal facts.

Comprehension Questions

With a general idea of the case in your mind, you can now read the case. As you are reading and after you finish reading, answer the following questions:

1. Summarize in your own words the facts of this case.
    a. Why did the police first suspect Boland of dealing in drugs? _____

    b. What steps did they take while investigating him? _____

2. What is your opinion about the police's conduct, for example that they observed the suspect and searched his garbage at night without a warrant? Does that seem like the police were acting justly and in good faith? _____

3. This case presents very interesting discussions of policy and of federalism. Under our system of federalism, all states have their own constitution. Yet, the court conducts a careful analysis under the Gunwall case before deciding whether the state grounds can be applied to the case and whether those constitutional grounds can provide greater protection than the federal law.
    a. What is the purpose of the Gunwall criteria? _____

    b. Why is it so important for the court to analyze these factors when a state can and does have its own laws and constitutions? Shouldn't the state be allowed to interpret its constitution as it wants? _____

    c. What are the two Gunwall criteria that the court examines? Summarize in your own words why, according to the majority decision, those criteria were met. _____

4. What policy arguments support extending a constitutional right to privacy to garbage left outside for collection? _____
_____
_____

5. And on the other hand, what policy arguments can be made *against* extending this right to garbage?
_____
_____

6. Look on page 1117 of the majority decision. You have learned that U.S. Supreme Court precedent is binding upon all state courts. But in this case, the court declares the U.S. Supreme Court case of Greenwood as an "important guide" to be followed. But the court chooses not to. Why in this case is the Supreme Court precedent only a "guide" and not binding?

7. Although written by only one judge, the dissenting opinion is quite passionate about the issue and how the majority has decided the case incorrectly.
    a. How does the dissent distinguish the ordinances that the majority claims show the privacy interest in garbage?
    b. How does the dissent interpret the phrase "private affairs?"
    c. Who has better support of other state courts with regard to this issue?
    d. Should the number of courts on one side of a decision matter? Is it a game of numbers?

8. What is your opinion about this case? Do you agree with the majority decision? Why or why not?

9. How is this case useful for our case of the City of Longworth? How can you use it for your client's arguments?

10. Is the case more helpful for the plaintiffs or the defendants? Why?

11. What arguments can you make to analogize or distinguish it from our case?

Language Focus — Pronunciation

You are an LL.M. student at a U.S. law school. To arrive at this point, you have studied English extensively, and you are well aware of the difficulties and perhaps absurdities of English spelling and pronunciation. This poem, attributed to T.S. Watt and first published in the Manchester Guardian in 1954, sums it up well. Can you pronounce all of the words in the poem? Perfecting the pronunciation of the words is not easy and will underscore how difficult English can be!

Brush Up Your English

I take it you already know
Of tough and bough and cough and dough.
Others may stumble but not you,
On hiccough, thorough, lough and through.
Well done! And now you wish, perhaps,
To learn of less familiar traps.
Beware of heard, a dreadful word

> That looks like beard and sounds like bird,
> And dead—it's said like bed, not bead.
> For goodness's sake, don't call it deed!
> Watch out for meat and great and threat:
> They rhyme with suite and straight and debt.
>
> A moth is not a moth in mother,
> Nor both in bother, broth in brother,
> And here is not a match for there,
> Nor dear and fear for bear and pear,
> And then there's dose and rose and lose—
> Just look them up--and goose and choose,
> And cork and work and card and ward,
> And font and front and word and sword,
> And do and go and thwart and cart.
> Come, come, I've hardly made a start.
>
> A dreadful language? Man alive,
> I'd mastered it when I was five.

The Boland case provides us a good example of an important distinction in pronunciation between a noun and a verb that are spelled the same, yet pronounced very differently.

> People reasonably believe that police will not indiscriminately rummage through their trash bags to discover their personal effects. Business records, bills, correspondence, magazines, tax records, and other telltale **refuse** can reveal much about a person's activities, associations, and beliefs.

Refuse as used here is a noun that means garbage. The pronunciation is /ˈref·jus/, and the stress is on the first syllable.

You are likely familiar with the verb *to refuse*. I refuse to do something that I don't want to do, or something that is uncomfortable. The pronunciation of the verb is /rɪˈfjuz/, and the stress is on the second syllable.

This pair of identical words — one a verb and the other a noun — follows a typical pattern: nouns take the stress on the first syllable, while verbs take the stress on the second syllable.

Here are two other words that are stressed differently, depending on whether they are used as a noun or a verb:

As a **noun**, the stress goes on the first syllable:

> I placed the object on the table.
>   /
> /ob ject/

But as a **verb**, the stress goes on the second syllable:

> I object to opposing party trying to introduce prejudicial evidence against my client.
> /
> / ob ject/

Here are some more pairs. Practice saying them out loud and make up practice sentences so you can practice where the stress is placed.

Conflict

Record

Permit

Research

Export

Recount

Suspect

There are many other pairs too! Do some searching online to find a list of them and then practice the pronunciation. Online dictionaries also have audio recordings of how words are pronounced if you are unsure and want to compare your pronunciation to that of a native speaker.

State v. Sweeney,
107 P.3d 110 (Wash. Ct. App. 2005).

Vocabulary and Legal Terminology

Methamphetamine: A synthetic, simulant drug often manufactured in homes or other places, known as meth labs.

Hopper: A container used for storing loose material such as grain or garbage.

To haul away: To carry away.

Floater: A person who moves from job to job within a company, fulfilling different job duties.

To clean out: To thoroughly clean the inside of something.

Seminal: Landmark.

Curb: The border of a street where the street meets a yard.

Dumpster: A large container for trash.

Pre-Reading Questions

Before you begin reading, skim the caption, synopsis and holdings and answer the following questions:
1. Is the case in federal or state court?
2. What motion was filed at the district court? Who filed it?
3. What did the district court decide with regard to the motion, and what effect did that ruling have on the case?
4. Who appealed?
5. What did the court of appeals decide?

Comprehension Questions

With a general idea of the case in your mind, you can now read the case. As you are reading and after you finish reading, answer the following questions:
1. Summarize in your own words the facts of this case. _____
_____
2. Which facts were particularly important for the court when reaching its decision that Mr. Sweeney's right to privacy had been violated? _____
_____

3. According to the defendant, the state was trying to "circumvent" his constitutionally-protected rights by asking another government employee — the garbage collector — to collect the garbage for the search.
    a. Do you think that the police asked the Refuse Department to obtain the garbage at the defendant's residence for this reason? Why or why not?_____
    _____

    b. How were the police trying to circumvent or go around his constitutional rights?
    _____
    _____

4. Many cities have private companies that do the garbage collection, so the garbage collectors are private employees and in no way are related to the city government, except that their employer has a contract with the city government.
    a. How might the case or its outcome change if the garbage collector were a private employee? _____
    _____

5. Under the state constitution, summarize the expectations of privacy that individuals have in the garbage that they have placed out for collection. Do they seem reasonable to you? Why or why not? _____
    _____

6. How is this case useful for our case of the City of Longworth? How can you use it for your client's arguments? _____
    _____

7. Is the case more helpful for the plaintiffs or the defendants? Why?_____
    _____

8. What arguments can you make to analogize or distinguish it from our case? _____
    _____

Language Focus — Vague Use of Pronouns

Look at this sentence from the Sweeney case (the internal quotation marks and citations have been omitted):

> The [Boland] court further noted that Mr. Boland's trash was in his can and sitting on the curb in expectation that it would be picked up by a licensed garbage collector. Significantly, the court determined that this fact leads us to the conclusion that ***it*** falls squarely within the contemplated meaning of a private affair.

Examine in particular the use of the pronoun *it* in the second sentence. What does the *it* refer to? As you know, *it* is a third person singular pronoun so must refer to a third person singular noun. What are the third person singular nouns that the pronoun *it* could refer to? Garbage can? Licensed garbage collector? The garbage being picked up by a licensed garbage collector? Or something else?

You might conclude that it isn't particularly clear which noun it refers to. An uncertain or vague use of pronouns, such as *he, she, it* and *they*, and some relative adjectives like *this, that, these* and *those*, can create confusion in English. A pronoun refers to a specific noun. Thus, when reading a sentence, the reader should understand immediately which noun the pronoun refers to. Good English is clear, including for pronoun use.

Examine the following sentences and the use of the pronoun in each. Determine whether the sentence is written properly for pronoun usage or whether the pronoun usage is vague. If you think the sentence should be edited and revised, articulate why. Then if you determine that it is necessary to revise it, write the revised sentence.

1. If you place the letter from opposing counsel in the client file, you can refer to it later.
2. The client told her attorney that when she hit the tree with her car, it was damaged.
3. They stole her wallet but didn't take her computer or leather jacket, and it was sitting on the table unattended.
4. Someone who recently left the building left their umbrella in the lobby.
5. The judge told the attorney in front of her client that the memorandum didn't follow the court's rule for formatting and for page length. She was very angry.

State v. Graffius,
871 P.2d 1115 (Wash. Ct. App. 1994).

Vocabulary and Legal Terminology

Tip: (here) A helpful piece of advice or information.

Gravel: Small rocks or stone.

Driveway: A road leading from a private home or structure to a public street.

Ajar: Partially open.

Fist-sized: About the size and shape of a closed fist.

Tainted by: Contaminated or polluted by.

Curtilage: The area connected to and surrounding a house.

Blinders: Pieces of leather put on a horse's face, next to his eyes, to prevent him from looking to the side and becoming distracted; also used in a figurative sense to describe a person who doesn't observe what is happening around him.

Pre-Reading Questions

Before you begin reading, skim the caption and first paragraph and answer the following questions:

1. Is the case in federal or state court?
2. What motion was filed at the district court? Who filed it?
3. What did the district court decide with regard to the motion, and upon what did the court base its ruling?
4. Who appealed?
5. What did the court of appeals decide?

Comprehension Questions

With a general idea of the case in your mind, you can now read the case. As you are reading and after you finish reading, answer the following questions:

1. Summarize in your own words the facts of this case. _____
2. State in your own words the issue before the court. _____

3. How can a police officer violate an individual's constitutional right to privacy when conducting a search in a public area? _____

4. State in your own words what the "open view" doctrine means. _____

5. State the factors that a court must consider when assessing whether a police officer exceeded the "open view" scope. _____

6. How does the court analogize the <u>Seagull</u> case to the case at hand? _____

7. Should an officer's training (and the fact that he/she is trained to be more observant than an average citizen) play a role in determining whether a search was unreasonable or not? Should the court compare police and an average citizen when assessing an officer's actions in general? Why or why not? _____

8. How is this case useful for our case of the City of Longworth? How can you use it for your client's arguments? _____

9. Is the case more helpful for the plaintiffs or the defendants? Why? _____

10. What arguments can you make to analogize or distinguish it from our case? _____

Language Focus — Precision in Vocabulary

One characteristic of good writing is economy and precision. When one precise word will do, why use two in its place? One precise, specific word conveys your idea more economically and more efficiently. An economic and precise use of a word can be found in the <u>State v. Graffius</u> case:

> The lid was ajar on one can, creating an opening 6–8 inches wide.

As you learned in the Vocabulary and Legal Terminology section, ajar means partially open. Instead of using two words — partially open — we can use one word, more precise and specific, to describe the same thing.

Which of the two following sentences do you think is better? Why?

> She is very pretty.
> She is striking.

On the next page is a list of verbs with a qualifying adverb or phrase. Each of these verbs + the descriptive adverb or phrase can be expressed in one precise, specific verb. The more specific and descriptive words you learn, the richer your vocabulary and the deeper your understanding of English will be. Complete the list on the next page. The first verb has been done for you as an example.

To hit someone hard: _____to strike, to beat_____

To speak softly: _____

To speak loudly: _____

To cry very loudly: _____

To run at top speed for a short distance: _____

To pull something with effort: _____

To break into many pieces: _____

To do something with difficulty: _____

To eat rapidly: _____

To swallow something quickly and in a large amount: _____

To drive fast: _____

To sleep lightly: _____

State v. Rodriguez,
828 P.2d 636 (Wash. Ct. App. 1992).

Vocabulary and Legal Terminology

<u>Receptacle</u>: A container for storing something such as garbage.

<u>Gurney</u>: A bed-like table upon which patients are transported to or within a hospital.

<u>Machete</u>: A large knife, originally from Central America and the Caribbean.

<u>Suppression hearing</u>: A motion hearing at which the court considers a party's motion to suppress evidence (i.e. to rule that the evidence is inadmissible).

Pre-Reading Questions

Before you begin reading, skim the caption and first paragraph and answer the following questions:
1. Is the case in federal or state court?
2. What motion was filed at the district court? Who filed it?
3. What did the district court decide with regard to the motion, and upon what did the court base its ruling?
4. Who appealed?
5. What did the court of appeals decide?

Comprehension Questions

With a general idea of the case in your mind, you can now read the case. As you are reading and after you finish reading, answer the following questions:

1. Summarize in your own words the facts of this case. _____

2. State in your own words the issue before the court. _____

3. What facts does the court use to distinguish the <u>Boland</u> case from the case at hand? List the facts here: _____

4. In distinguishing <u>Boland</u> from the <u>Rodriguez</u> case, what do you learn about the importance of using facts in your analysis? _____

5. How is this case useful for our case of the City of Longworth? How can you use it for your client's arguments?

6. Is the case more helpful for the plaintiffs or the defendants? Why?

7. What arguments can you make to analogize or distinguish it from our case?

Language Focus — What Order Do We Put Adjectives In?

In the State v. Rodriquez case, the court states, "*Mr. Martinez heard the child say something about light brown clothing, light brown pants and light brown shirt.*"

How does the meaning of the sentence change if I say instead: "*Mr. Martinez heard the child say something about brown, light clothing, brown, light pants and a brown, light shirt?*"

Analyze the sentences and determine how the meaning and the description of the clothing change by changing the order of the adjectives light and brown and by using a comma between the two adjectives.

The answer that you should have reached is that in the first sentence, the brown color of the clothing is light, as opposed to a dark color. We know nothing about the weight or type of fabric, only that the brown color of the fabric is light.

But in the second sentence, the brown and light are both referring to and describing the clothing (pants, shirt). The pants are brown, and the pants are also light (meaning the fabric is not heavy in weight). The order of the adjectives and the use of the comma tell the reader that both adjectives refer to the noun (clothing, pants or shirt).

The question then arises of how do we know what order to put adjectives in? If we have three adjectives to describe a noun, which adjective goes first? Second? And which goes third?

Compare these three sentences and determine which sentence uses a correct order of adjectives.

1. The attorney submitted into evidence a medium-sized, blue wool sweater that the victim had been wearing when she was assaulted.
2. The attorney submitted into evidence a wool, blue, medium-sized sweater that the victim had been wearing when she was assaulted.
3. The attorney submitted into evidence a blue, wool, medium-sized sweater that the victim had been wearing when she was assaulted.

In a sentence with two or more adjectives that modify a noun, the adjectives in English must follow a precise order when the adjectives denote attributes or characteristics of the noun.

1. Quantity or number
2. Quality or opinion
3. Size
4. Age
5. Shape
6. Color
7. Proper adjective (often nationality, other place of origin, or material)
8. Purpose or qualifier

For example, we say *a blue, American* car. The attributes are color (6) and place of origin (7) in the list above. We also say *three, beautiful, large American sports cars*. The attributes are quantity (1), opinion (2), size (3), place of origin (7), and purpose (8).

Unit 4: LLC/Partnership Dispute

Anest v. Audino,
773 N.E.2d 202 (Ill. App. Ct. 2002).

Vocabulary and Legal Terminology

Inter alia: (Latin) Among other things.

Directed finding: (also known as directed verdict) A jury verdict ordered by the court. In civil cases, a party may receive a directed verdict if the opposite side does not present a prima facie case or a necessary defense.[106]

Tortious interference with business expectancy: A civil claim brought when the plaintiff alleges that the defendant intentionally interfered in a contract or business relationship between the plaintiff and a third party.

Case in chief: The part of a trial in which the party presents evidence to support its claim.

To levy: To impose a tax or a fee.

Want of service: Lack of proper service.

Memorandum of Understanding: (also known as letter of intent) A preliminary written statement that memorializes the important terms and conditions of an agreement.

Payable: Debts owed by a business.

Constructive trust: A trust held to exist by a court of equity against a person who obtains or holds legal title to property through fraud, abuse of confidence, or some other unconscionable conduct, that is, title which in good conscience he should not hold.[107]

Accounting: Action to obtain a statement of account, to clarify the rights of parties in a shared asset.[108]

To usurp: To take something wrongfully and by force.

---

[106] *Directed Verdict*, Gilbert's Pocket Size Law Dictionary (3rd ed. 2014).
[107] *Constructive*, Gilbert's Pocket Size Law Dictionary (3rd ed. 2014).
[108] *Accounting, Action of*, Gilbert's Pocket Size Law Dictionary (3rd ed. 2014).

Pre-Reading Questions

Before you begin reading, skim the caption and first paragraph and answer the following questions:

1. Is the case in federal or state court?
2. Who are the parties in the case and what is their relationship?
3. What claims did the plaintiff bring against the defendant?
4. What did the defendant do in response?
5. What happened at the district court?
6. Who appealed?
7. What did the appellate court decide and do with the case?

Comprehension Questions

With a general idea of the case in your mind, you can now read the case. As you are reading and after you finish reading, answer the following questions:

1. Summarize in your own words the facts that led to the dispute.
2. What did Anest do that led Audino to claim that he had breached his fiduciary duty?
3. What reasoning did the district court give for the decisions it reached regarding the claims of breach of fiduciary duty and tortious interference with business expectancy? _____
4. What was the "business expectancy" that Audino interfered with? _____
5. What duty do members of an LLC owe towards the LLC and towards other members? _____
6. State in your own words what the "corporate opportunity doctrine" is: _____
7. In the case, locate the paragraph that includes the rules regarding the corporate opportunity doctrine. How many rules are there? _____
8. In this case, how did Anest violate the corporate opportunity doctrine? _____
9. How is this case useful for our fact pattern?
10. What rules or reasoning can you use from this case to help you analyze the Desert Salon Suites, LLC case?

Language Focus — Difficult Prepositions

Learning prepositions in a foreign language is very difficult. In this ESL Workbook, you will find six exercises on prepositions in acknowledgment that they are often one of the most difficult aspects of learning and perfecting a foreign language.[109] It is easy to confuse prepositions that are similar in meaning and use the wrong one.

---

[109] The following Grammar Review and Language Focus exercises deal with prepositions (including phrasal verbs): Maxell, Inc. v. Kenney Deans, Inc. (p. 26); Regency Oaks Corp. v. Norman-Spencer McKernan, Inc. (p. 52); Cook v. Rockwell Int'l Corp. et al., v. Nuclear Reg. (p. 76); Van Wyck v. Apsinwall (p. 146); and Bishop v. TES Realty Trust (p. 295). You are encouraged to review and complete the exercises for further practice.

As a learner of English as a second language, you probably think that native speakers never make mistakes with their preposition use, and that only other non-native speakers use the wrong preposition. If that is what you think, don't be so hard on yourself!

Look at the sentences below from the Anest case. In the sentences, find the mistake in preposition usage. After you have identified the incorrect preposition, change the preposition to the correct one and explain the rule for the correct usage of the prepositions. Write your answers below.

> After the emergency meeting of Precision Pour, Teichner testified that another meeting took place among Anest, Teichner, and Schilling, at which they agreed to exercise the exclusive distributorship offer. Thus, on December 9, BLM Technologies, L.L.C. (BLM Technologies), was formed. The members of BLM Technologies and their percentage interests are as follows: Anest, 40%; Iseberg, 10%; Schilling, 25%; and Teichner, 25%. Anest was the company's manager, and he testified that he put up the necessary funds to secure the letter of credit required for BLM Technologies to become the exclusive distributor of the BLM 2000 in the United States and Canada.

Incorrect preposition: _____

Why it is incorrect: _____

Correct preposition in its place: _____

You should have identified that the judge incorrectly used *among* and should have used *between*. *Between* and *among* are very similar in meaning, but we use *between* when we are talking about or choosing between distinct, separate items, even if there are more than two. When we are talking about things that aren't distinct or separate, we use *among*. Here are some examples:

> After graduation, Paul got job offers from five different firms and had to make a difficult choice between them.

> After graduation, among all of his classmates, Paul was one of the few who had multiple job offers.

> Between Paris, Rome and Berlin, which city do you want to go to?

> Budapest stands among the most beautiful cities in Europe.[110]

Thus, in the sentence from the Anest case, the judge incorrectly used *among* because the meeting was held between three individuals, all of whom are identified and distinct.

Below you will find other commonly confused preposition pairs. If you are unsure of the difference between the two prepositions, do some online research to discover the nuances between the words. Then write sample sentences that demonstrate your understanding of the two prepositions and the slight yet important differences between them.

---

[110] *Top Ten Most Beautiful Capitals in the World*, ABC News Point, http://www.abcnewspoint.com/top-ten-most-beautiful-capitals-in-the-world/ (last visited May 27, 2016).

Besides/Beside

Meaning of *beside*: _____
Sample sentence: _____
Meaning of *besides*: _____
Sample sentence: _____

Difference between the two: _____
_____

Around/About

Meaning of *around*: _____
Sample sentence: _____
Meaning of *about*: _____
Sample sentence: _____

Difference between the two: _____

Farther/Further

Meaning of *farther*: _____
Sample sentence: _____
Meaning of *further*: _____
Sample sentence: _____

Difference between the two: _____
_____

Of/From

Meaning of *of*: _____
Sample sentence: _____
Meaning of *from*: _____
Sample sentence: _____

Difference between the two: _____
_____

Gifford v. Gallano Farms, LLC,
Nos. 2-10-0055, 2-10-0355, 2011 WL 10109462 (Ill. App. Ct. May 18, 2011).

Vocabulary and Legal Terminology

<u>Integration clause</u>: A contract provision that states that the adopted writing or writings is the full and final expression of the agreement between the parties.[111]

<u>To supersede</u>: To take the place of someone or something.

<u>Motion to reconsider</u>: A request made to the court, asking that it reexamine a matter it has already decided.

<u>Residual trust</u>: A trust that receives property upon the testator's death.[112]

<u>Successor trustee</u>: The individual who adminsters a trust after the original trustee is no longer able to do so.[113]

<u>Easement</u>: The right to use, or limit the use of, part of the land owned by another for a special purpose. Its use must be consistent with the general use of the property by the owner.[114]

<u>Motion to stay</u>: A request made to the court, asking it to stop the legal proceedings, either temporarily or permanently.

Pre-Reading Questions

Before you begin reading, skim the caption, the synopsis and the holdings and answer the following questions:

1. Is the case in federal or state court? _____
2. What can you tell about the relationship between the parties, based only on the caption?
3. You likely concluded that the parties seem to be family members, at least the defendants as they all have the same last name. What initial reaction do you have when you see that a case involves family members suing other family members? _____
4. What claim did the plaintiff bring against the defendants and what relief did the plaintiffs seek?
5. What did the district court decide? _____
6. Who appealed? _____
7. What did the appellate court decide? _____

---

[111] *Integration*, Gilbert's Pocket Size Law Dictionary (3rd ed. 2014).
[112] *Trust*, Black's Law Dictionary (10th ed. 2014).
[113] *Trustee*, Black's Law Dictionary (10th ed. 2014).
[114] *Easement*, Gilbert's Pocket Size Law Dictionary (3rd ed. 2014).

Comprehension Questions

With a general idea of the case in your mind, you can now read the case. As you are reading and after you finish reading, answer the following questions:

1. Summarize in your own words the facts that led to the dispute in this case.
2. What were the three counts (causes of action, claims) that the plaintiffs brought against the defendants:
   a. _____
   b. _____
   c. _____
3. What facts did the plaintiffs allege to support the above claims?
4. What defenses did the defendants raise against the claims?
   a. According to the defendants, what were the plaintiffs estopped from doing or claiming? Why?
   b. According to the defendants, what had the plaintiff waived? Why?
   c. What facts did the defendants allege to support these defenses?
5. Why did the trial court rule that the defendants had not breached the operating agreement?
6. What did the trial court rule with regard to the fiduciary duty that the defendants owed the plaintiffs?
   a. With regard to renting the farmland at less than market value through October 31, 2003: _____
   b. With regard to the leasing of the farmland after the written lease expired: _____
7. How does the appellate court distinguish Anest and Labovitz from this case?
8. Why does the appellate court disagree with the trial court about the breach?
9. How is this case useful for our fact pattern?
10. What rules or reasoning can you use from this case to help you analyze the Desert Salon Suites, LLC matter?

Legal Focus — Standards of Review

While reading cases in your LL.M. program, you have likely encountered many times the term "standard of review." It is used in the Gifford case. Do you know what standards of review are and the purpose that they serve?

A standard of review is the legal scale used by an appellate court in weighing a claim of error.[115] A standard of review provides the degree of deference the decision under review (the trial court's or intermediate appellate court's) should receive.[116]

Four policies support the use of a standard of review as a type of test for appellate courts to follow, rather than giving discretion to analyze and decide the issues on appeal without any guidance on how to do so. First, a standard of review "balances the power among the courts," and helps the courts to have a "healthy" respect for other courts and for their authority.[117] Second, a standard of review increases

---

[115] Fields v. Saunders, 278 P.3d 577, 581 (Okla. 2012) (internal citations omitted).
[116] Id.
[117] Amanda Peters, *The Meaning, Measure, and Misuse of Standards of Review*, 13 Lewis & Clark L. Rev. 233, 238-239 (2009).

judicial economy.[118] If an appellate court were to review all of the questions of fact and law as if the lower court had reached no ruling and relitigate the case, valuable time and resources would be lost.[119] Third, a standard of review "standardizes the judicial process, ensuring that each appellate court examines the issues on appeal in the same way."[120] Fourth, a standard of review provides notice to parties of their chances on appeal as a potential appellant has a "better understanding" of what to expect on appeal.[121]

If a standard of review is low, it means that the appellate court will give little deference to what the trial court ruled and overturn the trial court's ruling if any error is found. In contrast, when there is a high standard of review, the appellate court will overturn the trial court's ruling only in cases of serious error. Even if the appellate court would have decided the matter differently, the decision won't be overturned.

Look at the following paragraph from the Gifford case and answer the following questions regarding the appellate standard of review and the appeal in that case.

> To prevail on a claim for breach of fiduciary duty, the plaintiffs were required to prove the existence of a fiduciary duty, that the defendants breached this duty, and that they suffered damages proximately caused by that breach. Neade v. Portes, 193 Ill.2d 433, 444, 250 Ill.Dec. 733, 739 N.E.2d 496 (2000). We review the trial court's determination as to the alleged breach of fiduciary duty pursuant to a manifest weight of the evidence standard of review. Bernstein and Grazian, P.C. v. Grazian and Volpe, P. C., 402 Ill. App.3d 961, 976, 341 Ill.Dec. 913, 931 N.E.2d 810 (2010). Under this standard, we may only conclude that the trial court's determination was against the manifest weight of the evidence if an opposite conclusion is clearly apparent or the trial court's findings appear to be unreasonable, arbitrary, or not based on the evidence. Id.

1. What alleged error was the appellate court reviewing on appeal?
2. Is this error a question of fact or of law?
3. What is the standard of review that the Gifford case used?
4. This is a high standard of review. What words indicate that?
5. Why is this standard of review high?

Standards of review can be divided according to whether the appellate court is reviewing questions of fact or questions of law.

Questions of fact

- Clearly erroneous: Also called clear error, this standard of review is used by appellate courts to examine a trial court's findings of facts.[122] This standard is quite deferential to the trial court's determinations.
- Substantial evidence: The substantial evidence standard is also used by an appellate court to review a trial court's factual findings, and under it, the trial court's determination will be reversed only if there is no substantial evidence to support it.[123] Many commentators have noted that no difference really exists between the substantial evidence and clearly erroneous standards.[124]

---

[118] Id. at 240.
[119] Id.
[120] Id.
[121] Id. at 241.
[122] Id. at 245.
[123] Id.
[124] Id.

Questions of law

- De novo: De novo is a Latin phrase that means "starting from the beginning" and it refers to the standard used by appellate courts to examine the trial court's application of the law. No discretion is given to the lower court's ruling and the appellate court examines the legal findings as if the trial court had not done so.[125]

- Abuse of discretion: This standard is the most deferential to the trial court and is used to review procedural matters decided by the trial court.[126] This is a very high standard, and a difficult one for appealing parties to overcome on appeal.[127] Thus, an appellant will likely frame his appeal on other issues rather than one that employs this standard to increase the chances of success.[128]

Constitutional law: If you have taken constitutional law, you have encountered other standards of review that courts use when determining the constitutionality of a law. Which standard or test is applied depends on the group that the law targets, or the right that is infringed upon.

- Strict scrutiny: Laws that treat people differently on the basis of race and color (a so-called "suspect classification"), or laws that infringe upon a fundamental right protected under the Constitution, such as the right to marry or to procreate, are examined under the strict scrutiny test. Under this standard, the law will be upheld only if it furthers a compelling governmental interest and is narrowly tailored to achieve that interest.[129]

- Rational basis: The standard that gives the most deference to congressional action is the rational basis standard. This standard is used when the group targeted is neither a suspect classification or a quasi-suspect classification, or when no fundamental right is infringed upon. A presumption of validity exists under this standard, and the law will be held constitutional so long as it bears a rational relation to some legitimate governmental interest.[130]

- Intermediate scrutiny: Intermediate scrutiny lies between the "extremes of rational basis review and strict scrutiny" and has generally been applied to discriminatory classifications based on sex or illegitimacy (the so-called "quasi-suspect" classification).[131] Under this standard, a statutory classification must be substantially related to an important governmental objective.[132]

---

[125] Id. at 246.
[126] Id. at 243-244.
[127] Id.
[128] Id.
[129] See, e.g., Regents of Univ. of Cal. v. Bakke, 438 U.S. 265, 267 (1978) (stating that "[r]acial and ethnic distinctions of any sort are inherently suspect and call for the most exacting judicial examination; such suspect classifications are subject to strict scrutiny and can be justified only if they further a compelling government purpose and, even then, only if no less restrictive alternative is available" when deciding whether state medical school's affirmative action program for admissions violated the Fourteenth and Fifth Amendments).
[130] See, e.g., Minn. State Bd. for Cmty. Colleges v. Knight, 465 U.S. 271, 288 (1984) (declaring that rational basis scrutiny applied because the alleged constitutional violation – state employees' exclusion from "meet and confer" committees regarding policy decisions – did not constitute an infringement on First Amendment rights because the rights to speak, associate, and petition do not require government policymakers to listen or respond to communications of members of the public on public issues).
[131] Clark v. Jeter, 486 U.S. 456, 461 (1988).
[132] Id.; see, e.g., Craig v. Boren, 429 U.S. 190, 199-200 (1976) (declaring Oklahoma statutes prohibiting the sale of 3.2% beer to males under the age of 21 and females under the age of 18 to be unconstitutional and implementing the intermediate scrutiny test, holding that the statistical evidence showing that males were more inclined to drink and drive was insufficient to justify discriminatory treatment afforded to males).

Azulay, Horn and Seiden, LLC v. Horn,
2013 IL App. (1st) 1120625 (Ill. App. Ct. Aug. 1, 2013).

Vocabulary and Legal Terminology

<u>Moot</u>: Without practical value or significance.

<u>Interlocutory appeal</u>: An appeal which does not resolve the controversy, but which is necessary for a later adjudication of the case on its merits.[133]

<u>Nitty-gritty</u>: The essential details of something.

<u>To stall</u>: To stop.

<u>Windup</u>: The process of closing down a business and settling all of its liabilities and obligations.[134]

<u>Genesis</u>: Beginning.

<u>Fuzzy</u>: Unclear.

<u>Bereft</u>: Lacking something.

<u>Abrasive</u>: Harsh or difficult to deal with (when used to describe a person).

<u>Nettlesome</u>: Causing difficulty or problems.

<u>Bald</u>: Plain or blunt.

Pre-Reading Questions

Before you begin reading, skim the caption and the first two paragraphs (¶ 1 and ¶ 2) and answer the following questions:

1. Is the case in federal or state court?
2. What is the relationship between the parties?
3. What else do you notice about the names of the parties in the caption?
4. Why didn't the minority member not give up or relinquish his interest in the LLC?
5. The parties tried to negotiate a settlement but were unsuccessful. What did the majority members do once the negotiations ended?
6. What did the trial court decide?
7. Both parties appealed.
    a. Why did the appellate court dismiss the appeal of the LLC/plaintiff?
    b. Why did the appellate court dismiss the appeal of the minority member?
8. As you read these two introductory paragraphs, what type of dispute do you think this is and what do you think that the appellate court thought of the parties and their litigation?

---

[133] *Interlocutory*, Gilbert's Pocket Size Law Dictionary (3rd ed. 2014).
[134] *Liquidate*, Gilbert's Pocket Size Law Dictionary (3rd ed. 2014).

Comprehension Questions

With a general idea of the case in your mind, you can now read the case. As you are reading and after you finish reading, answer the following questions:

1. Summarize in your own words the facts that led to the dispute in this case. _____

2. What claims did the plaintiff bring against the defendant, Stanley? _____

3. While reading the facts of this case, does it remind you about the Desert Salon Suites, LLC matter? If it does, how? _____

4. What was your impression of the attorneys as you read through the case? _____

5. Why was the motion for injunctive relief denied? _____

6. Why did the court rule that the issue of dissolution of the LLC was moot? _____

7. What advice does this case give to practicing attorneys and how they should prepare the pleadings that they file with the court? _____

8. If your advice to Anthony Becerra were to dissolve Desert Salon Suites, LLC and wind up its business, what guidance does this case provide? _____

9. What other guidance does the case provide with regard to the Desert Salon Suites, LLC matter? _____

Language Focus — Inference

Inference is defined as "a conclusion reached on the basis of evidence and reasoning; the process of reaching such a conclusion."[135] In English, we say that you "read between the lines" when you infer something from what you read, or find a meaning that is not explicitly stated. Writers don't always explain everything, and being able to make inferences is an advanced and complex skill that all expert readers should develop. When reading in a second language, making inferences is even more difficult because you might be unfamiliar with vocabulary or encounter difficult sentence structures, making the underlying, hidden sense of what you read harder to grasp. But nevertheless, making inferences is an important skill to hone.

The Azulay case is interesting because of inferences we can make about what both the trial court and appellate court judges thought about the litigants. The judges never explicitly tell the reader their opinions of them, but we can infer it through their choice of words and expressions.

Below you will find several sentences from the Azulay case, with questions for you to answer about the language choices and the inferences we can make from them. Complete the questions to test your ability to read between the lines.

---
[135] *Inference*, THE NEW OXFORD AMERICAN DICTIONARY (2001).

Azulay, Horn and Seiden, LLC v. Horn, 2013 IL App. (1st) 1120625 (Ill. App. Ct. Aug. 1, 2013)

Sentence 1

These interlocutory appeals arise from a dispute between attorneys practicing immigration law as members of an LLC, even though the nitty-gritty iteration of their travails is legally redolent of a four-spouse divorce.

1. What does the above sentence tell you about the court's opinion of the litigation and the litigants?
    a. That the parties were acting as other litigants in similar civil matters
    b. That the parties acted as they did when they were in family court and getting divorced
    c. That the parties were misbehaving and acting immaturely and unreasonably
    d. That the parties were slow in resolving the dispute and reluctant to settle

2. By comparing the parties to four spouses getting a divorce, the court means that the parties are:
    a. Being difficult and obstructive
    b. Getting upset and yelling at each other
    c. Happy to be ending their relationship
    d. Sad and depressed, as divorcing spouses often are

Sentence 2

When negotiations stalled, the majority members expelled Stanley from AHS through what can gently be described as "extrajudicial means" and thereafter sought a declaration that AHS was entitled to dissociate him.

1. From the above sentence, what can you infer about the methods that AHS used to expel Stanley from AHS?
    a. That the methods used were legal
    b. That the methods used were against the law
    c. That the methods were not recommended, but still legal
    d. That the methods used didn't involve the court but should have

2. When the court says that the means used to remove Stanley can be "gently" described as "extrajudicial," what rhetorical device does the court use to make that point?
    a. Irony
    b. Humor
    c. Mockery
    d. Praise

Sentence 3

The [trial] court also incisively note that although Stanley Horn would be regarded as abrasive and uncooperative, Ira Azulay, on both grounds, could see Stanley and raise him a couple of cards.

1. From the above sentence, what can we infer about Ira Azulay and his character?
    a. He is as difficult and aggressive as Stanley Horn.
    b. He is more difficult and aggressive than Stanley Horn.
    c. He is less difficult and aggressive than Stanley Horn.
    d. Unlike Stanley Horn, Ira Azulay is easy to deal with.

2. By stating that the trial court was "incisive" in noting that Stanley Horn was difficult to deal with, the court was:
    a. Criticizing the trial court for not observing Stanley Horn's character
    b. Praising the trial court for how observant it was
    c. Disagreeing with the trial court's assessment of Stanley Horn's character
    d. Affirming the trial court's factual findings about both Stanley Horn and Ira Azulay

Shrock v. Meier,
2012 IL App (1st) 111408-U (Ill. App. Ct. Mar. 19, 2012).

Vocabulary and Legal Terminology

<u>To seek leave to do something</u>: To ask permission to do something.

<u>Nominal</u>: Very small, minimal.

<u>To strike</u>: To dismiss, such as a complaint or causes of action.

<u>Unjust enrichment</u>: A civil claim brought when a defendant has obtained the benefits of the plaintiff's efforts or work, but without paying any compensation for such work or efforts. The plaintiff brings the claim to recover the gains that the defendant unjustly earned.

<u>To denigrate</u>: To criticize and attack another person's reputation.

<u>Rule 308(a) certification</u>: Rule 308 of the Illinois Civil Appeals Rules, stating when a trial court or a party can petition the state supreme court to answer a certified question of law.[136]

Pre-Reading Questions

Before you begin reading, skim the caption and the holding paragraph and answer the following questions:

1. Is the case in federal or state court?
2. Who are the parties in the case and what is their relationship?
3. What motion was filed in the district court and by whom?
4. What did the trial court decide with regard to this motion?
5. Who appealed?
6. What did the appellate court decide?

Comprehension Questions

With a general idea of the case in your mind, you can now read the case. As you are reading and after you finish reading, answer the following questions:

1. Summarize in your own words the facts that led to the dispute in this case.
2. Summarize the procedural history of this case, including the various motions that were filed and the orders issued.

---

[136] ILCS S. Ct. Rules, Rule 308.

3. This case states eight rules of LLCs and their management that are important for the Desert Salon Suites, LLC matter. First, identify the paragraph with those rules. Second, write those rules below:

   a. _____

   b. _____

   c. _____

   d. _____

   e. _____

   f. _____

   g. _____

   h. _____

4. Will this paragraph of rules be useful for your memo analyzing the Desert Salon Suites, LLC matter? Why or why not? _____

5. What arguments did the plaintiff raise in objection to the dissolution of the LLC? _____

6. How did the appellate court respond to those arguments? _____

7. Like the Azulay case, this case teaches us an important lesson about lawyering and what is expected of attorneys who appear in court. What is that lesson?

8. How is this case useful for our fact pattern?

9. What rules or reasoning can you use from this case to help you analyze the Desert Salon Suites, LLC matter?

Language Focus — Idiomatic Expressions

Look at the following sentence from the Shrock v. Meier case:

> [T]he Seller will take measures to ensure that such dealings [between the parties] are **at arm's length** and on commercially reasonable terms.

At arm's length is an idiomatic expression that means that in a commercial transaction, the parties are "independent and have equal footing and equal bargaining power."[137] It also has a literal meaning: to hold something away from the body, with the arm fully extended.

---

[137] *Arm's length,* MERRIAM-WEBSTER ONLINE DICTIONARY, http://www.merriam-webster.com/dictionary/arm's%20length (last visited May 2, 2016).

English has many idiomatic expressions, or expressions whose meanings cannot be inferred from the meanings of the words in the expression. All languages have idiomatic expressions; some of them are the same from language to language, while others are completely different. Idiomatic expressions are fun, yet also difficult to learn.

Knowing how to translate an idiomatic expression in another language can be difficult. In some cases, the expressions might be exactly the same and you can translate the expressions literally and still be understood. But more often than not, translating literally an idiomatic expression from your mother tongue into a second language can lead to confusion and hilarity as well. Languages often have expressions with the same meaning, but expressed in very different ways. Sometimes, an idiomatic expression in one language might not have an expression in another language, so you just have to translate the meaning instead.

Here are some other idiomatic expressions in English that use a body part in them, as does *at arm's length*:

To eyeball something: _____
To hand something to someone: _____
To mouth something to someone: _____
To eye something: _____
To elbow someone: _____
To stomach something: _____

Look up in a dictionary the meanings of these expressions. Do you have to translate the meaning of the English verb, or does your mother tongue also have an idiomatic expression to express the same concept? If your language does not express the meaning of the expression in the same way, what expression can you use?

Tully v. McLean,
948 N.E.2d 714 (Il. App. Ct. 2011).

Vocabulary and Legal Terminology

Receiver: A court-appointed custodian of assets that are subject to litigation or to a bankruptcy action. The receiver will hold and preserve property of the parties or of the bankrupt while awaiting the court's ruling. In the case of corporations, a receiver may not only manage the assets but will sometimes, upon the court's order, manage the operation of the business.[138]

To vacate: To cancel or make void, such as a judgment.[139]

To disgorge: To repay something illegally obtained, such as profits, pursuant to a court order.[140]

To step down as something: To resign.

Derivatively: Based on something else, another source.

To loot: To raid or steal.

To shore up: To strengthen or bolster.

Overdraft: A check drawn in an amount that exceeds the balance of funds present in the checking account.[141]

Overkill: Excess; more than what is needed or necessary.

Pre-Reading Questions

Before you begin reading, skim the caption, synopsis and holdings and answer the following questions:

1. Is the case in federal or state court?
2. Who are the parties in the case and what is their relationship?
3. What claims did the plaintiff bring against the defendants?
4. Who filed a motion in the district court?
5. What did the motion seek to do?
6. What happened procedurally at the district court?
7. Who appealed?
8. What did the appellate court decide?

---

[138] *Receiver*, GILBERT'S POCKET SIZE LAW DICTIONARY (3rd ed. 2014).
[139] *Vacate*, GILBERT'S POCKET SIZE LAW DICTIONARY (3rd ed. 2014).
[140] *Disgorgement*, BLACK'S LAW DICTIONARY (10th ed. 2014).
[141] *Overdraft*, GILBERT'S POCKET SIZE LAW DICTIONARY (3rd ed. 2014).

Comprehension Questions

With a general idea of the case in your mind, you can now read the case. As you are reading and after you finish reading, answer the following questions:

1. Summarize in your own words the facts that led to the dispute in this case.
2. What was the issue on appeal? _____
   _____
3. What reasoning did the trial court give for the damages that it awarded the plaintiff? _____
   _____
   _____
4. On what grounds was the plaintiff seeking to have the defendants dissociated from the LLC? ___
   _____
5. Why did the trial court find that the dissociation of the defendants from the LLC was warranted?
   _____
   _____
6. How is this case useful for our fact pattern?
7. What rules or reasoning can you use from this case to help you analyze the Desert Salon Suites, LLC matter?

Language Focus — Homophones, Homonyms and Homographs

There is no doubt about it – English pronunciation is difficult. Several other Language Focus exercises in this ESL Workbook focus on English pronunciation, highlighting not only its difficulty but also its importance in speaking English well.[142]

The Tully case presents a rather frequent conundrum in English pronunciation – homographs. A homograph is when two or more words have the same spelling, but are pronounced differently. Take a look at these two sentences from the Tully case. Can you identify the homograph in each one?

> Defendants brought motion to dissolve the LLC and to appoint a receiver to wind up LLC's business affairs.

> Pursuant to section 35–1(1) of the Act, "[a] limited liability company is dissolved, and its business must be wound up, upon the occurrence of [a]n event specified in the operating agreement."

The verb — *to wind   wound   wound* – has various meanings:
- to twist something around something else: *She wound the ribbon around her finger.*
- to make a device such as a clock or watch work by turning a key: *Most watches you buy run on batteries so you don't have to wind them.*
- to change directions repeatedly, such as a river or road: *The road wound through the mountains and along the river.*

The phrasal verb *to wind up* is used when discussing LLCs or corporations and the processes followed for concluding the entity's business. Note that you will see the verb written as two words (to wind up), as a compound word (to windup) and also as a hyphenated word (to wind-up).

---

[142] The Language Focus exercises for the cases Wood on Behalf of Doe v. Ashford (Section II, Unit 1 on page 126) and State v. Boland (Section II, Unit 3 on page 150) deal with pronunciation.

In terms of pronunciation, the verb is pronounced /waɪnd/ and the past tense and past participle as /waʊnd/. If you are unsure of the pronunciation, search an online dictionary that includes an audio of the pronunciation. The difficulty in pronouncing these verbs lies in the fact that both *wind* and *wound* are also nouns that are pronounced very differently than the verbs.

When describing the movement of the air — *wind* (noun) – we pronounce it as /wɪnd/. When we are injured, we receive a *wound*, pronounced as /wu:nd/. Online dictionaries will provide audio also of these words if you are unsure of the pronunciation. As with most words, the American and British pronunciations will vary.

Below are other pairs of homographs. To improve your vocabulary and your English pronunciation, first verify that you know the meanings of both words in each pair. Once you have done that, note the different pronunciation for each word, finding audio recording online or asking a friend who is a native speaker if you are unsure. To help you, the part of speech (noun, verb, adjective) has been indicated.

To lead (v.) and lead (n.)

Bass (n.) and bass (n.)

To sow (v.) and sow (n.)

To close (v.) and close (adj.)

To bow (v.) and bow (n.)

Moped (n.) and moped (verb - past tense of *to mope*)

To tear (v.) and tear (n.)

SECTION III

Unit 1
Restrictive Covenants and Preliminary Injunctions

Reed, Roberts Associates, Inc. v. Strauman,
353 N.E.2d 590 (N.Y. 1976).

Vocabulary and Legal Terminology

Cross-appeal: When both parties file appeals against the lower court's ruling.

Efficacy: The ability to bring about a desired result.

Lion's share: The largest or biggest part.

To strike off on one's own: To leave the company where one is employed to start one's own business.

Goodwill: (also good will) An intangible asset which represents the favorable attitude of clients or customers of a business toward the operation of the business.[143]

Usurpation: The act of wrongfully and forcefully taking something.

To fetter: To restrain.

To safeguard: To protect.

Surreptitious: Something done secretly.

To enunciate: To pronounce or state.

To pirate: To use without permission.

"An injunction would not lie:" "An injunction would not be properly issued."

To pilfer: To steal, usually things of little value.

Dun and Bradstreet's Million Dollar Directory: A publication (now also online) that lists information regarding public and private companies and their executives.

---

[143] *Goodwill*, Gilbert's Pocket Size Law Dictionary (3rd ed. 2014).

Reed, Roberts Associates, Inc. v. Strauman, 353 N.E.2d 590 (N.Y. 1976)

Pre-Reading Questions

Before you begin reading, skim the caption and first paragraph and answer the following questions:
1. Is the case in federal or state court?
2. Who were the parties in the case?
3. What claim did the plaintiff bring against the defendant?
4. The plaintiff filed a motion for a preliminary injunction, asking the court to stop the defendant from doing what?
5. What did the district court decide with regard to the motion?
6. Who appealed?
7. What did the appellate court decide?
8. On what grounds did the appellate court base its decision?

Comprehension Questions

With a general idea of the case in your mind, you can now read the case. As you are reading and after you finish reading, answer the following questions:
1. Summarize in your own words the facts of this case.
2. What reasons did the trial court give for both granting and denying the injunction?
3. In general, the enforcement of a restrictive covenant depends on what? _____
   _____
   _____
4. What policy reasons support the different approach that courts give to restrictive covenants in the context of the sale of a business and the context of an employer and employee relationship?
   _____
   _____
5. What are the competing interests at play with regard to restrictive covenants and employment situations?
6. The court states the test, consisting of four elements, for determining whether a restrictive covenant in an employment context is reasonable and enforceable. Write those four elements below:
   a. _____
   b. _____
   c. _____
   d. _____
7. In this case, the court concluded that Strauman was not a "key employee" whose "unique or extraordinary" services warranted the issuance of a non-competition agreement. What facts did the court use to support that conclusion?
8. How do those facts compare to our case?
9. What facts support the court's conclusion that the trial court erred in issuing the injunction to enforce the non-solicitation agreement?

10. How does this case compare to ours?

11. Is it useful for our fact pattern? Why or why not?

12. It is more useful for SDA or for Winsted? Why?

Language Focus — The Verb "To Strike"

In the facts section, the court in the Reed case states that "[a]fter 11 years with Reed, Roberts, Strauman decided to strike off on his own and formed a company called Curator Associates, Inc."

As you learned in the Vocabulary and Legal Terminology section, the verb *to strike off on your own* is an idiomatic expression that means to start your own business or independent activity. You might also see the phrase *to strike **out** on your own* (not off), and it has the same meaning. English has many idiomatic expressions that use the verb *to strike*, and this exercise will introduce you to some of them.

But before examining some of those idiomatic expressions, take this short quiz.

Which of the following is **not** a meaning of the word "strike?" (either the noun or the verb)

1. To hit strongly or forcefully

2. To organize that workers collectively stop working in protest of working condition

3. To tap or hit lightly something

4. In baseball, to swing and miss a ball when at bat

5. To succeed in knocking down all pins in bowling

6. A sudden attack, especially a military one

7. To occur suddenly and with damaging effects, especially a natural disaster such as a hurrance or tornado

8. A disadvantage that makes it difficult for someone to succeed

Of all the possible answers, only #3 — to tap or hit lightly — is not a meaning of strike, as either a noun or a verb. This quiz is an example of how frustating English can be for non-native speakers, as you see how many different meanings one word can have. It also shows you the richness of the vocabulary.

Likewise, the word *strike* can also make up many different idiomatic expressions. How many of the following expressions are you familiar with? After each expression below, you will find a blank space. Write the definition of the expression and a sample sentence that demonstrates your understanding of it.

1. To strike out:[144] _____

_____

2. To strike up a conversation: _____

_____

---

[144] You will find more than one meaning of this phrasal verb.

3. To strike while the iron is hot: _____
   _____

4. "It strikes me that..." _____
   _____

5. "Three strikes and you're out:" _____
   _____

6. To go on strike: _____
   _____

BDO Seidman v. Hirshberg,
712 N.E.2d 1220 (N.Y. 1999).

Vocabulary and Legal Terminology

Overbroad: Excessively broad.

Liquidated damages: An amount of money specified in a contract to compensate a party for injuries suffered because of a breach of contract by the other party to the agreement.[145]

Patronage: Support given to a business or organization by its clients or customers.

Pretrial discovery: Discovery such as depositions done before a trial is conducted.

To aver: To claim or allege.

Ancillary agreement: An agreement that is additional or supplemental.

Cognizable: Easily identifiable.

To obviate: To avoid or prevent.

Tripartite: Consisting of three parts.

Parity: The state of being equal.

To turn something on its head: To deal with something in a completely different and unexpected way.

Scant: Barely sufficient.

To cure: To solve a problem.

To militate: To have an effect on something.

To forestall: To stop something from happening.

Pre-Reading Questions

Before you begin reading, skim the caption and first paragraph and answer the following questions:
1. Is the case in federal or state court?
2. What motion was filed at the district court? Who filed it?
3. What did the district court decide with regard to the motion, and what effect did that ruling have on the case?
4. Who appealed to the appellate court and what did the court decide?

---

[145] *Liquidated Damages*, Gilbert's Pocket Size Law Dictionary (3rd ed. 2014).

5. Who appealed to the New York Court of Appeals?
6. What did the New York Court of Appeals decide?
7. What happened with the case after the court of appeals issued its decision?

Comprehension Questions

With a general idea of the case in your mind, you can now read the case. As you are reading and after you finish reading, answer the following questions:

1. Summarize in your own words the facts of this case that led to the dispute.
2. What arguments did the defendant make in response to his former employer's allegations that BDO had lost one hundred clients to the defendant?
3. The central issue here, as the court says, is the "reimbursement clause," or the provision that allows for liquidated damages. It isn't a restrictive covenant in the sense of a non-competition or non-solicitation agreement, but the court says that "in its purpose and effect," it is a non-competition agreement. Why?
4. Write the three-prongs of the test applied by New York courts to determine the reasonableness of a non-competition agreement.
    a. _____
    b. _____
    c. _____
5. The Gelder Medical Group and Kaprinski cases are important in the court's analysis, and the court distinguishes those two cases from the case at hand. How does the court distinguish the cases and the facts of the cases?
6. What "legitimate interests" is SDA seeking to protect with the non-competition and non-solicitation agreements that it required its employees to sign?
7. How does this case compare to ours?
8. Is it useful for our fact pattern? Why or why not?
9. It is more useful for SDA or for Winsted? Why?

Legal Focus — Citations and Sources

Citations, defined as "reference[s] to a legal precedent or authority, such as a case, statute, or treatise, that either substantiates or contradicts a given position,"[146] are an important part of U.S. legal writing. We include citations so that the reader can check what we have written and ensure that we haven't misstated or misrepresented anything. Citations are a way to verify.

It is common in U.S. legal writing to cite every sentence in a legal document. The citation might be to a primary sources such as a case, statute, rule, or regulation, or to a secondary source like a treatise, law review article, newspaper article or legal encyclopedia. We also cite to discovery responses (interrogatories, documents, and deposition transcripts) or to pleadings in a case. In the United States,

---

[146] *Citation*, BLACK'S LAW DICTIONARY (10th ed. 2014).

there are two systems of legal citation: the Bluebook and the Association of Legal Writing Directors, both of which are also manuals that include detailed explanations and examples of how we cite every type of source imaginable, from administrative cases to the constitution of Zambia and everything in between. As a U.S. lawyer and law student, you are expected to cite correctly, and correct citations are a part of good legal writing. You likely have studied or will study one of the legal citation formats during your LL.M. program.

In many cases that you read, you will find citations just to the "usual" sources — statutes and other cases. However, the BDO Seidman case is unusual because it includes citations to many different sources, both primary and seconday authorities. The case also presents a good opportunity to examine citations of different sources so you can better understand citations in U.S. legal writing and then replicate them in your own legal writing.

Citation 1

Author's name. Per the Bluebook, the author's full name should be included first on a citation. Here, the court only uses the last name.

The title of the article, which is always in italics

Blake, *Employee Agreements Not To Compete*, 73 HARV. L. REV. 625, 629, citing, *inter alia*, *Mitchel v. Reynolds*, 1 P. Wms. 181, 24 Eng. Rep. 347 [QB 1711]

This part of the citation tells you the name of the law review that the article appears in – The Harvard Law Review.

Tables 13.1 and 13.2 of the Bluebook contain abbreviations of institutions, periodicals, and other common words.

The first number – 73 – is the volume number of the Harvard Law Review that the article appears in, and the second number – 625 – tells you the page on which the article begins. The third number – 629 – is instead the page that the author is citing. This cite is often called a "pin cite" since it indicates the exact page that is cited, like the author took a stick pin and placed it on the page for the reader to see.

The second part of the citation (after citing) is interesting because the court is citing an English case from 1711! The case, Mitchel v. Reynolds is cited in two reporters: The Peere Williams' and the English Reporter. The QB stands for Queen's Bench.

While early American court decisions often cited English cases because American jurisprudence hadn't had the chance to develop, nowadays it is rather unusual to see U.S. courts citing cases from foreign courts.

BDO Seidman v. Hirshberg, 712 N.E.2d 1220 (N.Y. 1999)

Citation 2

Technical Aid Corp. v. Allen, 134 N.H. 1, 8, 591 A.2d 262, 265–266; Blake, *op. cit.*, at 648–649; Restatement [Second] of Contracts § 188).

Here, the first part of the citation is a court decision. You know this: (1) because of the "v." between the parties' names, and (2) because of the second part of the citation – 134 N.H. 1 and 591 A.2d 262.

The second part of any citation to a court decision tells you information about where the decision can be found (in hard copy, not online).

Before the internet, court decisions could only be found in books called reporters. You can still find them in your law school library. The N.H. stands for the New Hampshire Reporter. You need to be familiar with the abbreviations of U.S. states to know what state it refers to. Table 1 of the Bluebook provides that information. Like the citation for the law review article, the Technical Aid decision begins on page 1 of the 134th volume of the New Hampshire Reporter, and the court is citing to page 8.

The second reporter cited is the A.2d – the second edition of the Atlantic Reporter. State court decisions are published in two reporters – a state one and a regional one, which includes decisions from states in the same geographic area. The Technical Aid decision can be found in volume 591 of the Atlantic Second Reporter, staring on page 262. In the case, the court is citing to pages 265-266 (the pin cite).

The final part of the citation is to a secondary source –the second edition of the Restatement of Contracts. When citing to the Restatement, we always note the edition, as well as the section, identified with the § symbol.

The op. cit. means "opera citato," a Latin phrase that means "the work already cited." Here, it refers the reader to pages 648-649 of the previously cited Blake article.

Citation 3

Education Law § 7404[1], [2], [3]; 8 NYCRR 70.1); they must pass a written examination (Education Law § 7404[1], [4]; 8 NYCRR 70.3); and they are subject to mandatory continuing education requirements (Education Law § 7409; 8 NYCRR 70.6). Their professional conduct is regulated by the Board of Regents under statutory disciplinary procedures (Education Law §§ 6509–6511). Moreover, there is a national code of professional conduct for certified public accountants which provides that "[m]embers should accept the obligation to act in a way that will serve the public interest, honor the public trust, and demonstrate commitment to professionalism" (American Institute of Certified Public Accountants Code of Professional Conduct § 53, art. II). The foregoing factors closely correspond to the criteria for a learned profession listed in *Matter of Freeman*, 34 N.Y.2d 1, 7, 355 N.Y.S.2d 336, 311 N.E.2d 480.

The first citations in the highlighted lines can be difficult to understand if you are not familiar with the New York state laws (NYCRR or New York Code, Rules and Regulations). Each state names its statutes in a different way, and knowing how to cite to those sources can be challenging. The Bluebook includes in Table 1.3 summaries for each state, telling you how to cite to its court decisions, statutes and also rules and regulations. Here, the New York Education Law is cited as well as the NYCRR.

Sometimes, we cite different authorities and sources. The Bluebook provides you the format for every type of citation imaginable, from online sources to emails, personal interviews and foreign sources. Here, the court is citing a professional code of conduct for CPAs (certified public accountants), much like the ABA Model Rules of Professional Conduct. The section number (53) and the article (II) are cited.

Note that three reporters are included in the last citation – the New York Second Reporter, West's New York Supplement and the North Eastern Reporter. Table 1 (T1) of the Blue Book includes information on citations formats for all U.S. jurisdictions, and by referring to this table you can find how to cite to a state court, statute or rule, or a federal statute, agency or regulation.

Kanan, Corbin, Schupak, Aronow, Inc. v. FD International, Ltd.,
797 N.Y.S.2d 883 (N.Y. Sup. Ct. 2005).

Vocabulary and Legal Terminology

<u>Order to Show Cause</u>: An order issued by a court requiring a party to explain or justify something to the court.

<u>To induce</u>: To cause someone or something to do something.

<u>In accord with</u>: In agreement with.

Pre-Reading Questions

Before you begin reading, skim the caption, synopsis and holding and answer the following questions:
1. Is the case in federal or state court?
2. What court issued this decision: trial court, appellate court or state supreme court?
3. What claims were brought against the defendants?
4. What motion did the plaintiff file, and what was the plaintiff seeking to accomplish with the motion?
5. What did the district court decide with regard to the motion?
6. What happened after the court issued its decision regarding the motion?

Comprehension Questions

With a general idea of the case in your mind, you can now read the case. As you are reading and after you finish reading, answer the following questions:
1. Summarize in your own words the facts of this case that led to the dispute.
2. Write below the three-prong test that courts apply when analyzing a motion for a preliminary injunction:
   a. _____
   b. _____
   c. _____
3. Why are courts careful when issuing an injunction?
4. For the injunction to be issued, SDA must show that it is likely to succeed on the merits. On the merits of what? _____
5. What irreparable harm might Winsted suffer if the injunction were issued in the litigation against SDA?
6. What irreparable harm might SDA suffer if the injunction were not issued?

7. How do you balance the harms that SDA and Winsted will suffer through the imposition of the injunction?
8. What is the Reed standard? _____
   _____
9. How does the Reed standard apply to our case? _____
   _____
10. How was the Reed standard modified in the BDO Seidman case? _____
    _____
11. How does the BDO Seidman standard apply to our case? _____
    _____
12. Why does the court determine that the plaintiffs are not entitled to a preliminary injunction against the defendants?
    a. _____
    b. _____
    c. _____
    d. _____
    e. _____
13. How does this case compare to ours?
14. Is it useful for our fact pattern? Why or why not?
15. It is more useful for SDA or for Winsted? Why?

Language Focus – Legal Analysis

Legal analysis is the heart of legal writing. Facts are important, as are the rules and the rule statements, but unless you analyze those facts and apply the law to them, you aren't doing your job as a lawyer and as a legal writer. However, how that analysis is carried out and communicated can vary from country to country and from culture to culture. What is expected of U.S. legal analysis is likely different than the legal analysis that you were trained to do in your home country.

Legal writing in the United States is "writer-responsible," meaning that the writer is mainly responsible for communicating his or her ideas to the reader.[147] It is not the reader's job to understand what the writer is trying to say; the responsibility instead lies upon the writer to explain to the reader in clear and concise language what he is trying to say.[148] Conciseness and clarity are highly valued in U.S. legal writing. U.S. writers don't "hide the ball" when explaining something but are rather direct and explicit; they get to the point of the letter, memo or document they are writing rather than including a long introduction or lengthy background information.[149] Moreover, when discussing a complex topic, an expert English writer will explain the topic in an easy-to-understand way so that the reader can understand the first time she reads the text.[150] If a reader is not able to fully understand a writer's meaning, he or she is not impressed but rather views the writing as confusing and unclear.[151]

---

[147] Laurel Currie Oates & Anne Enquist, Legal Writing Handbook: Analysis, Research and Writing, 843 (2014).
[148] Id.
[149] Id.
[150] Id.
[151] For additional information on the differences between legal writing in the United States and other cultures, see generally id. at 843 – 856.

Contrast these expected and admired characteristics of U.S. legal writing with the legal writing that lawyers in your home country strive for. Are the expectations different? If they are, how are they different? It is important to keep in mind different expectations and characteristics of legal writing in your home country and the U.S. when writing papers or other assignments for your classes in your LL.M. program.

Below you will find a paragraph from the BDO Seidman case. The paragraph is included in this Language Focus because it provides an example of good analysis: a conclusion well supported by cited authority. The writer just doesn't state the conclusion but also provides the support for it.

Read the paragraph and answer the following questions about the legal writing and analysis.

> BDO urges that accountancy is entitled to the status of a learned profession and, as such, the *Karpinski* and *Gelder Medical Group* precedents militate in favor of the validity of the restrictive covenant here. We agree that accountancy has all the earmarks of a learned profession. CPAs are required to have extensive formal training and education (Education Law § 7404[1], [2], [3]; 8 NYCRR 70.1); they must pass a written examination (Education Law § 7404[1], [4]; 8 NYCRR 70.3); and they are subject to mandatory continuing education requirements (Education Law § 7409; 8 NYCRR 70.6). Their professional conduct is regulated by the Board of Regents under statutory disciplinary procedures (Education Law §§ 6509–6511). Moreover, there is a national code of professional conduct for certified public accountants which provides that "[m]embers should accept the obligation to act in a way that will serve the public interest, honor the public trust, and demonstrate commitment to professionalism" (American Institute of Certified Public Accountants Code of Professional Conduct § 53, art. II). The foregoing factors closely correspond to the criteria for a learned profession listed in *Matter of Freeman*, 34 N.Y.2d 1, 7, 355 N.Y.S.2d 336, 311 N.E.2d 480.

1. In the paragraph, what is the conclusion that the court is supporting through its analysis?
2. What five facts does the court use to support that conclusion?
    a. _____
    b. _____
    c. _____
    d. _____
    e. _____
3. Is this analysis well done? Why or why not? _____
4. What does this paragraph tell you about how you should do your legal analysis? _____
5. Identify in the paragraph all of the sources that the court uses to bolster its analysis.
6. Must good analysis be supported by sources or legal authority? Why or why not? _____

Kanan, Corbin, Schupak, Aronow, Inc. v. FD International, Ltd., 797 N.Y.S.2d 883 (N.Y. Sup. Ct. 2005)

Now you will read a paragraph from the Kanan decision, which also provides a good example of the type of legal analysis that you should aim to write. Once you have read the paragraph, answer the questions below.

> Under the first prong of its test, the *Reed* court determined that the vice-president's alleged use of the consultancy's "customer-list" was not actionable because the names and contact information of current and potential customers were easily ascertainable from public sources. *Id.* at 308, 386 N.Y.S.2d 677, 353 N.E.2d 590. Further, the court held that the defendant's intimate knowledge of plaintiff's business operation did not meet the "unique or extraordinary" standard. Rather, the court stated that where knowledge is not deemed a protectable trade secret and there has been no misappropriation, an employee should not be inhibited from realizing his professional potential. *Id.* at 309, 386 N.Y.S.2d 677, 353 N.E.2d 590.

1. Identify two conclusions reached by the Reed court, which the Kanan court cites and references.
   a. _____
   b. _____
2. What facts does the court use to support those conclusions? _____
   _____
3. Why does the Kanan court cite the Reed case? (you will likely have to refer to the complete decision) _____
   _____
4. Is the citation that the Kanan case made to the Reed decision helpful? Why or why not? _____
   _____
5. What would make the citation more helpful to determine how the Reed case is analogous or distinguishable from the Kanan case? _____
   _____
6. In comparing the analysis in the first paragraph from the BDO Seidman case and the second paragraph from the Kanan case, what rule can you take away about what makes good legal analysis? _____
   _____

Veramark Technologies, Inc. v. Bouk,
10 F. Supp. 3d 395 (W.D.N.Y. 2014).

Vocabulary and Legal Terminology

Removal to federal court: To transfer a claim brought in state court to federal court when the claim has jurisdictional reasons for being heard in federal court: federal matter jurisdiction or diversity jurisdiction.

To enjoin: To stop or prevent.

To raid: To carry out a surprise search or attack.

To be intertwined: To be closely connected together.

Seminal: (of a work, event, movement or person) Influential.

Title insurance: Insurance that is purchased to protect against defects in the title to real property.

To submit: (here) To allege or claim.

Conclusory: Without supporting evidence.

To trump: To be more important than something else.

To buttress: To support.

Infirmity: Weakness.

Pre-Reading Questions

Before you begin reading, skim the caption, synopsis and holdings and answer the following questions:
1. Was the case first decided in state or federal court?
2. What claims did the plaintiff bring against the defendant?
3. Why did the defendant ask to have the case transferred (removed) to federal court?
4. What motion was filed?
5. What did the district court decide with regard to the motion and why?

Comprehension Questions

With a general idea of the case in your mind, you can now read the case. As you are reading and after you finish reading, answer the following questions:

Veramark Technologies, Inc. v. Bouk, 10 F. Supp. 3d 395 (W.D.N.Y. 2014)

1. Summarize in your own words the facts of this case that led to the dispute.
2. Write below the four-prong test that courts apply when analyzing a motion for a preliminary injunction:
    a. _____
    b. _____
    c. _____
    d. _____
3. What arguments did the plaintiff in the Veramark Technologies case make as to why the court should issue a preliminary injunction against Bouk? _____
4. This case provides a good example of how a party can cite a case, but the case is not really applicable or relevant (p. 402). The plaintiff cited several cases in support of the proposition that the enforcement of a non-solicitation agreement is insufficient to protect an employer's goodwill. Find the cases that the plaintiff cited, but that the court rejected as being inapplicable. How does the court distinguish those cases and show that they aren't applicable? _____
5. This case also provides a good example of how a case, Ticor Title Insurance v. Cohen, is compared to the case at hand to show how Bouk was not a "unique" employee. What facts does the court use to compare the employee in Ticor to the case at hand? _____
6. Why did the court in the Veramark Technologies case reach a different conclusion than the Ticor court and conclude that Bouk was not a "unique" employee? _____
7. How does the Ticor case compare to ours? Is Winsted "unique" under the Ticor reasoning? Why or why not? _____
8. Is this case useful for our fact pattern? Why or why not?
9. It is more useful for SDA or for Winsted? Why?

Language Focus — Definite and Indefinite Articles

The use of articles (definite and indefinite) in English is challenging for ESL speakers. The rules have lots of exceptions, and the best way to learn when we use and don't use an article is through practice. Here are some general rules of thumb.

When you are writing or speaking and ask yourself whether you need to include an article with a noun, go through this analysis:
1. Ask yourself whether the noun is a countable or uncountable noun.
    a. Countable nouns are just what the name says they are: nouns that we can count. A table. A car. A house. I can count the number of tables in a room, so table is a countable noun.
    b. Uncountable nouns can't be counted: Air. Dirt. Grass.
    c. Some nouns can be both, but they are exceptions: *Coffee is an important commodity in Central American countries.* (uncountable) *I drink two coffees a day* (countable because I mean two cups of coffee).

2. **Countable**:
    a. If you have a countable noun and you are using the noun in the singular, you must have an article with the noun. Whether you use the definite (the) or the indefinite (a/an) article depends on the sense of the sentence.
        1) *I would like to adopt a cat.* Here, I am not talking about a particular or specific cat, but just a cat in general. So I use the indefinite article. NOT: *I would like to adopt cat.*
        2) *I would like to adopt the cat that I saw last week at the Animal Humane Society.* Here, I am talking about a specific cat (the one I saw last week), so I use the definite article.
        3) We use *one* instead of *a/an* when we want to emphasize the number, but if the number is not important, then we use a/an. *My sister has two dogs, but we've got one cat.* Or: *How many pets have you got? We've got one horse now but we used to have two.*
    b. If you have a countable noun and you are using the noun in the plural, you use an article only if you are referring to specific things. If you are speaking in general, you don't use the article:
        1) *When we were traveling in Italy last year, we noticed how small the cars were.*
            Here, I am speaking about specific cars: the Italian ones that we saw last year. I am not talking in general about cars, but about specific ones, so I use the definite article.
        2) *Cars create a lot of pollution.*
            Here, I am speaking in general about cars, so I use no article. The rule is if I am speaking in general about a countable noun, I don't use an article but use the noun in the plural. Some examples:
            (1) *Dogs make great pets, but cats are easier to care for.*
            (2) *Horses were the main means of transportation until cars became mass produced and more affordable.*
            (3) But contrast here: *The cars manufactured at the beginning of the 20th century were very dangerous compared to the cars manufactured today.*

3. **Uncountable:**
    a. If the noun you are using is uncountable, you use the definite article only when speaking about a specific item or thing, and the noun is singular:
        1) *The grass in our yard really needs to be cut!*
        2) *The coffee they grow and harvest in El Salvador is considered some of the best in the world.*
    b. If the noun you are using is uncountable, you use no article only when speaking in general about the thing:
        1) *You don't see grass in Arizona or in other Southwestern states.*
        2) *Without fresh air, you will get sick.*
    c. You don't use the indefinite article with an uncountable noun, unless used in a countable sense:
        1) NOT: *You don't see a grass in Arizona.*
        2) *I would like a coffee, please.*

d. If you want to make an uncountable noun countable, we often add "a piece of" or some other phrase:

    1) A piece of information
    2) A piece of advice (not advices)
    3) A blade of grass
    4) A piece of luggage

e. **Uncountable nouns can never be plural**.

Below you will find three paragraphs from the <u>Veramark Technologies</u> case. The articles have all been deleted, and blanks have been put in front of all nouns. Your task is to complete the paragraph (without looking at the original text of the case!) by adding definite or indefinite articles where appropriate. Remember that just because there is a blank space before a noun doesn't mean that an article necessarily must be added.

_____ Mr. Bouk began his employment with _____ Veramark on March 3, 2008, as _____ Vice President of Customer Services. Veramark is _____ provider of _____ Telecom Expense Management software and services, which means that it "helps _____ businesses manage _____ lifecycle of _____ communications expenses across _____ diverse business units, geographies, etc." Veramark subsequently became _____ wholly owned subsidiary of plaintiff Calero, which was formed in 2013.

_____ Mr. Bouk ultimately held _____ position of Veramark's Vice President of Sales. According to Plaintiffs, Mr. Bouk was _____ Veramark's highest ranking sales executive, serving as Veramark's "senior-most executive point of contact with _____ key customers and channel partners...." Mr. Bouk's base salary exceeded $157,000 and he also received _____ "substantial commission and _____ bonus compensation, Restricted Stock Awards, _____ stock options and other employee benefits."

Shortly before commencing _____ employment, Mr. Bouk entered into _____ Employment Agreement with Veramark dated _____ January 25, 2008 ("the Agreement"). _____ Agreement, which is governed by _____ New York law, contains _____ various provisions with respect to _____ post-employment conduct by Mr. Bouk. Specifically, Mr. Bouk agreed not to use or disclose _____ information defined as "Confidential" under the terms of _____ Agreement, and to return all such information upon _____ termination of his employment. Mr. Bouk also agreed that for _____ 12 months following _____ termination of his employment, he would not compete with _____ Veramark, he would not solicit _____ Veramark employees, and he would not solicit _____ Veramark customers.

Scott, Stackrow & Co. v. Skavina,
780 N.Y.S.2d 675 (N.Y. App. Div. 2004).

Vocabulary and Legal Terminology

To assert: To argue.

To militate: To have an effect on something.

Pre-Reading Questions

Before you begin reading, skim the caption, synopsis and holding and answer the following questions:

1. Is the case in federal or state court?
2. What claim did the plaintiff file against the defendant?
3. What motion was filed at the district court? Who filed it?
4. What did the district court decide with regard to the motion and what effect did that ruling have on the case?
5. Who appealed?
6. What did the New York Appellate Division decide?

Comprehension Questions

With a general idea of the case in your mind, you can now read the case. As you are reading and after you finish reading, answer the following questions:

1. Summarize in your own words the facts of this case that led to the dispute.
2. When you read the sentence stating the Appellate Division's decision — refusing to partially enforce the non-solicitation agreement to apply only to the clients that the defendant worked with while employed at plaintiff — were you surprised that even partial enforcement was determined to be overly broad? Why or why not?
3. What were the terms of the non-solicitation agreement at issue in this case?
4. What were the plaintiff's arguments as to why the non-solicitation agreement should be enforced?
5. Why did the court in this case refuse to even partially enforce the non-solicitation agreement?
6. What factors are considered when a court decides whether to partially enforce a restrictive covenant?
    a. _____
    b. _____
    c. _____

7. What is the BDO Seidman rule and why is it so important in the analysis of restrictive covenants? _____
_____
_____

8. Of the factors listed in question #6 above, are any present in our case? If so, which and what facts support that conclusion? _____
_____

9. How does this case compare to ours?
10. Is it useful for our fact pattern? Why or why not?
11. It is more useful for SDA or for Winsted? Why?

Language Focus — Parallel Construction

Parallel construction, also called parallelism, uses the same pattern of words (nouns, verbs, phases or clauses) to show that two or more ideas enjoy the same level of importance.[152] Parallel constructions lend clarity, elegance, and symmetry to what you say or write.[153] In persuasive writing, parallel constructions can add to the persuasiveness of your argument.

Great orators throughout history have used parallelism as a rhetorical device. Examine the following quotes and identify the parallel constructions.

> I came, I saw, I conquered.[154] — Julius Caesar

> Let every nation know, whether it wishes us well or ill, that we shall pay any price, bear any burden, meet any hardship, support any friend, oppose any foe to assure the survival and the success of liberty. – President John F. Kennedy, 1961 inaugural address

> We have seen the state of our Union in the endurance of rescuers, working past exhaustion. We've seen the unfurling of flags, the lighting of candles, the giving of blood, the saying of prayers — in English, Hebrew, and Arabic. President George W. Bush in speech to the nation on September 20, 2001, following the 9/11 terrorist attacks

Parallelism is not just for politicians and great orators, though. Look at this sentence from the Scott, Stackrow & Co. case. What is the parallel construction?

> Accordingly, we cannot say that Supreme Court erred in declining to partially enforce the employment agreement or in granting defendant's motion for summary judgment dismissing the complaint.

---

[152] *Parallel Structure*, PURDUE ONLINE WRITING LAB, https://owl.english.purdue.edu/owl/resource/623/01/ (last visited May 2, 2016).

[153] David S. Goldstein, Ph.D., *Parallel Construction*, UNIVERSITY OF WASHINGTON, http://faculty.washington.edu/davidgs/ParallelConstruc.pdf (last visited May 2, 2016).

[154] Of course, Caesar wasn't speaking in English when he used this parallelism. In Latin, his famous words are "Veni, vidi, vici."

The parallel construction is the use of "erred in declining" and "[erred] in granting." Although the "erred" is not repeated with the second gerund, it is understood. By reading the sentence, you know that there are two things that the Supreme Court did not make a mistake about: (1) declining to partially enforce the employment agreement and (2) granting defendant's motion for summary judgment.

We often use parallel constructions with words like *or, and, not only...but, neither...nor, both...and* and *either...or* or with a list, which can be made up of nouns, verbs, phrases or clauses.

When you write a parallel construction, you must make sure that you are consistent with the forms (in the example above, gerunds):

> Accordingly, we cannot say that Supreme Court erred <u>in declining</u> to partially enforce the employment agreement or <u>to grant</u> defendant's motion for summary judgment dismissing the complaint.

This sentence is incorrect because the form is not the same on both sides of the *or* — the gerund is not repeated and the second form is an infinitive.

Below you will find sentences with parallel constructions, some of them written correctly and others incorrectly. Your task is to analyze the sentences to determine which are correct. If the sentence is incorrectly written, correct the bad or faulty parallelism.

1. Before going home, Paula went to the grocery store, the library and to the gym.
2. You can do many things on the Internet: research class assignments, read about anything imaginable, go shopping and even stay in contact with long-lost friends and family.
3. Before appearing in court the first time, the attorney imagined that the judge would not be late for the hearing, that opposing counsel would be difficult to deal with, and that he would be asked many questions by his client.
4. The senior partner told the law clerk, who was a first-year law student, that she should study a lot for the bar, that she should network with practicing attorneys and to become skilled at writing outlines.
5. The stress of practicing law creates unhappy lawyers who will yell at anyone else doing something they don't like or just says the wrong thing.
6. The facts demonstrated that the City of West Rapids acted appropriately when it revoked Mr. Frank's license to operate a restaurant and closing the restaurant: he served spoiled meat on several occasions, failed to properly clean the kitchen and his servers did not wash their hands after going to the bathroom.
7. Specifically, the Magistrate applied improper legal standards in deciding the Title IX elements of loss of educational opportunities and deliberate indifference, ignoring precedent. [155]

---

[155] This sentence is from a brief filed in the case, <u>Sanches v. Carrollton-Farmers Branch Independent School District,</u> 647 F.3d 156 (5th Cir. 2011) and is included in materials prepared by Ross Guberman of Legal Writing Pro, LLC and author of various books on legal writing, including Point Made: How to Write Like the Nation's Top Advocates.

Merrill Lynch, Pierce, Fenner & Smith v. Dunn,
191 F. Supp. 2d 1346 (M.D. Fla. 2002).

Vocabulary and Legal Terminology

<u>Inter alia</u>: (Latin) Among other things.

<u>Motion to vacate</u>: A motion asking the court to void an order or judgment.

<u>Temporary restraining order</u>: (TRO) A remedy granted temporarily by the court only in exceptional circumstances when the court cannot hold an immediate hearing. A TRO is granted to prevent further immediate and irreparable injury to the person seeking the order. The order may be granted without advance notice to the adverse party and lasts only until the court holds a hearing.[156]

<u>Status quo</u>: (Latin) The existing state of affairs; the condition of things at a certain time.[157]

<u>To avail</u>: To use or take advantage of something.

Pre-Reading Questions

Before you begin reading, skim the caption and first paragraph and answer the following questions:

1. Is the case in federal or state court?
2. The case was filed in Florida, but all the case law we have been reading is from New York. Why do you think that a Florida case is included here?
3. Who are the parties in the case?
4. What claims were brought against the defendants?
5. What motions were brought at the district court and by whom?
6. What did the district court decide with regard to the motions?
7. What happened after the court granted the plaintiff's motion?

Comprehension Questions

With a general idea of the case in your mind, you can now read the case. As you are reading and after you finish reading, answer the following questions:

1. Summarize in your own words the facts of this case that led to the dispute.
2. What type of agreements did the defendants sign? _____
3. What were the important terms of those agreements? _____

---

[156] *Temporary Restraining Order*, Gilbert's Pocket Size Law Dictionary (3rd ed. 2014).
[157] *Status Quo*, Gilbert's Pocket Size Law Dictionary (3rd ed. 2014).

4. The court concluded that the plaintiff was likely to succeed on the breach of contract claims brought against the defendants. Why? _____

5. In this regard, why did the court conclude that the plaintiffs had legitimate business interests to protect with the non-solicitation and non-disclosure agreements? _____

6. Why did the court conclude that the plaintiff would suffer irreparable harm if the injunction were not issued? _____

7. Why did the court find that the defendants would suffer less harm if the injunction were issued than the plaintiff if it were not? _____

8. What public policy arguments did the court consider when deciding to issue the injunction? ___

9. How does this case compare to ours?
10. Is it useful for our fact pattern? Why or why not?
11. It is more useful for SDA or for Winsted? Why?

Language Focus — Past Tenses: Past Simple, Past Continuous and Past Perfect

Generally, when describing the facts in a case or client matter, we use past tense verbs, often past simple, past simple continuous, or past perfect.

The past simple is used to describe a past action that is completed in the past. While it can be used to describe an action that took place several times, the important point to remember is that the action described is finished and completed and has no connection to the present. We often use temporal references like *last Friday, in 2011,* or *yesterday morning* when using the past simple.

We form the past simple of regular verbs with *-ed* — walked, jumped, opened — while irregular verbs must be memorized.[158]
- At 10:00 this morning, I met with my new client.
- Last Friday, I was in court.
- I decided that I no longer wanted to drive to work so I began taking the bus last summer.

The past continuous is also used to describe an action in the past, but a longer one, over a period of time, that was interrupted by another past action, either in time or as a real interruption. While the past continuous also has no connection with the present, we use the continuous tense to emphasize the past action and to emphasize that it was taking place when or while something else happened.

We form the past continuous with two parts: *was/were* + verb-*ing*:
- When I was reading the newspaper, my client called.
- My colleagues were talking loudly so I wasn't able to concentrate.
- While the woman was sleeping, she suffered a heart attack.

Instead, the past perfect is used when we are talking about actions in the past, and we want to describe a past action that occurred before another past action. By using the past perfect, the listener understands which past action happened before the other one.

---

[158] To test your knowledge of irregular past tenses, see the Language Focus exercise with the case Slater v. Douglas County (Section III, Unit 3) for a table of irregular verbs.

We form the past perfect with *had* + past participle:
- I had already heard the news about the landmark Supreme Court decision when my friend Pam mentioned it to me.
- Before going to law school, I had never studied so much in my life.
- Had you ever been in court before becoming a lawyer?

Below you will find two pieces of text, one from the Merrill Lynch case and another from the Veramark Technologies case. Each has the verbs in the past tense deleted. The verb is supplied for you in parentheses; you just need to decide whether the verb needs to be written in the past simple, past continuous or past perfect tense. After you complete the paragraphs, you can check your answers in the cases. The first sentence is done for you as a sample.

Merrill Lynch case:

On Friday, March 1, 2002, Defendants (to resign) resigned from their employment with Plaintiff and (to join) joined a competing firm, Salomon Smith Barney, Inc. Prior to their resignations, each defendant (to use) _____ Plaintiff's computers and (to print) _____ out confidential customer information. Defendants (to remove) _____ this information from Plaintiff's office and (to send) _____ it to a third party who (to use) _____ the information to create solicitation letters. Immediately after Defendants resigned, the solicitation letters (to be) _____ mailed to Plaintiff's customers. The solicitation letters (to encourage) _____ Plaintiff's customers to transfer their business to Salomon Smith Barney, and the letters (to contain) _____ account transfer forms to facilitate the transfer of the customers' accounts.

Additionally, after Defendants (to resign) _____, they (to use) _____ Plaintiff's confidential customer information to telephone Plaintiff's customers and encourage them to transfer their accounts to Salomon Smith Barney. (Doc. No. 5). Defendants also (to arrange) _____ some personal meetings with Plaintiff's customers after their resignations.

In response, on March 4, 2002, Plaintiff (to file) _____ suit against Defendants and (to seek) _____ a temporary restraining order and a preliminary injunction. For the reasons (to discuss) _____ below, the Court grants Plaintiff's motion for a preliminary injunction.

Veramark Technologies case:[159]

On or about January 17, 2014, Mr. Bouk (to notify) _____ Plaintiffs of his intention to resign his employment, providing 30 days' notice pursuant to the terms of the Agreement. In his resignation letter, Mr. Bouk (to advice) _____ that he (to accept) _____ a position with Cass, but he (honor) _____ his "commitment to Veramark to not solicit or approach any Veramark customers or employees during the coming year." Plaintiffs allege that prior to receiving this notice, they (to offer) _____ to increase Mr. Bouk's annual compensation to in excess of $290,000, and that after (to receiving) _____ his resignation, they (to offer) _____ a further increase to more than $350,000 annually. Mr. Bouk disputes Plaintiffs' claims, instead contending that his position with Veramark (to be) _____ insecure after the change in ownership involving Calero, and that it (to be) _____ only after he announced his resignation that Plaintiffs orally (to offered) _____ to increase his salary.

---

[159] In this paragraph, there are two "trick" verbs that are in the past tense, but different than the three past tenses presented here.

Lucente v. International Business Machines Corp., 310 F.3d 243 (2nd Cir. 2002).

Vocabulary and Legal Terminology

Transfer of action: To move a case from one district or court to another.

Motion for reconsideration: Similar to an appeal, asking the court to reexamine its prior decision.

Cross-appeal: When both parties appeal the lower court's decision and file appeals at the same time.

Incentive compensation plan: An arrangement between an employee and employer under which part of the employee's salary is based on performance and is not guaranteed.[160]

Ominously: Threatening, suggesting that something bad is about to happen.

Letter agreement: An agreement or contract, but in the format of a letter.

Bizarre: Strange.

Anticipatory repudiation: (also called anticipatory breach) The breaking of a contract after it has been entered into but before the actual time of performance arrives. In some jurisdictions, the aggrieved party has a right to sue for breach once the repudiating party states his intention not to perform.[161]

To bar: To stop or prevent.

To opine: To state an opinion about something.

To nail down: To make something happen or to establish.

Tender: To give.

To hammer out: To produce or bring into being.

Dueling: Competing.

Bedrock: The most important principles that something is based on.

Undercut: To make something weaker.

To top out: To reach the highest amount of something, here salary or earning.

Naïve: Innocent.

---

[160] *Incentive Compensation*, MONEY-ZINE.COM, http://www.money-zine.com/definitions/career-dictionary/incentive-compensation/ (last visited May 10, 2016).
[161] *Anticipatory Breach*, GILBERT'S POCKET SIZE LAW DICTIONARY (3rd ed. 2014).

Lucente v. International Business Machines Corp., 310 F.3d 243 (2nd Cir. 2002)

Pre-Reading Questions

Before you begin reading, skim the caption and first paragraph and answer the following questions:

1. Was the case first filed in federal or state court?
2. What claim did the plaintiff bring against the defendant?
3. What did the defendant do in response to the complaint?
4. Why was the case removed to federal court and transferred to another state/district?
5. What happened procedurally once the case was in federal court?
6. What did the district court decide with regard to the motion, and what effect did that ruling have on the case?
7. Who appealed?
8. What did the court of appeals decide?
9. What happened with the case after the court of appeal's decision?

Comprehension Questions

With a general idea of the case in your mind, you can now read the case. As you are reading and after you finish reading, answer the following questions:

1. Summarize in your own words the facts of this case that led to the dispute, focusing in particular on those that concern Lucente's departure from IBM, as they are the important facts for our issue of the restrictive covenant.
2. Why does it matter to the court whether Lucente voluntarily resigned or whether he was involuntarily terminated? _____
3. State in your own words what the "employee choice doctrine" is: _____
4. Write below the three elements of the "employee choice doctrine:"
    a. _____
    b. _____
    c. _____
5. What facts did the appellate court find were in dispute regarding Lucente's departure from IBM and whether it was voluntary or not? _____
6. An employee can be terminated in what is known as "constructive discharge" or "constructive termination," defined in Black's Law Dictionary as "[a]n employer's creation of working conditions that leave a particular employee or group of employees little or no choice but to resign, as by fundamentally changing the working conditions or terms of employment; an employer's course of action that, being detrimental to an employee, leaves the employee almost no option but to quit." [162]
    a. How might Lucente argue that he was constructively discharged and thus the "employee choice doctrine" cannot apply?

---

[162] *Discharge*, BLACK'S LAW DICTIONARY (10th ed. 2014).

b. How can Winsted argue that she was constructively discharged?
c. If you represent Winsted, might this be a good argument to make? Why or why not?

7. Is this case useful for our fact pattern? Why or why not?
8. It is more useful for SDA or for Winsted? Why?

Language Focus – Tool Idioms[163]

An idiomatic expression is an expression whose meaning cannot be inferred from the meanings of the words. You are probably familiar already with some idiomatic expressions: To rain cats and dogs.[164] To pull someone's leg.[165] To hold your horses.[166]

The <u>Lucente</u> decision includes two colorful idiomatic expressions:

> The district court then opined that if Lucente were her client, "I would make damn sure that I could *nail down* my claim for two million dollars" by tendering payment to IBM for Lucente's remaining stock options.

> The parties were unable to *hammer out* a joint stipulation as to Lucente's stock option damages.

In these two sentences, the judge isn't really saying that she would take a hammer and pound a nail through the claim (especially since a claim isn't even a tangible thing!). Instead, the judge means that she would make sure that it would happen that she would get the claim by making the payment. *To nail down* means to make something happen.

Instead, in the second sentence, the parties were not really using a hammer to do any work, but were simply trying to finalize the agreement. *To hammer out* means to produce or to bring about.

To understand each of these expressions, it isn't sufficient to know what a hammer or a nail is; you need to go beyond the literal meaning of the words. Often that involves looking up the expression in the dictionary or asking a native speaker.

To nail down and *hammer out* are not the only idiomatic expressions in English using common, everyday tools. Below is a list of other expressions, each using a different tool. Your job is to complete the list with both the meaning of the expression and a sample sentence that demonstrates the meaning. The first expression has been done for you.

To hit the nail on the head

<u>Meaning</u>: to describe precisely the problem facing someone or something
<u>Sample</u>: My boss really hit the nail on the head when he identified the weaknesses in my legal argument. I knew that with his decades of experience, he would know what was wrong and give me good suggestions to improve it.

---

[163] Jamal Anwar Taha, *Tool Idioms in English*, Apr. 2013, https://www.academia.edu/6079678/tool_idioms_in_English; http://www.dailywritingtips.com/90-idioms-about-tools/ (last visited May 10, 2016).
[164] To rain heavily.
[165] To joke with someone.
[166] To be patient.

To be tough as nails

Meaning: _____
Sample: _____
_____

To put a nail in the coffin of something

Meaning: _____
Sample: _____
_____

To bury the hatchet

Meaning: _____
Sample: _____
_____

To call a spade a spade

Meaning: _____
Sample: _____
_____

To have an ax to grind

Meaning: _____
Sample: _____
_____

To put a wrench into something

Meaning: _____
Sample: _____
_____

To drill down

Meaning: _____
Sample: _____
_____

To have a screw loose

Meaning: _____
Sample: _____
_____

To screw around

Meaning: _____
Sample: _____
_____

To screw someone over

Meaning: _____
Sample: _____
_____

To screw something up

Meaning: _____
Sample: _____
_____

To have your head screwed on right

Meaning: _____
Sample: _____
_____

Zellner v. Conrad,
589 N.Y.S.2d 903 (N.Y. App. Div. 1992).

Vocabulary and Legal Terminology

Ophthalmologist: Medical doctor who specializes in care of the eye.

To come into being: To start to exist.

Declaratory judgment: A statement of the court declaring the rights and duties of the parties in a case or stating an opinion on a question of law without awarding relief.[167]

Letter of transmittal: A letter that usually accompanies a longer document such as an agreement, as here.

Execution: (here) Act of signing a document such as an agreement.

Sole support: The only person working and thus earning money to provide for one's family.

Radius: Straight line from the center of a circle to the circumference; often used in restrictive covenants to measure geographic restriction and usually calculated from the former employer's place of business.

Ancillary: Additional or supplementary.

Forbearance: The act of not doing something, such as enforcing a right.[168]

Pre-Reading Questions

Before you begin reading, skim the caption and first paragraph and answer the following questions:

1. Is the case in federal or state court?
2. Who are the parties in the case and what is their relationship?
3. Why is this case different from the other cases that we've read in this Unit with regard to who the plaintiff is?
4. What motions were brought at the district court and by whom?
5. What did the district court decide with regard to the motions?
6. Who appealed?
7. What did the appellate court decide and why?

---

[167] *Declaratory Judgment*, Gilbert's Pocket Size Law Dictionary (3rd ed. 2014).
[168] *Forbearance*, Black's Law Dictionary (10th ed. 2014).

Comprehension Questions

With a general idea of the case in your mind, you can now read the case. As you are reading and after you finish reading, answer the following questions:

1. Summarize in your own words the facts of this case that led to the dispute.
2. According to the plaintiff, why did he sign the non-competition agreement? _____
3. What were the relevant and important provisions of the non-competition agreement? _____
4. Why did the former independent contractor bring the claim when usually, it is the former employer who files suit against the employee for violating the restrictive covenant? _____
5. The court states in two different places in the decision that there are two issues that must be decided. Write those two issues below:
    a. _____
    b. _____
6. What is the split between states with regard to a restrictive covenant signed after an employee has begun working at an employer? _____
7. Why does the court decide that the better approach is to follow the states that do not require additional consideration when a restrictive covenant is signed after an employee starts working? _____
8. What is the consideration in this case? _____
9. We learned in this case that in New York (and thus in Jefferson), a restrictive covenant doesn't need additional consideration if signed after employment has commenced. If Winsted were to claim that the agreement lacked consideration and if the court held that Winsted had not worked at SDA a "substantial time" to constitute consideration, what argument could SDA make that other, additional consideration does exist in the case? _____
10. How does this case compare to ours?
11. Is it useful for our fact pattern? Why or why not?
12. It is more useful for SDA or for Winsted? Why?

Language Focus – Conciseness[169]

Writing concisely or "tightly"[170] is a goal that all writers should have – whether they are writing legal English or "regular" English. Unlike some languages, English values short, tight, and concise sentences. Here are some quotes of famous writers that underscore this:

"If I had more time I would have written a shorter letter." — Blaise Pascal

"The most valuable of all talents is that of never using two words when one will do." — Thomas Jefferson

"Vigorous writing is concise. A sentence should contain no unnecessary words, a paragraph no unnecessary sentences, for the same reason that a drawing should have no unnecessary lines and a machine no unnecessary parts. This requires not that the writer make all his sentences short, or that he avoid all detail and treat his subject only in outline, but that every word tell." — William Strunk and EB White

Unfortunately, legal writing is often some of the least concise writing out there! You have no doubt read court decisions with long, convoluted sentences. Contracts and statutes have the same problem. It seems that many attorneys think that to sound "lawyerly," they have to write in long sentences with complicated structure, unnecessary words and difficult legal terminology.

Entire books have been written on the subject of how to write in clear, concise and "plain" legal English, and more can be said on the subject than can be covered in this short exercise. But some basic guidelines to improving your legal writing and to making it tighter recommend that you:[171]

- Omit needless words
- Keep your average sentence length to about 20 words
- Keep the subject, verb, and the object together – towards the beginning of the sentence
- Prefer the active voice to the passive voice
- Avoid multiple negatives

Zellner v. Stephen D. Conrad, M.D is not the best example of concise legal writing. If you scrutinize the decision, you can find many sentences and paragraphs that would benefit from careful revising and editing. Below is a paragraph from the Zellner decision (the citations have been omitted for ease of reading).

---

[169] The skill of "tightening up" your writing is a very important one for a good writer to develop, so much so that you will find another Language Focus exercise on this same topic (with some of the same introductory information) in Unit 4 of this same Section of the ESL Workbook (The Great Atlantic and Pacific Tea Co. v. Yanofsky). For more practice, you can do the exercise presented with the Great Atlantic case. Bryan Garner's book Legal Writing in Plain English is also a good resource with not just extensive explanations about how you can write more clearly and concisely, but also with practice exercises.

[170] While you might be familiar with the adjective tight to describe clothing that fits closely to the skin, we also use it to describe writing. *Tight writing* is writing that is "marked by control or discipline in expression or style; having little or no extraneous matter." MERRIAM-WEBSTER ONLINE DICTIONARY, http://www.merriam-webster.com/dictionary/tight (last visited May 2, 2016).

[171] These guidelines are from Legal Writing in Plain English by Bryan Garner and are the topics of some of the sections in the second chapter of his book. BRYAN A. GARNER, LEGAL WRITING IN PLAIN ENGLISH 17-31 (2001).

You are a clerk with the judge who wrote the Zellner decision. Before the decision is issued, the judge asks you to check his writing and edit it where necessary so that it is as concise and clear as possible, but without changing the meaning. Thus your task is to revise this paragraph to make it tighter. Once you have finished, you can compare your edits with the sample revised paragraph on the next page.

> We believe the latter position to be the better view. Because in at-will employment the employer has the right to discharge the employee (or, as here, an independent contractor providing services under a similar arrangement), without cause, and without being subject to inquiry as to his or her motives, forbearance of that right is a legal detriment which can stand as consideration for a restrictive covenant. It is certainly true that this detriment would have little meaning if the employer exercised his right to terminate the employment shortly after the execution of the agreement. However, where, as here, a relationship continues for a substantial period after the covenant is given, the forbearance is real, not illusory, and the consideration given for the promise is validated. Thus, "forbearance to discharge" and "continued employment" are but two expressions of the same legal detriment. Accepting the plaintiff's position would mean that the employer would have to fire the at-will employee and then immediately offer to rehire the employee on the condition that he or she sign the covenant in order to protect the covenant from a later attack that it lacked consideration. We will not encourage unnecessary legal dramatics.

With edits shown:

~~We believe t~~The latter position is ~~best to be the~~ better ~~view~~. ~~Because in at-will employment the a~~An employer has the right to discharge ~~the~~an at-will employee ~~(~~or, as here, an independent contractor ~~providing services~~ under a similar arrangement~~)~~, without cause, and without ~~being subject to inquiry as to his or her~~ the need to explain his motives~~.~~ Thus, forbearance of that right is a legal detriment ~~which~~ that can ~~stand as~~ constitute consideration for a restrictive covenant. ~~It is certainly true that t~~This detriment would have little meaning if the employer ~~exercised his right to~~ terminated the employment shortly after the ~~execution of the~~ agreement was signed. However, ~~where, as here,~~ when a relationship continues for a substantial period ~~after the covenant agreement it is~~ ~~signing given~~, the forbearance is real, ~~not illusory, and~~ as is the consideration ~~given for the promise is validated~~. Thus, "forbearance to discharge" and "continued employment" ~~are but two expressions of~~ represent the same legal detriment. Accepting the plaintiff's position ~~would~~ means that the employer would have to fire the at-will employee and then immediately offer to rehire ~~the employee~~ him on the condition that he ~~or she~~ sign the covenant in order to protect ~~the covenant~~ it from a later attack ~~that it lacked~~ of lacking consideration. We will not encourage unnecessary legal dramatics.

Without edits shown:

The latter position is better. An employer has the right to discharge an at-will employee or independent contractor under a similar arrangement without cause, and without the need to explain his motives. Thus, forbearance of that right is a legal detriment that can constitute consideration for a restrictive covenant. This detriment would have little meaning if the employer terminated the employment shortly after the agreement was signed. However, when a relationship continues for a substantial period, the forbearance is real, as is the consideration. Thus, "forbearance to discharge" and "continued employment" represent the same legal detriment. Accepting the plaintiff's position means that the employer would have to fire the at-will employee and then immediately offer to rehire him on the condition that he sign the covenant in order to protect it from a later attack of lacking consideration. We will not encourage unnecessary legal dramatics.

Ashland Management, Inc. v. Altair Investments NA, LLC,
869 N.Y.S.2d 465 (N.Y. App. Div. 2008).

Vocabulary and Legal Terminology

Conversion: Civil equivalent of theft; tortious act of depriving an owner of his property without his permission and without just cause. An illegal taking, detention, use, assumption of ownership, or destruction of the property of another all constitute conversion.[172]

Blatant: Very obvious.

High net worth individual: Individual who is worth a lot of money.

To divulge: To reveal or disclose.

To blind-side: To surprise someone in a very unexpected way.

To ascertain: To determine or conclude.

To discontinue without prejudice: To voluntarily dismiss a claim but with the right to re-commence it (without prejudice means that the claim can be filed again; with prejudice means it cannot).

To cross-move: When both parties move (here, for summary judgment) at the same time.

Is of no moment: Is unimportant or irrelevant.

Fiduciary duties of good faith and fair dealings: Duties that all employees owe their current employers; also found in commercial transactions.

Pre-Reading Questions

Before you begin reading, skim the caption, synopsis and holdings and answer the following questions:

1. Is the case in federal or state court?
2. What is the relationship between the parties in the case?
3. What claims did the plaintiffs bring against the defendants?
4. What motion was filed at the district court? Who filed it?
5. What did the district court decide with regard to the motion?
6. Who appealed?
7. What did the appellate court decide? Why?
8. Given what you have learned in the other cases, does the second holding — that the lack of

---

[172] *Conversion*, GILBERT'S POCKET SIZE LAW DICTIONARY (3rd ed. 2014).

a temporal restriction in a restrictive covenant does not render it unenforceable — surprise you? Why or why not?

9. Do you think that the court decided that the lack of a temporal restriction does not render it unenforceable because it was examining a confidentiality agreement rather than a non-competition agreement? Why or why not?

Comprehension Questions

With a general idea of the case in your mind, you can now read the case. As you are reading and after you finish reading, answer the following questions:

1. Summarize in your own words the facts of this case that led to the dispute.
2. List all of the facts that show that the defendants acted in bad faith and violated the duty that they owed their employer: _____
3. Are there any similar facts in our case to show that Rachael Winsted violated any duty that she owed to SDA? Why or why not? _____
4. Summarize in your own words what the district court (supreme court) prohibited in the injunction: _____
5. How does the court reason that the lack of a temporal restriction in the confidentiality agreement does not void the agreement?
6. How does this case compare to ours?
7. Is it useful for our fact pattern? Why or why not?
8. Is it more useful for SDA or for Winsted? Why?

Language Focus — Verbs Taking the Gerund (-ing) or the Infinitive

Here are two sentences from the Ashland Management case. Examine the italicized words in each sentence.

> Prior to January 2003, and while still employed by plaintiff, Jones and Obuchowski *started planning* Altair.

> According to plaintiff, these actions were in violation of defendants' fiduciary duty and confidentiality agreements, and *designed to increase* their visibility to plaintiff's clients immediately prior to their resignation so that they would be more likely to attract those clients.

Certain verbs in English are followed by the infinitive, while others are followed by a gerund (verb + *ing*). It is important to remember which verbs take the infinitive and which take the gerund to speak and write in a grammatically correct way. In a field like the law, it is especially important. Lawyers write many letters, briefs and memos, and you want to be sure that your work is error-free so that you are seen as credible, authoritative and reliable by clients, opposing counsel or a judge. Likewise, how we speak (vocabulary choices, grammatical mistakes and pronunciation) is important for the same reasons.

Verbs in English that are followed by an infinitive include:

agree	help	prefer
arrange	hope	promise
attempt	intend	tend
choose	learn	try
decide	like	refuse
expect	love	remember
fail	manage	want
forget	mean	would like
hate	plan	would love

Verbs that are followed by a gerund include:

admit	enjoy	love
avoid	fancy	miss
begin	finish	practice
consider	hate	remember
deny	imagine	risk
detest	keep	start
dislike	like	suggest

Examples of these verbs plus a gerund or infinitive include:

- I didn't want to *waste time watching* TV when I had so many pages to read for class.
- My brother *admitted to stealing* the neighbor's bike.
- We *finished painting* the garage just as it *started to rain*.
- They *happened to walk* into the store just as it was being held up.
- He *waited to see* the movie when it came out on DVD rather than pay full price at the movie theater.

You likely have noticed or learned that some verbs, such as like and love, can take either the infinitive or the gerund. As the website EnglishPage.com tells us:

> Although the difference in meaning is small with these particular verbs, and gerunds and infinitives can often be used interchangeably, there is still a meaning difference. Using a gerund suggests that you are referring to real activities or experiences. Using an infinitive suggests that you are talking about potential or possible activities or experiences. Because of this small difference in meaning, gerunds and infinitives cannot always be used interchangeably.[173]

---

[173] ENGLISHPAGE.COM, *Verbs Followed by Gerunds or Infinitives (Similar Meanings)*, http://www.englishpage.com/gerunds/gerund_or_infinitive_same_list.htm (last visited May 2, 2016).

Here are some examples:

- I love riding my bike. (I am expressing something that I always love doing)
- I love to ride a bike when it is warm and sunny out. (Here, it is something that I can possibly do because it is not always warm and sunny)
- Many lawyers love litigating cases when they have good facts and when the law is on their side. (Here, the sentence describes something that these particular lawyers always love doing)
- Most lawyers don't love to work on the weekends. (Here, it is a possible activity or experience)

However, there are some other verbs in English that have very different meanings, depending on whether they are followed by a gerund or an infinitive. Your task is to examine the three pairs of sentences below with the verbs *to forget*, *to stop* and *to regret* and answer the following questions:

- What is the difference of meaning between the two sentences?
- What rules can you draft for the different meanings when we use these verbs followed by an infinitive or a gerund?

She forgot to drink water.
She forgot drinking the twelve pack of beer.

I stop to drink a soda.
I stopped drinking soda.

I regret telling my boss my true feelings about my job.
I regret to inform you that I am resigning from my job.

Unit 2

Personal Jurisdiction and the Internet

Atkinson v. McLaughlin,
462 F. Supp. 2d 1038 (D.N.D. 2006).

Vocabulary and Legal Terminology

Diversity action: A claim filed in federal court based on the grounds that the parties are all residents of different states. Federal courts are courts of limited jurisdiction, and diversity jurisdiction is one of the ways that a federal court can hear a claim.

Tortious interference with business: A tort claim that alleges that the defendant intentionally interfered with the contractual or business relationship between the plaintiff and a third party.

To warrant: To justify.

Department: (here) A state or region in a country.

Surrogate: Substitute.

Innuendo: An indirect comment that suggests or implies something improper or unpleasant.

Insinuation: An statement that suggests something negative or derogatory.

"Smear" campaign: To smear means to spread gossip or rumors about someone; a "smear" campaign is a series of activities with the goal of harming someone's reputation through rumors and gossip.

Purposeful availment: In matters of personal jurisdiction, the rule that an out-of-state defendant must have availed, or used or taken advantage of the benefits of the forum state (in other words, had minimum contacts with the state) so that the constitutional due process rule is not violated by exercising jurisdiction over the defendant.

Aggregate: Formed by adding together two or more parts or elements.

"Sliding-scale:" A variable scale or way of measuring something, in this case the characteristics of interactivity of a website, with an interactive website at one end of the scale and a passive one at the other end.

Spectrum: A complete range of options.

Atkinson v. McLaughlin, 462 F. Supp. 2d 1038 (D.N.D. 2006)

Pre-Reading Questions

Before you begin reading, skim the caption, the synopsis and the holdings and answer the following questions:

1. Is the case in federal or state court?
2. What claims did the plaintiffs file against the defendants? Are these state or federal claims?
3. On what basis did the plaintiffs file the claim in federal court?
4. What motion was filed at the district court?
5. Was the motion granted?
6. What happened after the motion was filed and the court ruled on the motion?

Comprehension Questions

With a general idea of the case in your mind, you can now read the case. As you are reading and after you finish reading, answer the following questions:

1. Summarize in your own words the facts of this case that led to the dispute.
2. When a court considers whether to exercise jurisdiction over an out-of-state defendant, it must follow a two-step test. Write the two steps below:
   a. _____
   b. _____
3. Why does the court in the Atkinson case only analyze the second step of the above test?
4. In your own words, what does it mean that jurisdiction over an out-of-state defendant must not offend the "traditional notions of fair play and substantial justice?"
5. What are the two types of jurisdiction that a court can exercise over an out-of-state defendant:
   a. _____
   b. _____
6. Describe specific jurisdiction: _____
7. Describe general jurisdiction: _____
8. Why do courts require that an out-of-state or nonresident defendant "purposely avail" him or herself of the "privilege" of conducting activities within the state to then exercise jurisdiction over the defendant? _____
9. Even if a defendant has minimum contacts with the forum state, when might the court still decide *not* to exercise personal jurisdiction over it? _____
10. Write the five elements or prongs of the test of measuring whether a nonresident defendant has minimum contacts with the forum state.

a. _____
b. _____
c. _____
d. _____
e. _____

11. Is one of these factors determinative in the analysis of personal jurisdiction and minimum contacts? _____

12. In our Groovia v. SDA case, which state is the forum state? _____

13. Summarize the three types of websites that are presented in the case and first enumerated in the Zippo case.
    a. _____
    b. _____
    c. _____

14. Which type of website allows for the exercise of personal jurisdiction over an out-of-state defendant? _____

15. Based on what you have read so far, which type of website does SDA operate? _____

16. What argument does Atkinson make about why the court should have jurisdiction over the defendants? _____

17. What facts does the court use to conclude that the website in the Atkinson case is either passive or in the middle of the spectrum? _____

18. If the forum court decides that it cannot exercise personal jurisdiction over an out-of-state defendant, what options has the plaintiff got for suing the defendant? _____

19. How is this case useful for our case?

20. Is the case more helpful for SDA or Groovia? Why?

21. What arguments can you make to analogize or distinguish this case from our case?

Grammar Focus — Relative Pronouns: That or Which? Who or Whom?

A relative pronoun is a pronoun that introduces a relative clause. The name *relative pronoun* may not be familiar, but you will certainly recognize the relative pronouns in English: *who, which, that, whom, whomever, whose, when* and *where*. We call these words relative pronouns because they take the place of a noun (like all pronouns) and because they relate back to and define the noun that they replace.

We use the relative pronoun *who* when referring to a person:

- *The plaintiff, Patrick Atkinson ("Atkinson"), is a resident of Franklin **who** founded the God's Child Project in 1991 and serves as the executive director.*

- In this sentence, *who founded the God's Child Project in 1991,* is a relative clause.
- *Who*, the relative pronoun, is the subject of that relative clause.
- The relative pronoun and clause refer or relate back to the noun, the plaintiff, and provide additional information about him.

The relative pronoun *which* is used to refer to a thing:

- *Both categories of minimum contacts require some act by **which** the defendant purposely avails himself or herself of the privilege of conducting activities within the forum state, and thus invokes the benefits and protections of its laws.*

We use the relative pronoun *that* when referring to either a person or a thing:

- *The motion to dismiss **that** the defendant filed was not granted.*
- *The judge **that** heard the motion in the <u>Mink</u> case was later nominated to the 5th Circuit Court of Appeals.*

The relative pronoun should always follow the noun that it relates to or defines:

- *I am sending you the motion to dismiss, which I have signed.*
- NOT: ~~*I am sending you the motion to dismiss in this matter, which I have signed*~~.
    - In this sentence, the relative pronoun *which* refers to the motion to dismiss. Thus, the second sentence is incorrect because the relative pronoun follows the noun *matter*, which it doesn't refer to.

That, Which or Who?

From the rules above, you see that we use both *which* and *that* to refer to things, and both *who* and *that* to refer to a person. Thus, the first question we want to examine is how do you know whether you should use *who* or *that*, or *which* or *that*, since both can refer to a person or to a thing, respectively? The answer comes down to determining what type of relative clause you have in a sentence. There are two types: a restrictive and a non-restrictive relative clause.

Restrictive Relative Clause:

A restrictive relative clause provides essential information to a sentence, without which the sentence would not make sense to the reader or to the listener.

- *The judge that is hearing the case is usually pro-defendant.*
- *The books that are on the table are mine.*

In these sentences, the relative pronouns provide essential information for the understanding of the sentence. If I remove the relative clause and say *The judge is pro-defendant*, the reader won't know which judge I am referring to, and the sentence will mean that any judge, not just the one hearing the case, is pro-defendant.

In the second sentence, if I remove the relative clause, it means that all books are mine. That certainly isn't the case. Thus, the clause *that are on the table* is essential for understanding the sense of that sentence.

Note too that we can remove the relative pronoun when we have a restrictive relative clause:
- *The judge hearing the case is pro-defendant.*
- *The books on the table are mine.*

Non-Restrictive Relative Clause:

A non-restrictive relative clause, on the other hand, provides additional information in a sentence. Without that information provided in the relative clause, the sentence will still make sense to the reader or to the listener.
- *The judge, who is originally from Florida, was nominated to the bench in 1999.*
- *The table, which is made from oak, was handmade in 1955.*

In both of these examples, if you remove the relative clauses, the sentences still make sense. The relative clauses provide extra information for the reader, but non-essential information for understanding the sentence.

Note too that the non-restrictive clauses are surrounded by commas, unlike the restrictive clauses. In addition, unlike the relative pronouns with restrictive clauses, I cannot remove the relative pronouns in these sentences:
- NOT: ~~The judge, originally from Florida, was nominated to the bench in 1999.~~
- NOT: ~~The table, made from oak, was handmade in 1955.~~

Who or Whom:

Another question to examine is when you use *who* and when you use *whom*, since both refer to a person, but are used in very different grammatical situations.

The relative pronoun *whom* is used to refer to a person, but when that person is the object of a relative clause or of a prepositional phrase:
- *I argued the case in front of the judge **with whom** I graduated from law school.*
    - In this sentence, *with whom* is a relative clause introduced by a preposition. *With* is a preposition, and the object of that preposition is the relative pronoun. Because the relative pronoun is the object of the preposition, we use *whom*.
    - In everyday spoken English, we would instead say: *I argued the case in front of the judge that I graduated from law school with.*

- *The attorney **whom** my colleague saw at the courthouse is an old friend.*
    - In this sentence, *whom my colleague saw at the courthouse,* is the relative clause.
    - The subject of the clause is my colleague, who did the action of seeing.
    - The relative pronoun – whom – is instead the object of the verb *to see*: My colleague saw the attorney.
    - Because the relative pronoun is the object of the relative clause, we use whom.
    - In everyday spoken English, we would likely say: *The attorney that my colleague saw at the courthouse is an old friend.*

Below are sentences with the relative pronoun missing. Complete the sentences with the correct relative pronoun. The sentences are all from cases that you have read in this Unit. After you complete the sentences, you can check your answers by finding the sentences in the Commented Cases and Legal

Authorities book (open the electronic version and do a search to help find the sentences). You will likely see that the strict rules of which/that and who/that are not always followed, and your answers based on the rules might be different than what the court used.

1. With respect to general jurisdiction over a defendant, "a court may hear a lawsuit against a defendant _____ has 'continuous and systematic' contacts with the forum state, even if the injuries at issue in the lawsuit did not arise out of the defendant's activities directed at the forum."

2. A passive Web site that does little more than make information available to those _____ are interested in it is not grounds for the exercise [of] personal jurisdiction.

3. From July of 1997 to March of 1998, the defendants, James McLaughlin and Roberta McLaughlin ("McLaughlins"), volunteered for the God's Child Project in Guatemala through a Guatemalan-registered charity entitled Association Nuestros Ahijados, _____ was also founded by Atkinson.

4. Unlike sellers in online auctions, _____ may have limited control over those with whom they transact business, Go Satellite could have excluded website users who were residents in certain states.

5. The issue of exercising personal jurisdiction over a defendant ____ operates an Internet website without other contacts with the forum state is a question of first impression in the Fifth Circuit.

6. This direct contact results in an exchange of information between the website and the consumers _____ order the inkjet printer cartridges.

7. Plaintiff, a Louisiana resident, alleges that she learned about Dr. Revis through the website www.justbreastimplants.com ("JBI"), _____ Dr. Revis and SFPSA allegedly used "to solicit patients from across the country to come to Florida for breast augmentation surgery."

8. Personal jurisdiction "is 'an essential element of the jurisdiction of a district ... court,' without _____ the court is 'powerless to proceed to an adjudication.'"

9. First, she argues that defendants made contacts with Louisiana through JBI, _____ she characterizes as an "interactive website."

10. This case arose after the decedent, Lake Charles resident Phillip Gatte, sought the help of Ready 4 A Change, LLC, ("R4C") a Minnesota-based company _____ specializes in connecting people _____ desire affordable weight loss surgery with hospitals and doctors in Mexico _____ provide this surgery.

Mink v. AAAA Development, Inc.,
190 F.3d 333 (5th Cir. 1999).

Vocabulary and Legal Terminology

Patent pending rights: Rights given to someone after he or she has filed for a patent, but before it is granted.

Sales management software: A computer program or system that allows the user to manage all aspects of a sales job (leads, sales made, client contact information, etc.).

Motion for reconsideration of the order: In federal court, pre-trial matters such as a motion to dismiss are handled and decided by a magistrate judge. If a party disagrees with the magistrate judge's decision on a motion, he can appeal to the district court judge for a reconsideration, which is like an appeal but within the district court. The party can then appeal to the court of appeals if he is not satisfied with the outcome of the motion for reconsideration.

De novo review: Standard of review for an appellate court, as if it were considering the issue for the first time.[174]

At the outset: Initially.

Pre-Reading Questions

Before you begin reading, skim the caption and first paragraph and answer the following questions:
1. Is the case in federal or state court?
2. What claims did the plaintiffs file against the defendant?
3. What motion was filed at the district court?
4. Was the motion granted?
5. Who appealed?
6. What did the court of appeals decide about the appeal and on what grounds?

Comprehension Questions

With a general idea of the case in your mind, you can now read the case. As you are reading and after you finish reading, answer the following questions:
1. Summarize in your own words the facts of this case that led to the dispute.
2. In the paragraph that begins "On November 7, 1997," what additional facts about the procedural history do we learn? _____

---

[174] For additional information about standards of review, see the Legal Focus exercise with the case Gifford v. Gallano Farms (Section II, Unit 4) on page 167.

3. From the paragraphs in which the court summarizes the facts of the case, what specific facts do we learn about the defendant's contacts with Texas? _____

4. Based on what you know so far, which type of jurisdiction might a Franklin court have over SDA in the dispute with Groovia, general or specific jurisdiction? Why? _____

5. Why did the court affirm the lower court's ruling dismissing the complaint against the defendant? _____

6. Are the facts in this case similar to or different from our case? How? _____

7. How is this case useful for our case, regardless of whether you represent SDA or Groovia?

8. Is the case more helpful for SDA or for Groovia? Why?

9. What arguments can you make to analogize or distinguish this case from ours?

Legal Focus: Tests in Legal Analysis

As you have been reading cases for your legal writing class or for other classes in your LL.M. program, you have no doubt noticed that courts in the United States use many tests when carrying out their legal analysis. In the Atkinson case, you were introduced to four tests:

1. The two-step framework for analyzing issues of personal jurisdiction
2. The five-part (or prong) test for measuring minimum contacts for purposes of asserting personal jurisdiction over a defendant
3. The totality of the circumstances (or aggregate) test to determine whether minimum contacts exist
4. A sliding-scale test applied in Internet cases to determine whether a website can be the basis for personal jurisdiction over a nonresident defendant

The tests are introduced as well in the Mink case, and you will see them in the rest of the cases that you will read for this Unit. You may have encountered other tests in cases you have read for other classes. For example, courts apply a balancing test when considering whether to admit evidence.

In constitutional law, you will learn about the Lemon test when reading about cases in which a government action is challenged as violating the First Amendment separation of church and state. The Lemon test says that courts generally uphold government action as long as the action or statute 1) has a secular legislative purpose; 2) has a principal or primary effect that neither advances nor inhibits religion; and 3) does not foster an excessive government entanglement with religion.[175]

The Miller test also involves the First Amendment but is applied when a court analyzes whether speech is obscene and thus not entitled to the constitutional protections that the First Amendment grants. Under the Miller test, speech is obscene if 1) the average person applying contemporary community standards would find that the work, taken as a whole, appeals to the prurient interest; 2) the work depicts or

---

[175] Lemon v. Kurtzman, 403 U.S. 602 (1971).

describes, in a patently offensive way, sexual conduct specifically defined by the applicable state law; and (c) the work, taken as a whole, lacks serious literary, artistic, political, or scientific value.[176]

Many other tests exist in the law in addition to those listed above, and when you are reading a case and encounter a test in the analysis, you should immediately highlight the test, make a note in the margin and include the test in your case brief. They are very important to your understanding of the law. A question we can ask ourselves is why they are so important.

Legal analysis tests provide a predictable and uniform way to analyze legal matters. This is one reason why courts create and also employ them: they are thought to lead to less ambiguity and less subjectiveness. Likewise, as a law student, a test provides you a clear and easy-to-follow structure for your legal analysis, and following the test will ensure that you cover each and every element of the issue you are analyzing. If your test is a five-prong test such as that for minimum contacts and you only have four sections in your legal analysis, you immediately know that something is missing and can quickly identify your mistake.

Because tests are made up of elements (or prongs), they also lend themselves to an outline format, which aids you in organizing the legal document that you are writing. For example, if you are writing a memo on personal jurisdiction, following the tests will help you write the outline:

Analysis for personal jurisdiction
1. Whether state will exercise personal jurisdiction under the long-arm statute
2. Whether the exercise of personal jurisdiction comports with due process
   a. Whether the defendant has purposefully availed himself of the benefits and protections of the state by establishing minimum contacts
      1) The nature and quality of the defendant's contacts with the forum state
      2) The quantity of such contacts
      3) The relation of the cause of action to the contacts
      4) The interest of the forum state in providing a forum for its residents
      5) The convenience of the parties
   b. Whether the exercise of jurisdiction does not offend the traditional notions of fair play and substantial justice

This outline was written with only the first two cases. As you continue reading the cases in this Unit, you will learn that there are other tests employed by the 5th Circuit in assessing personal jurisdiction, such as a three-prong test to determine whether specific jurisdiction exists.

With a complex topic like personal jurisdiction, or any other that you will deal with during your LL.M. program, studying and analyzing the tests and applying them to the facts will help your understanding of the law. Moreover, writing an outline from the tests will also help your understanding as it requires you to synthesize information from various sources.

---

[176] Miller v. California, 413 U.S. 15 (1973).

Carrot Bunch Co., v. Computer Friends, Inc.,
218 F. Supp. 2d 820 (N.D. Tex. 2002).

Vocabulary and Legal Terminology

Cybersquatting: Registering an internet domain name without a good faith intent to use the domain. Cybersquatting often involves registering a domain name that is the same or very similar to a company's name or trademark, with the intent of selling the name to the company.[177]

Anticybersquatting Consumer Protection Act: A federal law passed in 1999 that establishes a civil cause of action against a person who uses or registers a domain name that is confusingly similar to or dilutive of a personal or trade name.[178]

Lanham Act: A federal law passed in 1946 under President Harry Truman that provides a system for the registration of trademarks and regulates their use in commerce.[179]

Misappropriation: Wrongful or unauthorized use of property or funds (e.g., using trust funds other than for the beneficiary of the trust).[180]

Transfer of venue: To move a case from one jurisdiction (venue) to another.

Alias: A false or assumed identity.

Cease and desist letter: Letter sent demanding that the recipient stop a particular activity and threatening to take legal action if he or she does not.

Certified mail: Service offered by the U.S. Postal Service that provides proof (sufficient in court) that a letter was sent and received.

To find wanting: To find lacking.

Pre-Reading Questions

Before you begin reading, skim the caption and first paragraph and answer the following questions:

1. Is the case in federal or state court?
2. Who is the plaintiff and what claims did he bring against the defendant?
3. What had the defendant done to lead the plaintiff to file the claims against him?
4. What motion was filed at the district court? Who filed it?
5. What did the district court decide with regard to the motion?
6. What happened after the court ruled on the motion?

---

[177] *Cybersquatting*, Gilbert's Pocket Size Law Dictionary (3rd ed. 2014).
[178] 15 U.S.C. §1225(d) (2015).
[179] 15 U.S.C. § 1051 *et seq.* (2015).
[180] *Misappropriation*, Gilbert's Pocket Size Law Dictionary (3rd ed. 2014).

Comprehension Questions

With a general idea of the case in your mind, you can now read the case. As you are reading and after you finish reading, answer the following questions:

1. Summarize in your own words the facts of this case that led to the dispute. _____

2. What must be present in a nonresident defendant's activities that would lead a court to exercise personal jurisdiction over him? _____

3. In this case, how did the defendant "purposely avail" himself of doing business in Texas? _____

4. What minimum contacts did the defendant in this case have with Texas? _____

5. Do you think that SDA "purposefully availed" itself of doing business in Franklin? Why or why not? _____

6. What minimum contacts does SDA have with Franklin? _____

7. How is this case useful for our case, regardless of whether you represent SDA or Groovia? _____

8. Is the case more helpful for SDA or for Groovia? Why? _____

9. What arguments can you make to analogize or distinguish it from our case? _____

Language Focus — Find the Mistakes

Judges are people too, and like everyone, they make mistakes when they are writing their decisions. Below are two sentences from the Carrot Bunch case. Your task is to find the mistake in each sentence. Hint: if you are unsure, look at pages 97–100 of this ESL Workbook and review the rules in English for when we use capital letters.

1. A Federal court sitting in diversity may exercise personal jurisdiction only to the extent that it is permitted by the state long arm statute if exercising jurisdiction does not violate due process guaranteed by the Fourteenth Amendment.

2. In the Fall of 2000, Moglia used the aliases of "John Gailsworth" and "Curtis Peterson" to register many possible variations of Carrot Ink's trademarks "Carrot Ink" and "Carrot's Ink Cartridges" as domain names.

Instead the next four sentences, also taken from the Carrot Bunch case, have been modified and one or more mistakes have been added to the court's original language. Identify the mistakes and correct the sentences. The mistakes can be grammar, punctuation, style or vocabulary. You can check your answers by finding the original sentences in the case.

1. From 1998, Plaintiff operates a website, which markets and sells inkjet printer cartridges and refill kits. Carrot Ink has also been using and extensively promoting its "Carrot Ink" and "Carrot's Ink Cartridges" trademarks in connection with its website.

2. Defendant Moglia, an Oregon resident, is founder and owner of both Computer Friends and Carrots Inks. Defendant Computer Friends is an Oregon corporation, organized in 1985, that sells and distributes printer inkjet cartridges, inkjet refill kits, and other computer equipments in the Internet.

3. Plaintiff's council mailed Moglia a second cease and desist letter on April 9, 2001. Moglia rejected to take any action to remedy the alleged infringement and instead created a "Carrots Inks, Inc." website to sell the printer inkjet cartridges in competition against Carrot Ink.

4. To exercise personal jurisdiction over a nonresident defendant will not violate due process if two conditions will be met. First, the defendant must to have purposefully availed himself of the benefits and protections of the forum state by establishing minimum contacts with the forum state.

Ford v. Mentor Worldwide, LLC,
2 F. Supp. 3d 898 (E.D. La. 2014).

Vocabulary and Legal Terminology

Healthcare association: Group of organizations that provide health care.

Breast augmentation procedure: Surgery to increase (augment) the size of a woman's breasts.

To remove a case: To transfer a case from state to federal court.

Bilateral breast implant exchange: Removing the old breast implants on both breasts (bilateral) and replacing them with new implants.

Saline: A solution of salt water.

Preemption: A doctrine based on the Supremacy Clause of the U.S. Constitution (Article VI, clause 2) which holds that federal legislation overrides state legislation when both deal with the same subject matter.[181]

To shift: To move.

Paradigm: A typical example of something.

Unavailing: Unsuccessful.

Gravamen: The essential part or quintessence of a legal argument, grievance, charge, or cause of action.[182]

Pre-Reading Questions

Before you begin reading, skim the caption, synopsis and holdings and answer the following questions:

1. Who are the parties in the case and what is their relationship?
2. Why has the plaintiff filed the claim against the defendants?
3. Where did the plaintiff initially file the claim?
4. The defendants filed two motions. What were they?
5. Which motion was heard first and what did the court rule on it?
6. Which motion was subsequently heard? Was it heard in state or federal court?
7. What did the court rule on the second motion?

Comprehension Questions

With a general idea of the case in your mind, you can now read the case. As you are reading and after you finish reading, answer the following questions:

---

[181] *Preemption*, GILBERT'S POCKET SIZE LAW DICTIONARY (3rd ed. 2014).
[182] *Gravamen*, GILBERT'S POCKET SIZE LAW DICTIONARY (3rd ed. 2014).

1. Summarize in your own words the facts of this case that led to the dispute.
2. When does a court have general jurisdiction over a defendant? _____
   _____
3. What policy arguments support exercising general jurisdiction over a nonresident defendant? __
   _____
4. Find the cases that the court uses to analyze whether the court could exercise general jurisdiction over the defendants in this case. Using those cases, analogize and distinguish our case and determine whether you think that the Franklin court would have general jurisdiction over SDA. _____
   _____
5. Will Groovia be more successful arguing for specific or general jurisdiction over SDA? Why?
   _____
6. The exercise of personal jurisdiction over a nonresident defendant in a breach of contract case is an important part of the analysis in the <u>Ford</u> case. Is it relevant to our case? Why or why not?
   _____
7. Find the cases that the court uses when analyzing the exercise of personal jurisdiction in a breach of contract case. Using those cases, analogize and distinguish our case and determine whether you think that the Franklin court would have jurisdiction over SDA. _____
   _____
8. How is this case useful for our case, regardless of whether you represent SDA or Groovia?
9. Is the case more helpful for SDA or for Groovia? Why?
10. What arguments can you make to analogize or distinguish it from our case?

Language Review: Suffixes of –less and –ful

As you no doubt know, English uses prefixes and suffixes to change the meaning of a word. A prefix is a particle that goes at the beginning of a word such as *dis*, which has a negative meaning.

We take the word *like*, add the prefix *dis* and change the meaning to not liking: *I dislike studying for exams*. While not as strong as *to hate*, the simple addition of the prefix *dis* changes the meaning to a negative one. Likewise, we add suffixes to the end of the word to change the meaning. Here are some sentences from the <u>Ford</u> case with the suffixes highlighted.

- Personal jurisdiction an essential element of the jurisdiction of a district court, without which the court is **powerless** to proceed to an adjudication.
- If the plaintiff [is **successful** in satisfying] the first two prongs, the burden shifts to the defendant to defeat jurisdiction by showing that its exercise would be unfair or unreasonable.
- [Defendant] has [**purposeful** availment] of the benefits and protections of the forum state by establishing 'minimum contacts' with the forum state.

In the sentences, the suffix *–less*, which means without, is added to the noun power to produce an adjective — powerless — that means without power. Likewise, we can add the suffix *–ful*, which means with, to nouns to produce an adjective that means with something: successful, powerful, purposeful.

But the rule doesn't always work! Examine at the following sentences. Which sentences correctly use the suffix *–less* or *–ful*? Which do not? If the use of the suffix is incorrect, correct the sentence.

1. I have two cousins. One has been very successful in her chosen career; she earned her first million dollars before her 30th birthday. However, my other cousin has unfortunately been successless. In her career, she has closed two businesses, declared bankruptcy and been fired from many jobs.

2. It upsets me to see so many homeless people in American cities. I am thankful that I am homeful and not homeless.

3. Although many people are scared of my large dog, Oliver, he really is harmless. On the other hand, my sister's dog has bit three or four people and is quite harmful.

4. Dave thought that the picture he bought at the auction was an authentic Van Gogh and worthful; instead it is a worthless imitation.

5. Judge Smith's clerk is very helpful. Whenever you have a question, he answers you immediately and always goes out of his way to lend a hand. On the other hand, Judge Walker's clerk is helpless. He never answers the phone, never responds to email and never provides any help.

6. My grandfather was bald at age 25; my father was also hairless before his 30th birthday. But my sister is hairful, with thick, long hair that reaches her waist.

7. We weren't hopeless but instead were hopeful that our grandfather's surgery would be successful, based on what the doctor told us.

Gatte v. Ready 4 A Change, LLC,
No. 2:11-CV-2083, 2013 WL 123613 (W.D. La. Jan. 13, 2013).

Vocabulary and Legal Terminology

Sur-reply: In civil litigation, a party's response to his opponent's memorandum in opposition to the initial motion. Sur-replies are not allowed in most jurisdictions without the court's permission.[183]

Companion motion: A motion that is filed with another motion.

Parish: Subdivision of a state, used only in Louisiana; other states use county.

Contouring and body sculpting surgery: Surgery to remove excess fat and alter the shape of one's body.

Wrongful death lawsuit: Claim that alleges the defendant's negligence led to a person's death.

To dissect: (here) To examine and study something carefully.

To flesh out: To provide more information about something.

Undersigned: The person whose name is signed at the end of a document such as a letter or here, court decision.

Nonsensical: Without logical sense; nonsense.

Random: By chance; haphazard.

Fortuitous: Happening by chance or with luck.

To attenuate: To weaken or reduce the effect or strength of something.

To aver: To state clearly; allege; assert.[184]

Tenuous: Very weak.

To bootstrap: To do something on one's own rather than using the help or assistance of others.

In broad strokes: In broad or general terms.

Benchmark case: A landmark case.

Fleeting: Not lasting.

To cut or lean in favor: To be inclined to one's opinion or position.

---

[183] *Surreply*, BLACK'S LAW DICTIONARY (10th ed. 2014).
[184] *Aver*, GILBERT'S POCKET SIZE LAW DICTIONARY (3rd ed. 2014).

Pre-Reading Questions

Before you begin reading, skim the caption and the first three paragraphs and answer the following questions:

1. Is the case in federal or state court?
2. Who are the parties to the case, what is their relationship and why did the plaintiff file the claim against the defendants (each group — the R4C defendants and the Clinica defendants)?
3. Many motions were filed in this case.
    a. What motions did the R4C defendants file? What did the plaintiff do in response?
    b. What motions did the Clinica defendants file? What happened in response to the initial filing?
4. What did the court decide with regard to both of the defendants' motions?

Comprehension Questions

With a general idea of the case in your mind, you can now read the case. As you are reading and after you finish reading, answer the following questions:

1. Summarize in your own words the facts of this case that led to the dispute.
2. Which state is the forum state?
3. With regard to the R4C defendants, what arguments do the plaintiffs make as to why the court should have jurisdiction over them? _____
4. What arguments do the R4C defendants make in response as to why the court should not have personal jurisdiction over them and the case should be dismissed? _____
5. With regard to the Clinica defendants, what arguments do the plaintiffs make as to why the court should have jurisdiction over them? _____
6. What arguments do the Clinica defendants make in response? _____
7. Summarize in your own words the court's reasoning as to why the plaintiff failed to show that the court should exercise general jurisdiction over all the defendants. _____
8. What contacts did the defendants have with Louisiana? Why did the court find that those contacts were insufficient to exercise jurisdiction over the defendants? _____
9. List the facts that the court uses to determine that the website in <u>Gatte</u> is interactive in nature: _____
10. How does the court distinguish this case from others where the interactive nature of a website was *sufficient* to establish personal jurisdiction (unlike this case)?
11. Apply the above analysis to our facts, using the <u>Mink</u> and the <u>Gatte</u> cases to compare and contrast the facts of the SDA case.

12. How is this case useful for our case, regardless of whether you represent SDA or Groovia?
13. Is the case more helpful for SDA or for Groovia? Why?
14. What arguments can you make to analogize or distinguish it from our case?

Language Focus — Descriptive Verbs

The <u>Gatte</u> court uses very descriptive vocabulary in certain parts of the decision. For example, the court describes the plaintiff's analysis of the defendant's website by saying that "[the plaintiffs] **dissect** the language on the R4c website."

To dissect in this instance means "to examine and study something carefully." T*o dissect* also has another meaning: to cut up a dead animal, a plant or a dead body to study it and its internal parts.

We use dissect literally — *the medical study dissected the dead pig to study its cardiovascular system* — but also figuratively, as in picking apart word by word the language of contract or a website.

Here are other verb pairs that we can use both literally and figuratively. Write sentences showing both a figurative and a literal use of the verb. The first verb is done for you.

To fly:
- Literal: The birds flew within a few feet of our window.
- Figurative: I was so late this morning that I flew to catch the train!

To freeze:
- Literal: _____
- Figurative: _____

To explode:
- Literal: _____
- Figurative: _____

To crash:
- Literal: _____
- Figurative: _____

To die:
- Literal: _____
- Figurative: _____

To be in hot water:
- Literal: _____
- Figurative: _____

The Kelly Law Firm, P.C. v. An Attorney For You,
679 F. Supp. 2d 755 (S.D. Tex. 2009).

Vocabulary and Legal Terminology

Referral service: A service that provides leads for potential clients or customers in exchange for a fee.

To comport with: To be in agreement with.

Unjust enrichment: A civil claim brought when a defendant has obtained the benefits of the plaintiff's efforts or work, but without paying any compensation for such work or efforts. The plaintiff brings the claim to recover the gains that the defendant unjustly earned.

Mesothelioma: A form of cancer that affects the linings of the lungs and the abdomen.

Birth-injury lawsuit: A claim brought against a doctor or hospital, alleging that the medical provider's negligence led to injuries suffered by a baby.

To overstate: To exaggerate.

Actionable: An act or occurrence that provides grounds for a lawsuit.[185]

Pre-Reading Questions

Before you begin reading, skim the caption, the synopsis and the holdings and answer the following questions:

1. Is the case in federal or state court?
2. What is the relationship between the parties?
3. What motion did the defendants file?
4. Why was the motion denied?

Comprehension Questions

With a general idea of the case in your mind, you can now read the case. As you are reading and after you finish reading, answer the following questions:

1. Summarize in your own words the facts of this case that led to the dispute.
2. Where are the plaintiffs from? _____
3. Why do you think the plaintiffs decided to bring the claim in Texas and not New York? _____
_____
_____
_____

---

[185] *Actionable*, Gilbert's Pocket Size Law Dictionary (3rd ed. 2014).

The Kelly Law Firm, P.C. v. An Attorney For You, 679 F. Supp. 2d 755 (S.D. Tex. 2009) 229

4. Summarize in your own words the plaintiffs' arguments as to why the court should exercise jurisdiction over the defendants. _____

5. Summarize in your own words the defendants' arguments as to why the court should not exercise jurisdiction. _____

6. What facts does the court use in this case to show that there was a "purposeful availment" of the privileges of doing business in Texas? _____

7. How do those facts compare to ours?

8. The website in this case led to the finding of personal jurisdiction. Is the website similar to SDA's in our case? Different? How?

9. How is this case useful for our case, regardless of whether you represent SDA or Groovia?

10. Is the case more helpful for SDA or for Groovia? Why?

11. What arguments can you make to analogize or distinguish it from our case?

Language Focus — Revising and Editing: Plain Legal English

Legal English is not usually known for its high quality. Legal writing is often wordy, uses legal jargon (legalese) and often has overly complex and complicated syntax. Some lawyers think that they need to write in long, convoluted sentences to "sound like a lawyer" and to impress their clients, judges or opposing counsel. But it doesn't need to be this way!

Over the past few decades, a Plain English Movement has been underway. As stated on the Plain English website written and maintained by the U.S. government, Plain English is "communication your audience can understand the first time they read or hear it." [186] On October 13, 2010, President Barack Obama signed into law the Plain Writing Act of 2010, which requires that federal agencies use "clear Government communication that the public can understand and use."[187]

You might be wondering what is plain English. As legal writing expert Bryan Garner states,

> The phrase certainly shouldn't connote drab and dreary language. Actually, plain English is typically quite interesting to read. It's robust and direct — the opposite of gaudy, pretentious language. You achieve plain English when you use the simplest, most straightforward way of expressing an idea. You can still choose interesting words. But you'll avoid fancy ones that have everyday replacements meaning precisely the same thing.[188]

Some tips for writing in plain English:[189]

- Omit excess words (for example, don't use an expression that uses two, three or four words when you can express the same thing in one word)

---

[186] PLAINLANGUAGE.GOV., http://www.plainlanguage.gov/whatisPL/ (last visited May 2, 2016).
[187] Plain Writing Act of 2010, PL 111-274, 124 Stat 2861, Sec. 2.
[188] BRYAN A. GARNER, LEGAL WRITING IN PLAIN ENGLISH xiv (2001).
[189] Many resources exist for plain English. The plainlanguage.gov website is a good place to start, with a checklist available at http://www.plainlanguage.gov/howto/quickreference/checklist.cfm. The tips in this list are from the plainlanguage.gov website. Likewise, Bryan Garner's book, Legal Writing in Plain English, is another excellent resource.

- Use the active rather the passive voice
- Use short sections and sentences
- Use concrete, familiar words
- Avoid technical jargon or "legalese"

Below you will find some of the sentences from the affidavits that the parties submitted in the Kelly Law Firm case. Parts of them are written in language that you would expect from a law firm, and not in what would be considered Plain English. Revise the sentences to make them more concise and follow the guidelines of Plain English.

1. Original: Defendant Calliope Media, L.P., is an inactive California limited partnership that merged into Calliope Media, Inc., prior to the filing of this action.

   Your rewrite:_____

2. Original: After considering the possibilities of the types of services Defendants claimed it could provide, Defendants and I negotiated and then entered into two contracts, which are similar to the Agreements at issue herein, whereby Defendants would provide their services to our firm in Franklin.

   Your rewrite:_____

3. Original: However, as the sole contracting party, these leads were sent only to me at my Houston, Texas office for a period of approximately six weeks before Plaintiff Woska of Oklahoma and Weiss of New York, having joined this venture, began to receive these leads jointly with The Kelly Law Firm, at each of their firms' offices.

   Your rewrite:_____

4. Original: It is not disputed that the contracts were negotiated and executed between Calliope and Kelly.

   Your rewrite:_____

5. Original: The plaintiffs have provided a sworn declaration from Todd Kelly, the owner of The Kelly Law Firm, describing the events leading up to the litigation:

   Your rewrite:_____

Percle v. SFGL Foods, Inc.,
356 F. Supp. 2d 629 (M.D. La. 2004).

Vocabulary and Legal Terminology

"Soul in Yo Bowl:" Soul food is traditional southern African-American cuisine; *yo* means *your*.

Jambalaya: A spicy dish from Louisiana and typical of Louisiana cuisine (called Cajun or Creole) consisting of shrimp, chicken and vegetables.

Smokey Robinson: An American rhythm & blues (R&B) singer and composer.

To appropriate: To take possession of property without permission.

"Roll out" schedule: A schedule for introducing a product or service to the public.

Evidentiary hearing: Hearing in both the criminal and civil system at which the parties present evidence.[190]

Paramount: Of greatest importance.

Pre-Reading Questions

Before you begin reading, skim the caption and first two paragraphs and answer the following questions:
1. Is the case in federal or state court?
2. Who is the plaintiff and what claims did he bring against the defendant?
3. What had the defendant done to lead the plaintiff to file the claims against him?
4. What motion was filed at the district court? Who filed it?
5. What did the district court decide with regard to the motion?
6. What happened after the court ruled on the motion?

Comprehension Questions

With a general idea of the case in your mind, you can now read the case. First read only to the heading *Section II. Law and Analysis* and answer the following questions:
1. Summarize in your own words the facts of this case that led to the dispute. _____
   _____
2. What are the plaintiff's arguments as to why the defendants are liable for the various claims brought against them? _____
   _____

---

[190] *Hearing*, BLACK'S LAW DICTIONARY (10th ed. 2014).

3. What arguments does the plaintiff make as to why the Louisiana court should have jurisdiction over the defendant? _____
_____
_____

4. What arguments does the defendant make to rebut those of the plaintiff? _____
_____
_____

5. Without reading the court's analysis, analyze the facts of this case, using the law and rules that you have read and analyzed in the past cases. Should the court exercise personal jurisdiction over SFGL Foods? Why or why not?

6. Do you agree with the court's ruling of dismissing the complaint? Why or why not?

Now continue reading the court's analysis, from *Section II. Law and Analysis* to the end of the case, and answer the following questions:

7. How does the court characterize the website in this case?
8. How does the Zippo sliding-scale test apply here?
9. How do the facts in this case compare to ours?
10. How is this case useful for our case, regardless of whether you represent SDA or Groovia?
11. Is the case more helpful for SDA or for Groovia? Why?
12. What arguments can you make to analogize or distinguish it from our case?
13. How similar was your analysis to the analysis that the court made?

Language Focus — Slang

The trade name that was the subject of the dispute in the Percle case — *Soul in Yo Bowl* — is a perfect example of slang. Slang is defined as "a type of language that consists of words and phrases that are regarded as very informal, are more common in speech than writing, and are typically restricted to a particular context or group of people."[191] In this case, *yo* is an American slang abbreviation for the possessive adjective *your*.

Yo is also a slang greeting and interjection. "Yo, Adrian!" is an iconic phrase from the Rocky films starring Sylvester Stallone that were hugely popular during the 1980s. You might have heard law students or other people using it: "Yo, what are you doing tonight? Wanna go to a movie?"

In fact, you have likely heard lots of slang during your stay in the United States and during your LL.M. program. Slang varies from generation to generation, and from group to group. As a second language learner, it can be hard to know when to use slang, and part of language learning is not only learning the meaning of a new word or phrase, but also understanding the proper context that a word or phrase should be used in, the register of the word or phrase, and any hidden meanings, such as cultural ones.

Here are some general tips about using slang:

---

[191] *Slang*, THE NEW OXFORD AMERICAN DICTIONARY (2001).

1. <u>Don't use slang unless you are 100% sure of its meaning, its register and any "hidden" meanings</u>

   For example, some words once commonly used may be no longer acceptable. While not slang, examples of such words in American English are retarded, crippled or colored, all of which are now considered insensitive or offensive. Instead, we now use mentally disabled or challenged, disabled, and black or African American.

   As an example of slang, the "N-word," is one of the worst racial epithets and vulgar terms to call another person in the United States, yet you hear the term in rap music and among some socio-economic and ethnic groups that consider its usage acceptable.[192] Be aware that even though you may hear a word, that alone doesn't mean that you should use it.

2. <u>Don't use slang specific to a group or generation unless you are part of it</u>

   Similarly, learn which groups (e.g. ethnic, age) use a particular slang term, and unless you are part of that group, don't use it. Few things sound less appropriate than an adult using slang that is popular among teenagers. Even sports have slang, used among those who practice the sport and are fans of it. If someone who is not a fan of the sport uses that slang, he risks looking silly.

3. <u>Learn which slang is "essential" American slang and learn the meanings and usage of those terms</u>

   Although there is a lot of slang that is particular to one group, as stated above, there is also as much slang that is considered essential to American English and is used by almost all age groups. To understand Americans and "real" American English, make sure you know the meanings of some of the "essential" American slang words:[193]

   a. Cool
   b. Awesome
   c. To hang out
   d. To get dumped
   e. Dunno
   f. To have a blast

   These six words are hardly the only essential, or most common, slang terms used in American English, and you will likely come up with your own list of "essential" slang during your LL.M. program.

4. <u>If you choose to use slang, use it when appropriate and learn alternate expressions</u>

   Like many things in life, there is a time and a place for everything, including slang. Many language learners choose not to use slang because they don't feel comfortable enough with their English to use words that show an intimate familiarity with the language. But if you are comfortable enough with your English that you choose to use slang, use it when appropriate. An appropriate use of slang would be when talking with friends or in a more informal setting. In more formal settings, such as at law school, when meeting with a professor or in

---

[192] For further information about when the use of the "N-word" is acceptable, see Gene Demby, *Who Can Use the N-Word? That's the Wrong Question*, NATIONAL PUBLIC RADIO, http://www.npr.org/sections/codeswitch/2013/09/06/219737467/who-can-use-the-n-word-thats-the-wrong-question (last visited May 2, 2016).

[193] For more essential American slang, see the complete list at FLUENT U ENGLISH LANGUAGE AND CULTURE BLOG, http://www.fluentu.com/english/blog/american-english-slang-words-esl/ (last visited May 2, 2016).

any job setting, slang is not the best linguistic choice to make. In a more formal setting, use a standard English word or expression instead.

For example, of the above examples of "essential" American English slang, you would likely not say to your law school professor: "My girlfriend dumped me over the weekend." Instead, it would be best to replace the verb *to get dumped* and say, "My girlfriend broke up with me over the weekend." Instead of saying, "That is awesome!" when the judge tells you that she will grant your motion, you would likely say "That is wonderful news!" instead.

Slang is everywhere. So even if you choose not to use it, it is important that you learn it so that you can easily understand those around you and follow conversations and discussions.

Tempur-Pedic International, Inc. v. Go Satellite, Inc.,
758 F. Supp. 2d 366 (N.D. Tex. 2010).

Vocabulary and Legal Terminology

<u>In personam</u>: An action taken against a person which involves his personal rights and is based on jurisdiction over him as opposed to seeking a judgment against property (in rem).[194]

<u>Forum non conveniens</u>: (Latin "inconvenient forum") Doctrine which allows a court which has jurisdiction over a case to decline to hear the case out of fairness to the parties if there is another court available which would be more convenient.[195]

<u>Bipartite</u>: Involving two separate parties.

Pre-Reading Questions

Before you begin reading, skim the caption, the synopsis and holdings and answer the following questions:

1. Is the case in federal or state court?
2. Who is the plaintiff and what claims did he bring against the defendant?
3. What had the defendant done to lead the plaintiff to file the claims against him?
4. What motion was filed at the district court? Who filed it?
5. What did the district court decide with regard to the motion?
6. What happened after the court ruled on the motion?

Comprehension Questions

With a general idea of the case in your mind, you can now read the case. As you are reading and after you finish reading, answer the following questions:

1. Summarize in your own words the facts of this case that led to the dispute.
2. Summarize in your own words the nature of the websites at issue in this case.
3. Summarize as well other facts included by the court regarding the defendant's activities in Texas.
4. In the court's analysis, what facts does the court use to reach the conclusion that the website in this case is interactive? _____
_____
_____

---

[194] *In Personam*, Gilbert's Pocket Size Law Dictionary (3rd ed. 2014).
[195] *Forum Non Conveniens*, Gilbert's Pocket Size Law Dictionary (3rd ed. 2014).

5. We have seen in two other cases that an interactive website, on its own, doesn't mean that a court can or will exercise jurisdiction. Why is this case different and what "extra" is present here to lead the court to exercise jurisdiction over the defendant? _____

6. What analysis does the court make to conclude that exercising jurisdiction will not offend the "traditional notions of fair play and substantial justice?" _____

7. Do you agree with the court's analysis? Why or why not?
8. How is this case useful for our case, regardless of whether you represent SDA or Groovia?
9. Is the case more helpful for SDA or for Groovia? Why?
10. What arguments can you make to analogize or distinguish it from our case?

Language Focus — To Break, Violate, Breach or Infringe?

To break, violate, breach and infringe: these words have similar yet not identical meanings. Because of this similarity, they are often confused by LL.M. (and J.D.) students and used incorrectly. Before doing an exercise that will require you to choose which of these four words correctly completes a sentence, let's look at the dictionary definitions of these four verbs:

- To breach: to break or fail to observe a law, agreement, or duty
- To break: violate or fail to observe a law or agreement
- To violate: to break or fail to conform to a law or agreement
- To infringe: to violate the terms of a law or agreement; to interfere with another person's rights

You will now complete ten sentences with either the word *to breach, break, violate* or *infringe*. The first sentence is from the Tempur-Pedic case; the other sentences are from other cases.

1. This is an action by plaintiffs Tempur–Pedic International, Inc. ("TP International"), Tempur–Pedic Management, Inc. ("TP Management"), Tempur–Pedic North America, LLC ("TP North America"), and Dan–Foam ApS ("Dan–Foam") against defendants Go Satellite Inc. ("Go Satellite") and Steven Hutt ("Hutt"), alleging that defendants _____ plaintiffs' trademark rights under the Lanham Act.

2. The evidence at trial was sufficient to permit the jury to conclude that the leaks in the apartment were an unsafe condition and that the landlord _____ its statutory duty to remedy the unsafe condition.

3. In its brief A & P alleges that Yanofsky _____ the section [of the statute] and that this constituted evidence of negligence.

4. There is nothing in the record to show that Brinson _____ the law, that he was driving with a suspended license or that the Officers believed he was driving with a suspended license.

5. Plaintiff alleged in its complaint that defendant willfully and intentionally _____ plaintiff's trademark rights to create customer confusion and to create the false impression that he was selling sheet metalworking products that were either manufactured or endorsed by plaintiff.

6. The mere fact that a party has _____ some law or ordinance does not make of him an outlaw entitled to no rights.

7. The court held that held that where landlord _____ the lease by failure to segregate security deposit, the tenant was under no obligation to comply with lease.

8. Instead, the question is whether the defendant _____ the contract he made with the court after the determination of guilt.

9. The District Court of Appeal held that trial court's denial of defendant's peremptory challenge _____ on his right to challenge any juror prior to time that jury is sworn and constituted per se reversible error.

10. There is an implied covenant of quiet enjoyment in every lease of real property. The covenant is between the lessor and the lessee. Any wrongful act of the lessor that interferes with the lessee's possession, in whole or in part, is a _____ of the covenant of quiet enjoyment.

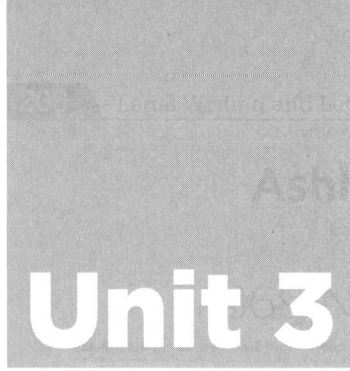

Unit 3

Title VII of the Civil Rights Act of 1964 and Religious Accommodations

American Postal Workers Union v. Postmaster General,
781 F.2d 772 (9th Cir. 1986).

Vocabulary and Legal Terminology

<u>Draft</u>: System by which young men (and in some countries women) are required to register for military service.

<u>To register for the draft</u>: To enroll in the military.

<u>Draft registration card</u>: Card filled by those registering for the draft.

<u>Draft registrants</u>: Those who register for the draft or enroll in the armed forces.

<u>Religious precept</u>: A general rule of a religious nature that regulates or orders behavior or thought.

<u>Bona fide</u>: Sincere, genuine, real.

<u>To incur</u>: To acquire or receive, often something unpleasant.

<u>To spell out</u>: To explain clearly in detail.

<u>In the wake of</u>: As a result of.

<u>To be incumbent upon (or on) someone</u>: To impose something as a duty on someone.

<u>Inapposite</u>: Inappropriate.

<u>To obviate</u>: To remove or eliminate.

Pre-Reading Questions

Before you begin reading, skim the caption and the first paragraph and answer the following questions:
1. Who are the parties?
2. Why do you think a union is the plaintiff when only individual employees can be discriminated against in employment?

3. Is the case in federal or state court? District or appellate court?
4. What mistake did the district court make in its holding?
5. What does it mean that the appellate court "reversed and remanded?"

Comprehension Questions

With a general idea of the case in your mind, you can now read the case. As you are reading and after you finish reading, answer the following questions:

1. What conflict did the plaintiff have between her job duties and her religion?
2. Summarize in your own words the reasoning that the district court used in reaching its holding.
3. This case introduces you to the burden-shifting test that exists in a religious discrimination claim under Title VII. Write it below.
    a. Step 1: _____
    _____
    _____
    b. Step 2: _____
    _____
    _____
    c. BUT IF Step 2 does not _____
    THEN _____
    _____
4. The case also tells you that an employer has to make a *negligible effort* in what situations?
5. Why is it important in a religious accommodation case that the accommodation preserves the "employment status" of the affected employee?
6. How might this case apply to our Singh v. Stray Dog Advertising case?
7. If you represent the plaintiff Singh, is this case helpful? How?
8. If you represent the defendant Stray Dog Advertising, is this case helpful? How?

Grammar Review — Phrasal Verbs

As you no doubt know, phrasal verbs, which are verbs that are composed of a verb plus one, two or even three particles or elements, are an important part of English. You probably know a lot of them already: To get up. To wake up. To stand up.

In those three examples, the verb is followed by the preposition *up*; together, they comprise the verb. Learning phrasal verbs can be difficult, but a helpful way to learn many of them is to find a group of verbs with something in common, such as the particle or element that follows the verb, and memorize them together.

The American Postal Workers case uses the phrasal verb *to spell out*.

> The reach of the obligation has simply never been **spelled out** by Congress or the EEOC.

Using a dictionary or your own knowledge, write the definitions of these other phrasal verbs with the particle *out*. Also write a sentence that uses the verb and that shows that you understand its meaning.

To speak out on something: _____

_____

To stand out from someone: _____

_____

To walk out on someone or something: _____

_____

To leave someone out of something: _____

_____

To figure out: _____

_____

To cross something out: _____

_____

Phrasal verbs are very common is spoken English, but used less often in more formal written English. Instead, language in a more formal document such as a client letter, office memo or brief should have a more formal register. Thus, if you have used a phrasal verb in one of these documents, you will probably want to find an alternative, more formal verb that has the same meaning.

Here is an example of how you can replace a phrasal verb with one that is more suited to formal English:

> The reach of the obligation has simply never been **spelled out** by Congress or the EEOC.
>
> *Revision with a non-phrasal verb:* Congress or the EEOC has never **specifically stated** what the "reach" of an employer's obligation is under Title VII of the Civil Rights Act of 1964.
>
> *To specifically state* is a good alternative to the verb *to spell out*. The meaning is the same, but the verb is more appropriate for a formal document.

Find an alternative for these phrasal verbs in the sentences that you wrote above, as well as the others.

To figure out: _____
_____

To stand out from someone: _____
_____

But it isn't always possible to find a good alternative, and in some cases, the phrasal verb might be the best choice.

Anderson v. General Dynamics Convair Aerospace Division,
589 F.2d 397 (9th Cir. 1978).

Vocabulary and Legal Terminology

Tenet: A main principle or belief of a religion.

Security clause: A provision in a collective bargaining agreement that requires employees to become union members as a condition of employment.[196]

Committeemen: Official union representative who handles grievances of union members at the beginning stages of the procedure.[197]

Conciliation: Mediation between two or more parties to resolve a dispute.

To proscribe: To prohibit someone from doing something.

Free rider: Someone who takes advantage of the benefits of something but without paying.

To grumble about something: (informal) To complain.

Pre-Reading Questions

Before you begin reading, skim the caption and the first paragraph and answer the following questions:
1. Is the case in federal or state court? District or appellate court?
2. What happened at the district court?
3. Did the appellate court agree with the district court's ruling?
4. What did the appellate court decide was not an undue hardship on the employer?
5. Look ahead to the second paragraph of the decision. What was the issue before the appellate court?

Comprehension Questions

With a general idea of the case in your mind, you can now read the case. As you are reading and after you finish reading, answer the following questions:
1. Briefly summarize in your own words the facts of the case.
2. Summarize in your own words the defendant's arguments at the district court.

---

[196] Society for Human Resource Management, *What is a Union Security Clause,* http://www.shrm.org/templatestools/hrqa/pages/whatisaunionsecurityclause.aspx (last visited May 2, 2016).

[197] Institute of Labor and Industrial Relations, University of Illinois, *Handling Grievances: An Outline for Union Shop Stewards and Grievance Committeemen,* https://www.ideals.illinois.edu/bitstream/handle/2142/26990/handlinggrievancoouniv.pdf?sequence=1 (last visited May 2, 2016).

3. What is the main rule to take away from this case? _____
_____

4. How can this case apply to our Singh v. Stray Dog Advertising case?

5. If you represent Singh, does this case seem helpful to you? Why?

6. If you represent Stray Dog Advertising, the case at first glance might seem to be detrimental to your client's argument. Why?

7. When you have a case that is or seems detrimental to your client, you need to try to distinguish it to show the court that your case is different and should have a different outcome. How could Stray Dog Advertising distinguish the Singh case from Anderson?

Language Focus — Frequently Confused Words

English has many homophones. A homophone is two or more words that have the same pronunciation or sound, but a different spelling and a different meaning, such as *see* and *sea*; *too, two* and *to*; *knows* and *nose*. Some words have the same spelling, but a different meaning, such as *rose* (the flower) and *rose* (the past tense of *to rise)*. These words are called homographs.[198]

Some words aren't necessarily homophones or homographs, but are very close in spelling and pronunciation so that it is very easy to confuse them. Here are some commonly confused words, some of which have similar but not identical meanings. Find the meanings of these words, and write example sentences with each word that show that you understand the different meanings of the words.

Insure – to secure or protect someone against something

> The parties also stipulated that Anderson had made known to his fellow workers, including his shop committeemen, that he would not join the Union and that he would not contribute to the Union, unless he could ***insure*** that his contributions went to a recognized charity.

Ensure - _____
Assure - _____

Affect - _____
Effect - _____

Tenet - _____
Tenant - _____

Principle - _____
Principal - _____

---

[198] See the Language Focus exercise with Tully v. McLean (Section II, Unit 4) on page 178 for additional information on homophones, homonyms and homographs.

Bhatia v. Chevron U.S.A., Inc.,
734 F.2d 1382 (9th Cir. 1984).

Vocabulary and Legal Terminology

<u>Gastight face seal</u>: On a face mask worn to prevent exposure to toxic fumes, the part that touches the person's face is so tight or close as to prevent the person from breathing the fumes.

<u>To file stipulated facts</u>: Stipulated facts are those facts that the parties agree to. They are often filed as part of litigation (often with a motion for summary judgment or at trial) so that the court knows which facts the parties do not dispute.

<u>De minimis</u>: From the Latin "*de minimis non curat lex*" ("the law is not concerned with trivial matters"), meaning unimportant or minimal.[199]

<u>Twofold</u>: Double or twice.

Pre-Reading Questions

Before you begin reading, skim the caption and the first paragraph and answer the following questions:
1. Is the case in federal or state court? District or appellate court?
2. What was the conflict between the employee's religion and his employment duties?
3. What happened procedurally at the district court?
4. What did the appellate court decide?

Comprehension Questions

With a general idea of the case in your mind, you can now read the case. As you are reading and after you finish reading, answer the following questions:
1. Summarize the facts of the case. _____
2. List the proposed accommodations that the employer made while engaging in the interactive process with the plaintiff, Bhatia. _____
3. What important rule is introduced in this case about when an employer can refuse an accommodation? _____
4. Why would it have been an undue hardship for Chevron to accommodate Bhatia? _____

---

[199] Oxford Online Dictionary, http://www.oxforddictionaries.com/us/definition/american_english/de-minimis (last visited May 2, 2016).

5. In this case, do you think that Chevron did more than it is required to do under the law? Why or why not? _____
_____

6. Does this case seem to set a standard for what future employers must do to comply with the law?
_____
_____

7. According to the court, how can a proposed accommodation impose more than a *de minimis* burden on an employer or on other employees? _____
_____

8. How is this case useful for our fact pattern of Singh v. Stray Dog Advertising? _____
_____

9. Is it more useful for the plaintiff or the defendant? Why? _____
_____

10. How can you analogize and distinguish this case from our facts? _____
_____
_____

Legal Focus: Public Policy

In law school, your professors often refer to *public policy arguments* while discussing the cases in class. Public policy can be defined as

> "A system of laws, regulatory measures, courses of action, and funding priorities concerning a given topic promulgated by a governmental entity or its representatives."[200]

Public policy is often difficult for LL.M. students to identify and articulate, perhaps because what is a priority for one government and one society is not for another, and LL.M. students often are not familiar enough with U.S. culture and society to easily identify the public policy arguments in the cases they read. Only by practicing can you get better at something, and that includes identifying public policy.

We learned in the Bhatia case that an employer can refuse an accommodation if it would impose an undue hardship, defined as more than a *de minimis* impact upon the employer or upon co-workers. *De minimis* means minimal. Thus, if a proposed accommodation has more than a small or minimal impact upon the employer or other employees, the employer can refuse it without violating Title VII.

Compare this standard to another federal anti-discrimination law, the Americans with Disabilities Act, which also requires employers to provide reasonable accommodations but to a disabled employee or job applicant. As under Title VII, an accommodation can be refused if it would impose an undue hardship upon the employer or upon co-workers, but under the ADA, an undue hardship is defined as "an action requiring significant difficulty or expense,"[201] a much more difficult standard to reach than that for religious accommodations under Title VII.

---

[200] Dean G. Kilpatrick, M.D., *Definitions of Public Policy and The Law*, NATIONAL VIOLENCE AGAINST WOMEN PREVENTION RESEARCH CENTER, https://mainweb-v.musc.edu/vawprevention/policy/definition.shtml (last visited May 2, 2016).

[201] 42 U.S.C. § 12111(10)(A) (2015). What is an undue hardship is determined by considering factors such as the nature and cost of the accommodation, the financial resources of the facility or the employer, the overall size of the business and the number of employees, as well as other factors. See § 12111(10)(B)(I) – (IV) for a complete list of the factors.

Think about the policy reasons behind these two laws, which impose the same duty on an employer (to offer a reasonable accommodation), but allow an employer not to do so for *very* different reasons: the accommodation would have a minimal impact (Title VII), or the accommodation would require significant difficulty or expense (ADA).

Think about the two laws:

1. Which law imposes a greater burden on employers?
2. Why do you think there are two different definitions in the two laws for the same term?
3. What policy reasons might be behind the different definitions for *undue hardship* that Congress created for Title VII and for the ADA?
4. Title VII of the Civil Rights Act was passed in 1964 (the amendment that defined religion to include religious practices and that imposed the duty of making reasonable accommodations was passed in 1972), while the ADA was passed in 1990. Do you think that has any impact on why there are two different standards? Why or why not?

Burns v. Southern Pacific Transportation Co.,
589 F.2d 403 (9th Cir. 1978).

Vocabulary and Legal Terminology

Enjoin: To prevent or stop someone from doing something.

Union dues and assessments: Money paid on a monthly basis to be a member of a union.

Brakeman: A railroad employee who assists the conductor in operating the train.

Injunctive relief: An injunction.

Contention: Argument or position.

Accord: (in a citation) A case that agrees with the proposition.

To open the gate to something: To lead to something happening (often, *to open the floodgates of litigation*).

To keep track of something: To maintain a record of something, such as expenses or in this case, the money paid to a charity.

Pre-Reading Questions

Before you begin reading, skim the caption and the first paragraph and answer the following questions:

1. Is the case in federal or state court? District or appellate court?
2. What happened at the district court?
3. Did the appellate court completely agree with the district court's ruling?
4. Which parts of the district court's ruling did the appellate court agree with? Why?
5. Which parts of the district court's ruling did the appellate court not agree with? Why?
6. What did the appellate court decide was not an undue hardship upon the employer?

Comprehension Questions

With a general idea of the case in your mind, you can now read the case. As you are reading and after you finish reading, answer the following questions:

1. Briefly summarize in your own words the facts of the case. _____
2. Summarize in your own words the defendant's arguments at the district court. _____
3. What is the main rule to take away from this case? _____
4. How can this case apply to our Singh v. Stray Dog Advertising case? _____

5. If you represent Singh, does this case seem helpful to you? Why? _____
6. If you represent Stray Dog Advertising, does this case seem helpful to you? Why? _____
7. This case introduces the phrase and defense of "opening the floodgates of litigation."
   a. What does that mean? _____
   b. Does that seem like a valid defense? Why or why not? _____

Language Focus — Synonyms

When writing and speaking in a legal context, lawyers use different vocabulary than non-lawyers would use. Law has specific terminology that lawyers are expected to use. However, we must also know how to express that legal term with a less technical term that a non-lawyer would understand. If we are speaking to our client or writing a letter to him or her, we likely wouldn't use terms like *de minimis* or *undue hardship* unless we first define them. Sometimes it is easier to simply find a different term.

Below are examples of words that lawyers use, with the non-legal, non-technical term that a layperson would use. Complete the table with the missing words and explain what nuance in meaning exists between the two verbs (if there is one). The first verbs have been done for you as an example.

The last two rows are blank. What four words can you include to complete the table?

Legal or More Formal Term	Non-Legal, More Everyday Term
To enjoin	To prohibit
To interrogate	To _____
To apprehend	To _____
To discharge (an employee)	To _____
To execute (a contract)	To _____
To	
To	

Note: there is nothing wrong with the more formal or technical-sounding verbs; they have a time and a place. The purpose of this exercise is to understand more deeply the slight differences in meaning and register between words that may appear on their face to be synonymous.

EEOC v. AutoNation USA Corp.,
52 Fed. Appx. 327 (9th Cir. 2002).

Vocabulary and Legal Terminology

Framework: Structure.

To short-circuit: To avoid, to get around or to evade.

To swap: To exchange something with someone.

Pre-Reading Questions

Before you begin reading, skim the caption and the first paragraph and answer the following questions:
1. Is the case in federal or state court? District or appellate court?
2. What was the motion before the district court?
3. Did the district court grant the motion? If so, on what grounds?
4. Who appealed and what did the appellate court decide?

Comprehension Questions

With a general idea of the case in your mind, you can now read the case. As you are reading and after you finish reading, answer the following questions:
1. What do the terms "bilateral cooperation" and "concomitant duty" mean? _____
2. Why are these terms important in this case? _____
3. Did the employee fulfill his duty? Why or why not? _____
4. What was the result of the employee's failure to meet his bilateral duty of cooperation? _____
5. Summarize in your own words the dissenting opinion and the difference between the majority and the dissent. _____
6. Which opinion do you agree with? The majority or the dissent? Why? _____
7. How does this case apply to the Singh v. Stray Dog Advertising case? _____
8. What rules or facts can you use in your arguments for your client? _____

Language Focus — Quotations and Quotation Marks

Quotation marks are one of the punctuation marks regularly used in legal writing.[202] Look at this sentence from the AutoNation case. Why are quotation marks used around the name "AutoNation?"

---

[202] See the Language Focus for the H.B. ex rel. v. Whittemore case (Section II, Unit 1) for explanations about periods, commas, semicolons and colons, and the Language Focus exercise with Cobai v. Young (page 81), which focuses on hyphens, en dashes and em dashes.

In this employment discrimination case, the EEOC appeals the district court's order granting summary judgment in favor of AutoNation USA Corporation ("AutoNation").

Here, the judge uses quotation marks because he is defining a term that will be used in the rest of the decision. Rather than repeating the entire name — AutoNation USA Corporation – the judge abbreviates it and uses just the shortened term "AutoNation." By including the term in quotation marks within parentheses, the reader knows that the term AutoNation stands for the entire name of the company.

We do the same in contracts:

> This agreement ("Agreement") is executed and effective this _____ day of _____, 20___, by and between Sam Jones ("Artist") and Columbia Records, Inc. ("Company").

In many contracts and legal documents, you will see the use of *hereinafter* or a longer phrase: (hereinafter "Artist"), or (hereinafter referred to "Company"). These extra words can and should be eliminated as they don't add to the sense of the sentence and are unnecessary legalese.

We also use quotation marks to indicate when we are including a direct quotation from another source. Look at this quotation from the AutoNation case:

> An employee, therefore, has a "concomitant duty . . . to cooperate in reaching an accommodation [under Title VII]." American Postal Workers, 781 F.2d at 777.

We know that the quotation in the original text (the American Postal Workers case) begins with *concomitant* and ends with *accommodation*. The use of the brackets [under Title VII] indicates to the reader that these words are not in the original and have been inserted into the quotation. We also know from the use of the ellipsis that words from the original text were omitted between *duty* and *to cooperate*, and if you were to reference the original text of the American Postal Workers case, you would find what those words were.[203]

We use brackets to indicate the change in the original even when only one letter has been changed, from upper to lower case or vice versa:

> But "[u]ndue hardship means something greater than hardship." Anderson, 589 F.2d at 402

The original in the Anderson case is "Undue hardship means something greater than hardship," with an upper case *U*.[204] Because the original text has been changed, the writer must indicate that.

Here is another example of a quotation from the AutoNation case with the original text modified, and with those modification indicated by brackets:

---

[203] See the Language Focus for the H.B. ex rel. v. Whittemore case (Section II, Unit 1) for an explanation of what an ellipsis is and when we use it.

[204] See Rule 5.2 of the Bluebook for additional information about substituting or altering the original language in a quotation. Rule 5.2, THE BLUEBOOK: A UNIFORM SYSTEM OF CITATION (Columbia Law Review Ass'n et al. eds., 20th ed. 2015).

The burden then shifts to the employer to "prove that [it] made good faith efforts to accommodate [the employee's] religious beliefs and, if those efforts were unsuccessful, to demonstrate that [it was] unable reasonably to accommodate his beliefs without undue hardship." EEOC v. Townley Eng. & Mfg. Co., 859 F.2d 610, 614 (9th Cir.1988) (citation omitted); see also 42 U.S.C. § 2000e-2(a)(1).

Sometimes when writing, you may choose to include a longer quotation. If a direct quotation is more than fifty words long, you format the quotation as a block quote. This is an example from the Anderson case from this Unit:

On April 3, 1972, however, the Union and General Dynamics entered into a collective bargaining agreement, which contained the following provision:

> Any employee on the Company's active payroll who is in the bargaining unit and is not a member of the Union on 3 April, 1972, shall, as a condition of continued employment in the bargaining unit, join the Union within ten (10) days after the thirtieth (30th) day following the effective date of this agreement, and shall maintain his membership as provided in Paragraph A above.

A block quote is formatted by:
1. Indenting the left and the right margin of the quoted material ½ inch (1.25 cm.),
2. Formatting the quote to single spaced (even if your document is double spaced), and
3. Not including quotation marks before the first word and at the end of the quotation. The block quote format tells the reader that this is a quotation, not the use of quotation marks.[205]

We all make mistakes when writing, and sometimes a quotation will include a spelling or grammatical mistake. Just as you must indicate when you omit or change words in a quotation, you also must indicate to the reader that the mistake is in the original text so that the reader knows that you didn't copy the text incorrectly. We identify a mistake in the original with the use of [sic]. This example is from the Trademark Properties Inc. v. A&E Television Networks case, included in Section I, Unit 3 – contract formation.

> He said in an e-mail to a representative of the third party production company "Charles isn't [employed by Defendant] anymore but that doesn't change the deal he and I cut prior to me even meeting you guys.... If you guys are participating with advertising, sponsorship, dvd sales, ectm [sic] without us, that was not what I was promised."

The quoted email should have said *etc.* but evidently, the writer's finger slipped from the period key on the keyboard to the *m* key. This is a frequent mistake that we all can make when typing, especially when done on a cell phone. That mistake is indicated with the [sic] immediately following the mistake in the quotation. *Sic* is Latin for thus and is the first word of the complete phrase *sic erat scriptum* ("thus it was written.").

We also use quotation marks to indicate a translation, as used in the above sentence with the phrase *sic erat scriptum*.

---

[205] In the original in the Anderson case, the block quote does include quotation marks, unlike what is suggested in the Bluebook and other style guides. See Rule 5.1(a), THE BLUEBOOK: A UNIFORM SYSTEM OF CITATION (Columbia Law Review Ass'n et al. eds., 20th ed. 2015).

Finally, we use quotation marks in other ways: to indicate a word or a phrase used as an ironic or sarcastic comment, as slang, or as an invented or coined expression. When doing so, use quotation marks only the first time the word is used.[206] Here is an example, taken again from the Trademark Properties case:

> Plaintiff is a South Carolina real estate broker who buys underpriced properties to renovate and sell, engaging in a process we are told is commonly known as "flipping."

The verb "flipping" is a coined usage, used to describe the activity of an investor when he purchases a home, usually remodels it, and sells it for a profit. For this reason, quotation marks are used around the word.

An ironic comment is one that means the something other than, and often the opposite of what is written. Sarcasm is the use of irony to mock. The ironic or sarcastic sense of a word or phrase is indicated with quotation marks:

> The judge was "thrilled" when the attorneys informed him that they had been unable to resolve yet another dispute about discovery.
> ➢ Here, it is said sarcastically that the judge was "thrilled" about another dispute. No judge likes it when attorneys are unable to resolve their discovery disputes, especially when it is "yet another" dispute.

> The one-paragraph "instructions" were really helpful to assemble the complicated furniture that we bought at the store.
> ➢ Here, the writer is using the term instructions ironically, since instructions of just one paragraph can't really be useful to assemble complicated furniture.

Slang is also indicated with the use of quotation marks:

> She replied with a text that said only "LOL."

> He called his girlfriend "bae," a slang word that is a term of endearment.

Slang is also indicated with italics, and whether you use italics or quotation marks is a personal preference.[207]

---

[206] Stefanie, *Quotation Mark Uses Other than Quotations*, APASTYLE.COM (citing Publication Manual of the American Psychological Association 91 (6th ed.)), http://blog.apastyle.org/apastyle/2013/02/quotation-mark-uses-other-than-quotes.html (last visited May 9, 2016).

[207] See, e.g., Katy Steinmetz, *This is What Bae Means*, TIME.COM, http://time.com/3026192/this-is-what-bae-means/ (last visited May 9, 2016) (stating "[t]hough this word was used in the 1500s to refer to sheep sounds, today *bae* is used as a term of endearment, often referring to your boyfriend or girlfriend.").

EEOC v. Townley Engineering & Manufacturing Co.,
859 F.2d 610 (9th Cir. 1988).

Vocabulary and Legal Terminology

Permanent injunction: An order issued by a court that requires someone to either do or stop doing something.

Devotional services: Religious services.

Prospective waiver: In advance, agreeing to give up your right to something, such as bringing a claim or filing a complaint.

To frame: (here) To draft or draw up a document.

Inception: Beginning.

Non-denominational: A church that is open to people of all religious faiths and religions.

To constructively discharge: When someone voluntarily quits his or her job, but because of intolerable conditions created by the employer, often with the intent of causing the person to resign.

Chilling effect: Discouraging others from doing something, often exercising their legal rights.

To strip: To remove.

Pre-Reading Questions

Before you begin reading, skim the caption and the first paragraph and answer the following questions:

1. Is the case in federal or state court? District or appellate court?
2. What was the motion before the district court?
3. Did the district court grant the motion? Can you surmise why?
4. Who appealed and what did the appellate court decide?
5. All the cases you have read so far have included an employee who had some religious practice that needed to be accommodated. Whose religious practice is at issue in this case?
6. The appellate court affirmed the district court's ruling, but sent it back to the district court so that the district court could do what?

Comprehension Questions

With a general idea of the case in your mind, you can now read the case. As you are reading and after you finish reading, answer the following questions:

1. Summarize in your own words the facts of the case.
    a. How would you define the family that owned the Townley Manufacturing Plant?
    b. What were the religious beliefs of the plaintiff, Pelvas?
    c. The devotional services held at the Townely Plant were non-denominational and included discussions of business matters. Given these two facts, should Pelvas had complained about attending?
    d. What did Townely tell Pelvas to do once he objected to the devotional services?
2. What accommodation did the plaintiff request? _____
_____
3. What were the defendant's arguments regarding the undue hardship that it would have suffered if it had granted the plaintiff's requested accommodation? _____
_____
4. Why does the court rule that an employee cannot "prospectively waive" his or her rights under Title VII? _____
_____
5. When can an employee waive his or her rights under a statute like Title VII?
6. How does this case apply to the Singh v. Stray Dog Advertising case?
7. What rules or facts can you use in your arguments for your client?

Language Focus — "Verbing"

English is a fun and also very flexible language. One example of such flexibility is *verbing*, or how we can use as a verb a word not traditionally used as one. In other words, we simply turn a noun or even an adjective into a verb.

Here is an example from the Townley case: "[W]e remand to permit the framing of [the] injunction more narrowly."

As a noun, a *frame* is an open structure that holds something like a photograph or a poster. But *to frame*, as a verb, means to structure.

Here are some other examples of nouns being used as verbs, sometimes in very creative ways!

To door — When I was riding my bike down the street, someone opened his car door without looking and I got *doored*.

Write sentences that demonstrate the meanings of these verbs, which also happen to be nouns.

To author - _____

To impact - _____

To dialogue - _____

To friend someone - _____

To table a motion - _____

A song was released in 2015 by the artists Charlie Puth and Meghan Trainor with the title, "Let's Marvin Gaye and Get It On." Here, the proper name Marvin Gaye is used as a verb. Marvin Gaye is an American rhythm and blues (R&B) singer, songwriter and musician. What do you think the verb and the name of the song mean?

Start paying attention to news articles that you read, to movies or television shows that you watch, or news stories or interviews that you see. What examples of verbing can you find?

International Association of Machinists & Aerospace Workers v. Boeing Co.,
833 F.2d 165 (9th Cir. 1987).

Vocabulary and Legal Terminology

Union initiation fees: Money that an employee must pay before joining a union.

Bargaining unit employee: An employee who is a member of a union.

Monies: Irregular plural of money; monies is usually used by legal or finance writers to talk about "individual sums" or "discrete sums" of money.[208]

Maxim of statutory construction: Principle of how statutes are interpreted.

Legislative history: Documents that are produced as a bill is debated and discussed before voted into law; used when one interprets a statute to determine the meaning of ambiguous terms.

To supplement: To add something to another.

To supplant: Supersede and replace.

To undermine: To damage or weaken.

Pre-Reading Questions

Before you begin reading, skim the caption and the first paragraph and answer the following questions:
1. Is the case in federal or state court? District or appellate court?
2. What was the motion before the district court?
3. Who appealed and what did the appellate court decide?
4. Why was arbitration an issue in this case?
5. This is the third case that has dealt with an employee refusing to pay union dues for religious reasons, and all three cases have found that it would not have imposed an undue hardship for the employer to excuse the employee from paying the union dues. What situation can you think of in which a court might conclude that excusing the employee from paying *would* create an undue hardship?

Comprehension Questions

With a general idea of the case in your mind, you can now read the case. As you are reading and after you finish reading, answer the following questions:

---

[208] Mignon Fogarty, *Money, Monies or Moneys?*, QUICKANDDIRTYTIPS.COM (Aug. 20, 2014), http://www.quickanddirtytips.com/education/grammar/money-monies-or-moneys#sthash.4l57vXjk.dpuf (last visited May 2, 2016).

International Association of Machinists & Aerospace Workers v. Boeing Co., 833 F.2d 165 (9th Cir. 1987)

1. This case deals with a specific issue that ours does not include: whether section 19 of the NLRA (National Labor Relations Act, a federal law regarding unionization) supersedes Title VII. Put the argument that both sides made with regard to this issue into your own words.

2. Put into your own words the court's ruling with regard to whether section 19 the NLRA supersedes Title VII. Why does this matter for this case?

3. What was the undue hardship that the employer alleged it would face if it had granted the accommodation?

4. Did the court agree?

5. How does this case apply to the Singh v. Stray Dog Advertising case?

6. What rules or facts can you use in your arguments for your client?

Grammar Review — Passive vs. Active Voice

It is well-settled that the rights **created by** Title VII are independent and separate from the rights **created by** the NLRA.

The verb **created by** is in the passive voice. A rule of thumb in English (i.e. a general rule) is that we prefer the active voice to the passive voice.

> Active voice: It is well-settled that the rights Title VII **creates** are independent and separate from the rights that the NLRA creates.

Compare the two sentences. Which one sounds better, the one written in the passive voice, or in the active voice? Why?

That we prefer the active voice to the passive voice is just a general rule. But all rules have exceptions, and this is one of those exceptions. So that begs the question: What are the exceptions when the passive voice is preferred? Generally, we prefer the passive voice when:

1. We don't know who the actor is (i.e. who did the action).
2. We want to deemphasize who did the action.
3. It is unimportant who did the action.

With those rules in mind, compare the following pairs of sentences, both of which express the same idea but one uses the active voice and the other the passive voice. Analyze the sentences and then determine which is better, the passive or active voice? Why?

Pair 1:
The book was read by my roommate over the weekend.
My roommate read the book over the weekend.

Pair 2:
The car was completely destroyed by the defendant in the crash.
The defendant completely destroyed the car in the crash.

Pair 3:

Someone stole my car!
My car was stolen!

Pair 4:

The verdict was issued by the jury after a lengthy deliberation.
The jury issued the verdict after a lengthy deliberation.

Pair 5:[209]

She got hired by one of the best law firms in the city.
She was hired by one of the best law firms in the city.

---

[209] Note that both of these sentences are passive. Is there a difference in meaning between them? If so, what?

Proctor v. Consolidated Freightways Corp. of Delaware,
795 F.2d 1472 (9th Cir. 1986).

Vocabulary and Legal Terminology

Triable issue (of fact): A fact that can be analyzed and decided by judge or jury.[210] The existence of a triable issue of fact is a reason to deny a motion for summary judgment as the jury or fact-finder should determine issues of fact.

Without prejudice: When a complaint is dismissed, but not on the merits and not barring subsequent action.[211]

Payroll clerk: Employee who assists an employer in ensuring that other employees are paid promptly and accurately.

To bump someone from a position: When an employee forcibly moves another employee from her job.

Grievance: Complaint, but generally a more formal one against an authority figure such as an employer or the government.

To withdraw (withdrew, withdrawn): To remove or take out (here, for consideration for a position).

To show up for something: To appear or be present.

To find reasonable cause: To determine that a reasonable person, when faced with the evidence, would conclude that the facts of a claim exist, or that a fact occurred.[212]

Unavailing: Unsuccessful.

Magistrate: Judge in the federal court system that assists the district court judges and hears pre-trial civil and criminal matters.

Pre-Reading Questions

Before you begin reading, skim the caption and the first paragraph and answer the following questions:

1. Is the case in federal or state court? District or appellate court?
2. What was the motion before the district court?
3. Was the motion granted?
4. Who appealed and what did the appellate court decide?

---

[210] *Triable*, BLACK'S LAW DICTIONARY, (10th ed. 2014).
[211] *Dismiss, dismissal*, GILBERT'S POCKET SIZE LAW DICTIONARY (3rd ed. 2014).
[212] *Probable Cause*, BLACK'S LAW DICTIONARY (10th ed. 2014).

Comprehension Questions

With a general idea of the case in your mind, you can now read the case. As you are reading and after you finish reading, answer the following questions:

1. Summarize in your own words the facts of the case.
2. Why is it important for this case that the plaintiff, Proctor, held different positions within the company? _____
_____
3. What arguments did the plaintiff make that her former employer failed to initiate good faith efforts to accommodate her religious beliefs? _____
_____
4. What arguments did the defendant make that it made those good faith efforts? _____
_____
5. How does the court find that a triable issue of fact exists? _____
_____
6. Did the plaintiff win her case and show that her employer discriminated against her?
7. How does this case apply to the Singh v. Stray Dog Advertising case? _____
_____
_____
8. What rules or facts can you use in your arguments for your client? _____
_____

Grammar Review — Prefixes

A prefix is a part of a word that is placed before another word and that can reveal a good amount of information about it, especially if you are unsure about its meaning. In the Proctor case, the court declared that it would "reverse and remand" the case to the lower trial. Conciliation was defined as "unavailing." In those words, the prefixes are *re-* and *un-*.

The dictionary definition of a prefix is "an element placed at the beginning of a word to adjust or qualify its meaning, e.g., *ex-, non-, re-* or (in some languages) as an inflection."[213] A prefix can make the term negative (kind vs. unkind), signal repetition (invent vs. reinvent), or indicate support (abortion vs. pro-abortion). Compatible prefixes can work and be joined together, such as when we use *un-* and *re-* in the word unrefundable.[214]

You are no doubt familiar with many prefixes in English, as well as many words that use prefixes. Prefixes can be useful to expand your vocabulary. As stated in the above definition, the prefix *un-* makes a word negative, such as unfriendly. The prefix *dis-* accomplishes the same purpose, such as words like disagree and discomfort.

Look at the three pairs of words below, one with the prefix *dis-* and one with *un-*. There is a subtle yet important difference between the words. What difference in meaning is there between the words?

---

[213] *Prefix*, THE NEW OXFORD AMERICAN DICTIONARY (2001).
[214] *Prefix*, DICTIONARY.COM, http://dictionary.reference.com/browse/prefix (last visited May 4, 2016).

Disinterested vs. uninterested

Dissatisfied vs. unsatisfied

Dislike vs. unlike

The prefix *in-* can also create some confusion as it can have two meanings, both in or inwards, such as the words *inland* or *income*. But *in-* can also have a negative or privative effect, such as with the words *inedible* and *incomprehensible*.

Look at these two words. What meaning does the prefix *in-* have? In or inwards, or negative?

Inflammable

Invaluable

Note as well that the prefix *in-* often takes on the spelling of *im-*, *ir-* and *il-* for phonetic reasons: impartial, immeasurable, illiterate, illegal, irreplaceable, and irregular.[215]

The *in-* become *il-* before *l*; *im-* before *b*, *m* or *p*; and *ir-* before *r*.[216]

---

[215] *In*, Dictionary.Com, http://dictionary.reference.com/browse/in- (last visited May 4, 2016).
[216] *In*, The New Oxford American Dictionary (2001).

Slater v. Douglas County,
743 F. Supp. 2d 1188 (D. Or. 2010).

Vocabulary and Legal Terminology

<u>Cross-motions for summary judgment</u>: In motion practice, when both parties file motions for summary judgment and claim that there are no genuine issues of material fact in dispute and that the court should issue judgment as a matter of law in its favor.

<u>Movant</u>: Party who files a motion with the court.

<u>Non-movant</u>: Party against whom a motion is filed and who opposes the motion.

<u>Stark</u>: Severe.

Pre-Reading Questions

Before you begin reading, skim the caption, synopsis and holding and answer the following questions:
1. Is the case in federal or state court? District or appellate court?
2. What was the motion before the district court?
3. Who filed the motion?
4. Was the motion granted?
5. Who appealed and what did the appellate court decide?

Comprehension Questions

With a general idea of the case in your mind, you can now read the case. As you are reading and after you finish reading, answer the following questions:
1. Summarize in your own words the facts of the case.
2. What steps did the defendant/employer take to accommodate the plaintiff in this case? _____
   _____
3. Why were those steps insufficient to meet the employer's duty under Title VII? _____
   _____
4. What didn't the employer do to find a possible accommodation for the plaintiff? _____
   _____
5. How is this case helpful if you represent the plaintiff, Singh?
6. How is this case helpful if you represent the defendant, Stray Dog Advertising?
7. How can you distinguish the <u>Slater</u> case from ours?

Legal Focus: Comparing Cases

The synopsis told us that the fact that the county failed to engage in the interactive process did not mean, on its own, that the county had violated Title VII. In other words, in some situations, when an employee has requested an accommodation, the employer can decide not to discuss a possible accommodation with the employee and still not violate Title VII.

But we learned in the Burns case that Title VII requires employers to take some steps in negotiating with an employee to reach a reasonable accommodation. There is no obligation to find an accommodation, but "initial steps" must be taken.

How do you square these two apparently contradictory statements?

Grammar Review — Irregular Verbs

English verbs are easier than those in many languages. We don't really have a subjunctive tense,[217] and our verb endings are very few (-s, -ed, -ing) so conjugating a verb in English is much easier than it is in other languages. However, that doesn't mean that English is an easy language to learn. All languages are difficult to learn, but often for different reasons. Irregular verbs can be difficult for language learners for the simple reason that they are irregular and must be memorized.

This sentence is from the Slater case.

> The County contends that it is entitled to judgment as a matter of law because it made an effort to accommodate plaintiff by offering to transfer her out of the Clerk's Office into another County position if an opening **arose**.

Below you will find a table of irregular verbs, with some of the verb forms missing. Complete the table. Search online for any verbs that you do not know and cannot complete.

Base Verb	Irregular Past	Base Verb	Irregular Past	Base Verb	Irregular Past	Base Verb	Irregular Past
Awake	awoke, awoken	Build		Grow		Swim	
Beat		Catch		Hang		Throw	
Bend		Dig		Hurt		Wear	
Bet		Dream		Lay		Win	
Bid		Drive		Lead		Write	
Bite		Fall		Lie		Bear	
Blow		Feel		Rise		Break	
Broadcast		Fly		Shut		Dive	

---

[217] The subjunctive tense can be seen in this construction: If I were you, I would go to law school. The grammatically correct form is "If I were you," although it is very common to hear people say "If I was you, I would go to law school." See the Language Focus with the case Soucek v. Banham (Section I, Unit 1) for additional information of when we use the subjunctive in English.

Tiano v. Dillard Department Stores, Inc.,
139 F.3d 679 (9th Cir. 1998).

Vocabulary and Legal Terminology

Pacesetter: A leader, someone who is in front of others.

Anniversary sale: Sale held at many department stores where shoppers can find many good bargains and large discounts.

De novo: Standard of review for an appellate court, as if it were considering the issue for the first time.[218]

Clear error: Upon review by an appellate court, a mistake in application of the law or in matters of fact made by the trial court that is unquestionably erroneous.[219]

Prima facie case: A case in which the plaintiff has presented sufficient evidence to entitle him to a decision by the judge or jury; a case which compels a favorable decision when no contrary or rebutting evidence is presented.[220]

Equal Employment Opportunity Commission: The federal agency charged with enforcing and interpreting Title VII of the Civil Rights Act of 1964 and other federal anti-discrimination statutes.

Secular: Not relating to religion.

Pilgrimage: A journey taken to a holy place.

Pre-Reading Questions

Before you begin reading, skim the caption and the first paragraph and answer the following questions:
1. This is an appellate court decision. Is the case in federal or state court?
2. What happened at the trial court? Was there a jury trial?
3. What did the trial court decide?
4. Who appealed and on what grounds?
5. What did the court of appeals decide?
6. Did all of the appellate judges agree about the decision?
7. What do we know about the employee's religious beliefs from reading the initial paragraph?

---

[218] For additional information about standards of review, see the Legal Focus exercise with the case Gifford v. Gallano Farms (Section II, Unit 4) on page 167.
[219] *Error*, Gilbert's Pocket Size Law Dictionary (3rd ed. 2014).
[220] *Prima Facie*, Gilbert's Pocket Size Law Dictionary (3rd ed. 2014).

a. What thoughts come into your mind as you think about this employee, her desire to go on a pilgrimage, and her claim that she had to go at a certain time?

b. Do your religious beliefs influence in any way how you view this case and the plaintiff's claims?

Comprehension Questions

With a general idea of the case in your mind, you can now read the case. As you are reading and after you finish reading, answer the following questions:

1. Highlight the general rules regarding Title VII and the claims brought alleging religious discrimination for failure to accommodate. Are these rules important for the Singh v. Stray Dog Advertising case? Why or why not?

2. Find in the case two other, more specific rules that are applicable to Title VII cases. Write them below.
   a. _____
   _____
   _____
   _____
   b. _____
   _____
   _____
   _____

3. Are these rules useful for our fact pattern? Why or why not? _____
   _____

4. What was your opinion about the employee as you were reading the case?

5. What was your opinion about the employer as you were reading the case?

6. Do you think that the appellate court decided correctly? Why or why not?

7. Why do you think one of the judges disagreed with the majority opinion? Do you agree with this judge? Why or why not?

8. Is this case useful for our fact pattern?
   a. Why or why not?
   b. Is it more useful for the plaintiff or the defendant? Why?

9. What arguments (if any) could be made that Singh's religious beliefs were not sincere?

Grammar Review — On, Onto, Upon, In, Into — What's The Difference?

As we have discussed in other Grammar Review sections, prepositions can be tricky when learning a second language and oftentimes require special attention and memorization.[221] To complicate matters even more, English has several preposition pairs that seem identical in meaning, but have slightly different meanings.

---

[221] See the Language Focus exercises with the cases Maxell v. Kenney Deans, Inc. (Section I, Unit 3) on page 58, Regency Oaks Corp. v. Norman Spencer McKernan (Section I, Unit 2) on page 37, Cook v. Rockwell Int'l Corp. et al. (Section I, Unit 4) on page 76, Van Wyck v. Aspinwall (Section II, Unit 2) on page 146, Anest v. Ardino (Section II, Unit 4) on page 163 and Bishop v. TES Realty Trust (Section III, Unit 4) for additional exercises on prepositions.

To illustrate, examine the highlighted prepositions in the following sentences from both the Tiano, Slater and Proctor cases:

> The district court did not indicate **upon** which evidence it based the finding that the temporal mandate was part of Tiano's bona fide religious belief.

> In Tiano's absence, her immediate supervisor, McGraw, spent significant time **on** the sales floor. The arbitrator denied her grievances, finding that Proctor "caused her own problem by bidding off her job **onto** a job which required Saturday overtime work

In these two sentences, what difference do you think there is between **on** and **upon**? Why might we use **on** in one sentence and **upon** in another? If necessary, use a dictionary to help you answer the questions and differentiate between the sentences.

Here are two other sentence pairs. Examine the highlighted prepositions:

> The jury sat **in** the jury box and listened intently to the testimony of both the plaintiff's and the defendant's witnesses.

> The jurors walked **into** the jury box, took their seats and listened to the closing arguments.

> The domestic partnership law was intended to go **into** effect January 1, 2008, but because of a court challenge, did not go into effect until February 4, 2008.

What do you note about the two sentences and the prepositions used? If you were to translate the sentences into your mother tongue, you might use the same preposition in both sentences. Why do we use two different prepositions in English?

Finally, examine these sentence pairs, paying particular attention to the prepositions used. What differences do you note between the sentences, the actions and the prepositions used?

> The snow from the defendants' roof slid **onto** the plaintiff's house and into their backyard.

> All of the attorney's files are **on** her desk.

Having reviewed the above sentences, what general rules can you construct about the prepositions **on/onto** and **in/into**? What general rules can you make about the use of **on/upon**?

EEOC Consent Decree EEOC v. Razzoo's, L.P., No. 3:05-cv-00562 (N.D. Tex. June 16, 2006).

Vocabulary and Legal Terminology

<u>Adjudged</u>: Adjudicated or decided by a court.

<u>Federal deductions</u>: Federal taxes taken from an employee's paycheck for programs such as Social Security.

<u>Registry</u>: A book where official lists are kept.

<u>Conspicuous</u>: Easy to see.

<u>To deface</u>: To destroy.

<u>To bear</u>: (here) To pay.

Pre-Reading Questions

Before you begin reading, answer the following questions:
1. What is a consent decree?
2. When is a consent decree issued?
3. Who issues a consent decree?
4. How is a consent decree different from a settlement agreement?

Comprehension Questions

With a general idea of the case in your mind, you can now read the consent decree. As you are reading and after you finish reading, answer the following questions:

1. Paragraphs 3 and 4 limit the duration of the Consent Decree to two years and provide that during that term, "Defendant is enjoined from denying employees a reasonable accommodation" or "from discriminating against them on the basis of religion."

    Under Title VII, the Defendant is legally obligated not to discriminate. Does it seem superfluous to include this in the consent decree? If you had written it, would you have included it? Why or why not?

2. The Defendant is also ordered, in Paragraph 5, to create an "anti-discrimination policy." Many businesses have employee handbooks or employee manuals that include the provisions and policies that Defendant is now required to put into place.

    Does your country mandate employers to have an employee handbook? Or is it customary like here?

3. Review the facts of this case (in the comment at the beginning). Is this case useful for our fact pattern?
    a. Why or why not?
    b. Is it more useful for the plaintiff or the defendant? Why?
    c. How could you use this case and what arguments could you make with it, regardless of which side you represent?

Language Focus — Translating Legalese into "Regular English"

Legalese is defined as "the formal and technical language of legal documents."[222] The dictionary entry says not only that the term is "informal," but even that it is "derogatory."[223] Some people call it legal jargon. Legalese is the use of phrases like *hereinafter or herein*. It is how we think lawyers often write: in long, convoluted sentences that must be translated into everyday English in order to be understood.

Why do lawyers write this way? Some lawyers write in legalese because it is how lawyers have always written, and they think that is how lawyers are supposed to write. Some lawyers write in legalese because they think it sounds more "lawyer-like." Others think that their clients expect that type of writing, and might think they aren't getting their money's worth if the document is too easy to read.

Over the past years, there has been a growing movement away from legalese and towards legal English that is clear, concise and easy to follow. This movement is known as The Plain English Movement. In 2010, President Barack Obama signed into law the Plain Writing Act of 2010, which requires federal agencies to use "clear Government communication that the public can understand and use."[224] In 2011, he went one step further and issued an executive order that mandated that federal regulations be written in a way that is "accessible, consistent, written in plain language, and easy to understand."[225]

Writing in plain legal English doesn't mean that your writing will be boring, or that you won't be able to communicate all the legal nuances or meanings that you need as an attorney. What it means is that your clients will no longer need a translator to read a legal document. Why not join the movement?[226]

Here are two paragraphs from the Consent Decree, both of which are good (or bad?) examples of legalese. You have been asked by your friend, a non-lawyer, to translate the paragraphs into "normal" English. How would you do that?

---

[222] *Legalese,* THE NEW OXFORD AMERICAN DICTIONARY (2001).
[223] Id.
[224] Plain Writing Act of 2010, PL 111-274, 124 Stat 2861, Sec. 2. More information about the Plain English Act can be found at Plain Language: It's the Law, PlainLanguage.Gov http://www.plainlanguage.gov/plLaw/ (last visited May 30, 2016).
[225] Exec. Order No. 13563, 79 Fed. Reg. 3,821 (Jan. 18. 2011) The Plain Writing Act of 2010 is also discussed in the Language Focus exercise in the case The Kelly Law Firm P.C. v. An Attorney for You in Unit 2 of this Advanced Section.
[226] For additional practice in eliminating legalese and writing in plain legal English, see the Language and Legal Focus exercises with the following cases: Miller v. Carnation Co. (Section I, Unit 4) on page 78, Kowalchuk v. Stroup (Section I, Unit 3) on page 50, Hallock v. State of New York et al. (Section I, Unit 2) on page 29, Hendricks v. Tubbs (Section I, Unit 4) on page 101, The Kelly Law Firm, P.C. v. An Attorney for You (Section I, Unit 2) on page 236, and Buckley v. Litman (Section II, Unit 2) on page 140.

Paragraph 1: *This Court has jurisdiction of the subject matter of this action and the parties, venue is proper, and all administrative prerequisites to the EEOC's filing of this action have been met. The parties stipulate to the Court's jurisdiction.*

Your rewrite: _____
_____
_____
_____

Paragraph 12: *The terms of this Consent Decree shall be binding upon the EEOC and Defendant, its agents, officers, employees, servants, successors, and assigns, as to the issues resolved herein.*

Your rewrite: _____
_____
_____
_____

This paragraph of a union collective bargaining agreement is part of the <u>Anderson v. General Dynamics Aerospace Division</u> case. You represent the union and have been asked to write this provision in a way that all the employees can understand. How can you rewrite this provision to be clearer and easier to understand? (Hint: writing an IF/THEN statement may be a good way to start)

> Any employee who is a member of and adheres to established and traditional tenets or teachings of a bona fide religion, body, or sect which has historically held conscientious objections to joining or financially supporting labor organizations shall not be required to join or financially support any labor organization as a condition of employment; except that such employee may be required ... to pay sums equal to such dues and initiation fees to a nonreligious, nonlabor organization charitable fund.

Your rewrite: _____
_____
_____
_____

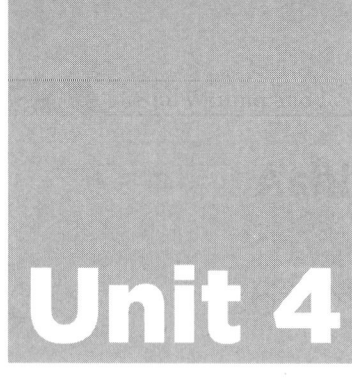

Unit 4 Premises Liability

Statutes

M.G.L.A.
186 § 15 and § 19

Vocabulary and Legal Terminology

To preclude: To bar or prohibit.

To exonerate: To clear someone from blame or responsibility.

Appurtenance: Something that is attached or belongs to something else of greater value, such as a barn or a fence to the land it is on.[227]

Comprehension Questions

As you are reading and after you finish reading the statute, answer the following questions:
1. According to this statute, certain provisions of leases can be considered void and against public policy. What must be the aim of the provision for it to be void?
2. Why would the legislature decide that this type of provision is against public policy?
3. Let's say that this statute has not been passed, and that landlords are allowed to include this type of provision in a lease.
    a. The landlord is sued for injuries that a guest suffers while on the rented property, and the guest recovers $100,000 in damages. What can the landlord do to recover this money?
    b. The tenant is injured because the stairs in the building collapse while she is walking up them. What can the tenant do to recover compensation for her injuries and losses?
4. In sum, the statute says that a landlord can be held liable for any injuries suffered "on or around" the leased premises, on an elevator or stairway or in an elevator, as well as on "other appurtenances" used in connection with the rented property. Explain why the landlord would or would not be liable for injuries someone suffered:
    a. In the detached garage that the tenant also rents from the landlord, but for an amount separate from and in addition to the monthly rent.

---
[227] *Appurtenance*, Gilbert's Pocket Size Law Dictionary (3rd ed. 2014).

b. On the sidewalk that is in front of the building.
c. In the swimming pool that is on the apartment building grounds.
d. In a tool shed in the backyard of a house that a tenant rents.
e. On the public street that the apartment building is located on, but immediately in front of it.

Language Focus: Reading Statutes

For both native and non-native speakers, reading a statute can be very difficult. Many reasons exist why it is so difficult:

1. Long, run-on sentences

The statute M.G.L.A. 186 § 15 has 127 words, all in one sentence! That is a run-on sentence, and run-on sentences are always hard to understand because it is easy to lose your place as you read through the sentence and try to remember how it started and where it takes you. Many English writing experts (and not just of legal English) stress the importance of conciseness and recommend that sentences have fifteen to twenty words.[228] Sentences with twenty-five words are considered difficult to understand, and twenty-nine words or more, very difficult.[229] Imagine a sentence with 127 words! It is almost impossible to understand.

2. Repetition, or two or three words to express the same thing

A statute like this requires a broad knowledge of vocabulary as more than one word is used to express the same idea, concept or action. Four verbs, all with similar meanings, are used to state what type of provision is prohibited: one that *indemnifies* the lessor or landlord, or *holds* the lessor or landlord *harmless*, or *precludes* or *exonerates* the lessor or landlord.

You might not be sure if preclude and exonerate are the same thing or whether you should take the time to look one or both of them up in the dictionary. Another example of two words used to express the same concept is the use of lessee or tenant and lessor or landlord.

This repetition adds to the difficulty in understanding the sense because it increases the number of words. And the longer a sentence is, the more difficult it is to understand and follow.

3. Separation (and 104 words) between the subject of the sentence (any provision of a lease or other rental agreement) and verb (shall be deemed void)

This distance between the subject and verb, which usually follow each other immediately in English, requires mental effort to remember what the subject was by the time that you get to the verb that accompanies it.

---

[228] See, e.g., RUDOLF PLESCH, PH.D., THE ART OF PLAIN TALK 51 (1st ed. 1946); MARTHA FAULK & IRVING M. MEHLER, THE ELEMENTS OF LEGAL WRITING: A GUIDE TO THE PRINCIPLES OF WRITING CLEAR, CONCISE, AND PERSUASIVE LEGAL DOCUMENTS 5-6 (1994); BRYAN A. GARNER, A DICTIONARY OF MODERN LEGAL USAGE 793 (2nd ed. 1995).

[229] A very easy sentence has 8 or fewer words; an easy sentence 11 words; a fairly easy sentence 14 words; standard sentence 17 words; a fairly difficult sentence 21 words; a difficult sentence 25 words; and a very difficult sentence 29 or more words. Plesch, *supra* at n.228 at 51. Literary English runs to about 20 words per sentence, and scientific English about 30 words per sentence. Id. at 52. The average sentence length of briefs filed in the New York Courts of Appeals has been climbing since the late 1980s. From 1979 to 1988, the average words per sentence was 15.9, while in the 1999-2008 decade, the average number of words per sentence had jumped to 34.7. Ian Gallacher, "*When Numbers Get Serious: A Study of Plain English Usage in Briefs Filed Before the New York Court of Appeals,*" 46 SUFFOLK U. L. REV. 451, 478 (2013).

So the question is how do you make it easier to read a statute, or a contract provision?

A useful first step to tackling a statute like this is dividing the long sentence into shorter segments or phrases. You can do this by taking note of the first and last word of each phrase, and putting those words into one sub-section of the larger sentence.

As you read the statute (copied below at the bottom of the page), you come to the word *whereby*. You know that *whereby* means "by which," and is a relative pronoun that must refer to and define the noun that it follows. So in other words, *whereby* starts a new sub-section of the long sentence, one that modifies the first part of the sentence. The main part of the first section of the sentence is in bold, italicized font (below).

The second sub-section of the long sentence begins with "the effect of which." The word "effect" should give you a clue that an effect has to be of something, so you should immediately ask yourself what word in the previous sentence the effect refers to. Here, it is the effect of the provision of a lease. By replacing "of which" with "of the provision of the lease" will make it easier to follow the remaining part of that sub-section, which includes a series of verbs. When you get to the end of the series and arrive at the last "or," you should slow down and pause, mentally arriving at the end of that sub-section (2).

Reflecting internally that you've reached the end of another sub-section of that very long sentence will help you maintain the sense of where you are, how the parts work together, and what the sentence means. When you arrive at the "for" — the beginning of the next sub-section (3) — your mind should return to the first verb in that list — indemnify — and if you know that we say "indemnify for something," you know that the list includes the types of indemnification included.

On your own, finish sub-sections (4), (5) and (6). Here are a couple of questions to help you:

1. Language-wise, what tells you that the next sub-section (5) begins with the preposition on?
2. What helps you to identify sub-section (4) as the list that begins with "from" and ends with "landlord?"
3. What tells you that the last sub-section of the very long sentence begins with the verb shall, where (6) begins?

(1) ***Any provision of a lease or other rental agreement relating to real property*** whereby a lessee or tenant enters into a covenant, agreement or contract, by the use of any words whatsoever, (2) ***the effect of which is to indemnify the lessor or landlord or hold the lessor or landlord harmless, or preclude or exonerate the lessor or landlord from any or all liability*** to the lessee or tenant, or to any other person, (3) ***for any injury, loss, damage or liability*** arising (4) ***from any omission, fault, negligence or other misconduct of the lessor or landlord (5) on or about the leased or rented premises*** or on or about any elevators, stairways, hallways or other appurtenance used in connection therewith, (6) ***shall be deemed to be against public policy and void.***

Regardless of how you read a statute or a very long sentence, realize that it isn't easy, even for a native-speaker. There are other ways to also aid you in understanding a complex statute.

You can rewrite a statute as an if/then statement. Writing a statute as an if/then statement is useful because it requires you to understand the language of the statute, and makes you simplify it. You can't write an if/then summary of a statute if you don't understand what it means.

IF a tenant or other person is hurt while on leased property (including on stairs, in elevators, hallways or other common areas) AND
IF the injury is because of the landlord's negligence or failure to act AND
IF in the lease the tenant promises to indemnify or hold harmless the landlord for the injury or loss suffered

THEN the lease violates public policy and is void.

When you write an if/then statement for your own understanding and for studying, realize that it doesn't matter if you don't put each and every word into your if/then statement. For example, you can understand the sense by including only the verb to indeminfy and to hold harmless, rather than all four in the original, as you can also understand the sense by only including landlord rather than landlord or lessor.

Try to parse apart the long four sentences that make up the other statute that is included with the Unit:

M.G.L.A. 186 § 19

§ 19. Notice to landlord of unsafe condition; tort actions for injuries resulting from uncorrected condition

A landlord or lessor of any real estate except an owner-occupied two- or three-family dwelling shall, within a reasonable time following receipt of a written notice from a tenant forwarded by registered or certified mail of an unsafe condition, not caused by the tenant, his invitee, or any one occupying through or under the tenant, exercise reasonable care to correct the unsafe condition described in said notice except that such notice need not be given for unsafe conditions in that portion of the premises not under control of the tenant. The tenant or any person rightfully on said premises injured as a result of the failure to correct said unsafe condition within a reasonable time shall have a right of action in tort against the landlord or lessor for damages. Any waiver of this provision in any lease or other rental agreement for residential use shall be void and unenforceable. The notice requirement of this section shall be satisfied by a notice from a board of health or other code enforcement agency to a landlord or lessor of residential premises not exempted by the provisions of this section of a violation of the state sanitary code or other applicable by-laws, ordinances, rules or regulations.

Cases

Young v. Garwacki,
402 N.E.2d 1045 (Mass. 1980).

Vocabulary and Legal Terminology

Judgment Notwithstanding the Verdict: A judgment by the court in favor of one party notwithstanding the jury's verdict in favor of the other party.[230] The common abbreviation is JNOV.

Railing: A structure made of a rail or piece of wood that serves as a barrier or for support, such as on a balcony or a stairway.

To give way: To collapse or fall from pressure or weight, here because of the decayed condition of the wood.

To reserve: (here) When a court does not answer and resolve an issue and saves the matter for a future decision.

Agrarian: Agricultural.

To turn on: (here) To depend on something.

To cede: To yield.

Caveat emptor: A Latin phrase that means "Let the buyer beware" to mean that the buyer assumes the risk that an item (or rental property here) has defects. Similar to an item being sold "as is."

Nonfeasance: Failure to perform a duty which one is obliged to perform.[231]

To exculpate: To clear or tend to clear of alleged guilt.[232]

Pre-Reading Questions

Before you begin reading, skim the caption and the first paragraph and answer the following questions:
1. Is the case in federal or state court?
2. What happened to lead the plaintiff to file the original complaint?

---

[230] *Judgment*, GILBERT'S POCKET SIZE LAW DICTIONARY (3rd ed. 2014).
[231] *Nonfeasance*, GILBERT'S POCKET SIZE LAW DICTIONARY (3rd ed. 2014).
[232] *Exculpate*, GILBERT'S POCKET SIZE LAW DICTIONARY (3rd ed. 2014).

3. Who were the defendants?
4. What happened at the trial court? Who did the court enter judgment for and why?
5. Who appealed?
6. How did the case arrive at the Massachusetts Supreme Court?
7. What did the supreme court decide?

Comprehension Questions

With a general idea of the case in your mind, you can now read the case. As you are reading and after you finish reading, answer the following questions:

1. Summarize the facts that led to the dispute.
2. What did the rental agreement between the landlord and the tenant state with regard to repairs?
3. Why did the jury find that the landlord was not liable for the injuries that the plaintiff suffered?
4. As stated in the comments with the case, this decision rests upon policy considerations as well as legal grounds (case law and statutory). Summarize the policy concerns that:
   a. Supported the original doctrine that stated that a landlord was liable for injuries that occurred on the premises only if he was negligent in maintaining the common area, but not the rented premises. _____
   b. Imposed upon landlords a duty of reasonable care towards everyone who entered onto his property. _____
   c. Prohibits landlords from signing an agreement with a tenant that limits or eliminates the landlord's liability for injuries that occur on his property. _____
5. Before the Young decision, when could a landlord be liable for injuries that resulted from repairs that he did or didn't do on the rented property? _____
6. Before the Young decision, when could a plaintiff bring a breach of contract claim against a landlord? When could he bring a tort claim? _____
7. Do you agree with the shift in policy towards the holding articulated in the Young decision? Why or why not?
8. Is this case useful for our fact pattern?
   a. Why or why not?
   b. Is it more useful for the plaintiff or the defendant? Why?
9. This case deals with residential landlords. Do you think that the holding also applies or should apply to commercial landlords? Why or why not?
10. Should there be a different standard for liability for commercial and residential landlords? Why or why not?

Language Focus — Modal Verbs

Modal verbs are those verbs in English that indicate likelihood, ability, permission and obligation. You are no doubt familiar with them already.

The verbs have subtle differences in meaning and also behave differently than other words, increasing the difficulty in truly mastering them. Here is a quick review of the verbs and their meanings.

Must — to be obliged or required to do something, such as by a law. It is also used to express a personal obligation. *Must* is always followed by the verb root (the infinitive without *to*, never by the infinitive).

    Examples:

        I really must go. NOT: ~~I really must to go~~.

        The new law says that you must have a driver's license to purchase cigarettes.

NOTE: *Must* is used only in the present and future, never in the past. To express an obligation in the past, you must use *to have to*.

    Examples:

        Before the legislature passed the law back in the 1990s, you didn't have to wear a seatbelt when driving.

        I told my sister that I really had to go home because I wanted to study for my final exams.

To have to — to be required to do something, but a more general obligation, and one imposed from an external source. *To have to* is always followed by the verb root.

    Examples:

        He has to turn in his paper by this Friday.

        Our refrigerator stopped working! We'll have to call a repair person right away so that the food doesn't go bad.

    NOTE:

        Although *must* and *to have to* have similar meanings when used in an affirmative sense, they have very different meanings when used as a negative.

        You must not drive. You've had too much to drink.
            ➢ Here, *must not* means that it is forbidden to drive.

        You don't have to drive me to work. I can take the bus.
            ➢ Here, *don't have to* expresses a negative necessity. In other words, "It isn't necessary for you to drive me to work. I can take the bus."

Need — need is what is called a semi-modal verb because we use it at times as a modal verb, but other times use it as a regular or main verb. When used as a modal verb, it takes the verb root, not the infinitive, and is used mostly in the negative to express the lack of an obligation or necessity. It is similar in meaning to *to have to* as a negative.

Examples:

You needn't drive me to work. I can take the bus.
- ➢ Here, *needn't* expresses a negative necessity. In other words, "It isn't necessary for you to drive me to work. I can take the bus."

He needn't worry about losing his job. The firm has a lot of client work to be completed.
- ➢ Here, *needn't* means that it isn't necessary for him to worry about losing his job.

NOTE: Like *must*, we don't use *need* in the past tense when using it as a modal verb. Instead, we use *to have to*.

While I greatly appreciated the favor, you didn't have to drive me to work yesterday. I could have easily taken the bus. But thanks anyway!

Should — used to indicate an obligation or to express advice.

You should practice writing more often if you want to improve your writing.

You really should call your parents more often.

In the past, you use *should have + past participle*.

When I was in law school, I should have studied more.

I should have reviewed my notes better before taking the exam. I probably would have done better.

May/Might — we use *may/might* to talk about various situations:

To talk about a possible situation: *It looks like it might rain.*

To politely ask for permission to do something: *May I go to the restroom?*

To politely give someone permission to do something: *You may go now.*

To express a wish or hope: *May he rest in peace!*

May and *might* are similar in meaning, but have subtle differences.[233] *Might* is less likely to happen than *may*:

I might go to the movies tonight, but I am really tired so I'll probably stay home.

I may come with you but I have another chapter to read so I'll let you know. (more likely than the above example).

To make matters worse, we often use may and might interchangeably, and which is used can depend on the speaker.

---

[233] *May or Might*, Oxford Dictionaries, http://blog.oxforddictionaries.com/2013/04/may-or-might-whats-the-difference/ (last visited May 30, 2016).

Both follow the same form in the past:

> I might have gone if you had called me earlier. (but you didn't)
>
> I may have gone if you had called me earlier.

Can/Could — we use *can/could* to express ability and permission. *Can* is present tense while *could* is conditional and the past tense of *can*.

> Can you come to my office this afternoon at 2:00?
>
> Could you come to my office this afternoon?
>
> Last year, I could have travelled more if I had had the time.

Look at these sentences from the Young case that use modal verbs:

> The traditional approach to landlord-tenant law was that the landlord **might have been** liable for negligent maintenance of common areas but was not generally liable for the negligent maintenance of the premises themselves.
>
> We said that the status of the person visited, landowner or lessee, **should not affect** the visitor's right to personal safety or the landowner's obligation reasonably to maintain premises in his control.
>
> Henceforth, landlords as other persons **must** exercise reasonable care not to subject others to an unreasonable risk of harm.
>
> Ordinarily, absent a contractual agreement or the tenant's permission, the landlord **can** neither inspect for defects nor make repairs on the rented premises.

Now look at these sentences and the highlighted words or phrases. What verbs can you replace the boldface phrases with? Be sure to put them in the proper tense.

> According to the judge's report, the landlord had made no express agreement to keep the premises in repair, although he testified **he considered it his obligation** to repair the porch railing.
>
> The landlord **was under a separate and limited duty** toward each tenant and the tenant's visitors **to exercise reasonable care** to maintain the common areas in a condition not less safe than they were, or appeared to be in, at the time of the letting to the particular tenant.
>
> If a landlord fails to correct the condition within a reasonable time, the tenant or any person rightfully on the premises **has a tort action** against the landlord for injuries sustained. (here, replace the phrase *has a tort action* with a modal verb + another verb).

Knowing how the court ruled in the Young case, complete the following sentences with modal verbs.

The court concluded that the landlord _____ the deck, but because he didn't, he was liable for the plaintiff's injuries.

Because of this decision, landlords _____ repair dangerous conditions in the area leased to the tenant and under the tenant's control or be held liable for any injuries suffered as a result of that dangerous condition.

Before this decision, a landlord _____ repair anything in the area leased to the tenant unless there was an express agreement.

Humphrey v. Byron,
850 N.E.2d 1044 (Mass. 2006).

Vocabulary and Legal Terminology

Joint application for direct appellate review: A form filled out and submitted by both parties asking the appellate court to review the trial court's decision.

Pre-printed form: (here) A standard template that you can purchase to use as the basis for a contract, with standard terms and conditions.

Basement: The floor of a building that is underground.

Workers' compensation benefits: Funds paid to workers for injuries or illnesses arising out of or in the course of employment, regardless of whether the injury was due to the fault or negligence of the employee.[234]

To overthrow: (here) To overturn or reverse.

To outweigh: To be greater in importance or value.

Pre-Reading Questions

Before you begin reading, skim the caption and the background and holding paragraphs and answer the following questions:

1. Is the case in federal or state court?
2. What happened to lead the plaintiff to file the original complaint?
3. What was the relationship between the plaintiff and the defendant?
4. Why do you think that the injured employee only brought a claim against the landlord and not his employer too, since the employer leased the building where he was injured? In contrast, in the Young case, the plaintiff named two defendants – the landlord and the tenant. Why the difference?
5. What happened at the trial court?
6. Who appealed?
7. What did the supreme court decide?

Comprehension Questions

With a general idea of the case in your mind, you can now read the case. As you are reading and after you finish reading, answer the following questions:

---

[234] *Workers' Compensation Laws*, Gilbert's Pocket Size Law Dictionary (3rd ed. 2014).

Humphrey v. Byron, 850 N.E.2d 1044 (Mass. 2006) 281

1. What is the issue in front of the court? _____
2. What role does the <u>Young</u> decision play in this case? _____
3. What did the rental agreement between the landlord and tenant state with regard to repairs and to the space that the tenant was entitled to access? Why is this important for the court? _____
_____
4. What arguments did the plaintiff make as to why the defendant should be liable for his injuries?
_____
5. What policy reasons support the "significant differences" between commercial and residential tenancies? _____
6. What are some of the differences between commercial and residential landlords, as explained by the court? _____
7. Small businesses are often treated differently and more favorably than larger business as to not impose an unreasonable burden.
    a. What policy arguments does the defendant make based on the fact that the landlord is a small business? _____
    b. Does the court agree with these arguments? Why or why not? _____
    c. Do you agree? Why or why not? _____
    d. Can you think of reasons or situations why a small business should be treated differently and more favorably? _____
8. What issue does the court reserve for a future decision? Why might this issue be important for our case? _____
9. Is this case useful for our case?
    a. Why or why not? _____
    b. Is it more useful for the plaintiff or the defendant? Why? _____
    c. Can you analogize or distinguish the facts from our case? How and why can the facts and holdings be useful? _____

Legal Focus — Citations and Signals

An introductory signal is a word or an abbreviation of a word or a phrase that tells the reader why the writer has cited a certain legal authority such as a statute, case or secondary source. A signal will clarify the usefulness of the source for the reader in understanding the text indicated by the signal.

Rule 1.2 of the Bluebook includes a complete explanation of all the signals used in U.S. legal writing.[235] Understanding the meaning of different signals and when they are used is not only useful for your own legal writing, but will also deepen your understanding of the cases that you read for your classes.

Examine the following paragraph from the <u>Humphrey v. Byron</u> case.

> Prior to our *Young* decision, Massachusetts adhered to the common-law rule of let the lessee beware: "The tenant took the premises as he found them." *Young v. Garwacki, supra* at 165, 402 N.E.2d 1045, citing *Gade v. National Creamery Co.*, 324 Mass. 515,

---
[235] Rule 1.2, THE BLUEBOOK: A Uniform System of Citation (Columbia Law Review Ass'n et al. eds., 20th ed. 2015).

> 518, 87 N.E.2d 180 (1949). "[D]uring the term of the rental, 'there could be no tort liability for nonfeasance in the absence of an agreement, for consideration, that the landlord would keep the premises in a condition of safety, and make all repairs without notice.'" *Young v. Garwacki, supra* at 166, 402 N.E.2d 1045, quoting *DiMarzo v. S. & P. Realty Corp.*, 364 Mass. 510, 513, 306 N.E.2d 432 (1974). As to residential tenancies, we did away with this "ancient law," *Young v. Garwacki, supra* at 168, 402 N.E.2d 1045, and adopted the rule that "landlords as other persons must exercise reasonable care not to subject others to an unreasonable risk of harm."

In the above paragraph, the first thing that you note about the citations and the signals is that there are no signals! Sometimes, we don't need a signal when we cite a source. According to the Bluebook, we use no signal when the cited authority "(i) directly states the proposition, (ii) identifies the sources of a quotation, or (iii) identified an authority referred to in the text."[236]

A point you want to note in the quotation that begins with the word "during" is the use of the brackets [ ] around the letter "d." It may seems strange and make the sentence hard to read, but writers use brackets in that way to indicate that in the original text, the word was not the first word of the sentence and was written with a lower-case d ("during.") The writer added the upper-case D since it is the first word of the quotation. If you change a quotation, you always have to let your reader know.[237]

Another point to note is how the second citation of the Young decision quotes the DiMarzo case. The first case that is quoted – Young v. Garwacki – is noted with the use of the double quotation marks ("), while the quotation from the second case – DiMarzo v. S & P Realty Corp. – is indicated with the single quotation mark ('), so from 'there could be...to without notice.'" The use of the single and double quotation marks at the very end of the sentence tells you the quotation from both cases ends there. You must be very careful when using quotation marks. Rule 5 of the Bluebook provides more detailed information about quotations.

Here is another paragraph from the Humphry v. Byron case:

> As the *Chausse* language suggests, Massachusetts case law recognizes a distinction between the leased premises themselves and "common" or "appurtenant" areas outside the leased premises, such that ordinarily, the tenant is responsible for the leased premises and the landlord, perhaps jointly with the tenant, is responsible for common or appurtenant areas. See, e.g., *Tuchinsky v. Beacon Prop. Mgt. Corp.*, 45 Mass.App.Ct. 469, 470, 698 N.E.2d 1291 (1998) ("By designation in the lease, the elevator lobby [where the accident occurred] was part of the leased premises. It was not common area and was not used by anyone except [the commercial tenant] and its invitees.... The allegedly unsafe door was not in a common area. It was *within* the leased area, and it was not in an area *appurtenant* to the leased area" [emphasis in original]; landlord of multitenant commercial building not liable for injury to tenant's employee); *Monterosso v. Gaudette,* 8 Mass.App.Ct. 93, 97–100, 102, 391 N.E.2d 948 (1979) (commercial landlord and one tenant in multitenant building not entitled to directed verdicts on negligence claims; evidence warranted findings that both landlord and tenant exercised control over appurtenant area where

---

[236] THE BLUEBOOK: A UNIFORM SYSTEM OF CITATION R. 1.2(a) 58 (Columbia Law Review Ass'n et al. eds., 20th ed. 2015).
[237] See the Language Focus with the case EEOC v. AutoNation USA Corp. (Section III, Unit 3) on page 257 for additional information about quotations and quotation marks, as well as information about how to modify quotations.

accident occurred). Gateway leased the entire building from the landlord, including the stairway where Humphrey's accident occurred. It was Gateway's responsibility to keep the leased premises safe, as nothing in the lease imposes this responsibility on the landlord.

Here, you first note the use of the signal "See, e.g." followed by the citation to the Tuchinsky v. Beacon Property Management Company case, as well as cites to several other cases that follow. If we examine the citations and the signals, we can learn many interesting things. First, "e.g" is a Latin phrase that means "exempla gratia," or simply "for example." So anytime you see that phrase, you know that the authority is provided as an example of *the* proposition that the cited case stands for. So in this example, the cases cited (Tuchinsky, Montrerosso) both stand for the proposition that Massachusetts case law recognizes this distinction between the leased premises, which is under the tenant's control, and the common areas, which are under the control of the landlord and the landlord and the tenant may both be responsible for.

The Bluebook states that *e.g.* is used when the "[c]ited authority states the proposition; other authorities also state the proposition, but citation to them would not be helpful or is not necessary."[238] 'E.g' may also be used in combination with other signals, or preceded by a comma, such as in the paragraph above. The 'see' is used instead of no signal when the cited authority is not "directly stated by the cited authority but obviously follows from it."[239]

The final point worth noting in this paragraph is the use of the two parentheticals that follow the citation to the Tuchinsky case. A parenthetical is a phrase included between two parentheses, and parentheticals follow the actual citation to the case. Parentheticals are very useful when you are reading cases and provide a wealth of information that you can use to better understand the issue being discussed.

See Rule 10.6 of the Blubeook for complete information about using parentheticals with cases, but in a nutshell, you want to include a parenthetical when the reason for citing an authority is not immediately clear to the reader and the additional information provided in the parenthetical can help explain the utility of the source (such as the citation to the Monterosso case) or to provide a quotation from the case that also provides additional information (such as the citation to the Tuchinsky case, which includes both a direct quotation and additional information provided by the writer/court (the last part of the parenthetical that begins "landlord of multitenant commercial building . . . .")).

Parentheticals and citations are easy to skip over and ignore when you read cases. But if you realize the helpful information that they can provide, the insight into the issues being discussed in a case, and the springboard that they can be for your own research (just click on one and read it to learn more), you will stop skimming over them and start reading them as carefully as the rest of your cases.

Check out Rule 1.2 in the Bluebook for additional information on other signals not covered here.

---

[238] Rule 1.2, THE BLUEBOOK: A UNIFORM SYSTEM OF CITATION (Columbia Law Review Ass'n et al. eds., 20th ed. 2015).
[239] Id.

Monterosso v. Gaudette,
391 N.E.2d 948 (Mass. App. Ct. 1979).

Vocabulary and Legal Terminology

Directed verdict: A jury verdict ordered by the court. In civil cases, a party may receive a directed verdict if the opposite side does not present a prima facie case or a necessary defense.[240]

Causally negligent: Stated of a defendant when his actions and his negligence were the cause of the plaintiff's injuries or loss.

Landing: (here) The area between flights of stairs.

Special verdict: Special finding by the jury on each material issue of the case, leaving the application of the law to the court (e.g., in a negligence case, the jury finds that defendant was driving too fast under the circumstances).[241]

To frame (the discussion): To construct.

Light fixtures: A device used to create light with a lightbulb.

Trap door: A door that covers or hides an opening in the floor or the ceiling.

Drape: A cloth or piece of fabric placed in front of windows or here, at a doorway, to conceal what is behind.

To freshen up: To make oneself feel fresher and cleaner such as by changing clothes or taking a shower or bath.

Adjacent to: Next to.

Uncontroverted: Undisputed.

To discharge (here): To fulfill, as in a duty.

Pre-Reading Questions

Before you begin reading, skim the caption and first three paragraphs and answer the following questions:

1. Is the case in federal or state court?
2. What happened to lead the plaintiff to file the original complaint?
3. What was the relationship between the plaintiff and the defendants?

---

[240] *Directed Verdict*, Gilbert's Pocket Size Law Dictionary (3rd ed. 2014).
[241] *Special Verdict*, Gilbert's Pocket Size Law Dictionary (3rd ed. 2014).

4. Motions:
    a. Who filed motions?
    b. When were the motions filed?
    c. What motions did they file?
    d. Which motions did the court grant?
    e. What happened after the motions were decided?
5. What did the jury decide and what did the court do after the jury issued its verdict?
6. When the plaintiff appealed, what errors did he claim that the trial court made?
7. What did the appellate court hold?
8. After the appellate court issued its decision, what happened to the case?

Comprehension Questions

With a general idea of the case in your mind, you can now read the case. As you are reading and after you finish reading, answer the following questions:

1. What arguments did Gaudette make concerning her liability for the customer's injuries? _____

2. A tenant has a duty to warn those in the space that he rents about dangerous conditions on the premises. Does that duty exist only to conditions within the area that the tenant leases or is under his control? If not, when does the tenant have that duty? _____

3. Does that rule seem fair to you? Why or why not? _____

4. What facts indicate that the landing area was leased to Gaudette? Did the court decide whether the landing area was part of the leased premises? _____

5. Look at the paragraph that begins (c) Huston's motion for directed verdict. In this paragraph, does the court conclude that Huston was negligent and thus liable for the customer's injuries? If not, what does the court conclude? _____

6. Is this case useful for our case?
    a. Why or why not? _____
    b. Is it more useful for the plaintiff or the defendant? Why? _____
    c. Can you analogize or distinguish the facts from our case? How can the facts and holdings be useful? _____

Grammar Review — Describing Repeated Past Actions or Habits

We use many different tenses to describe past actions in English — past simple, past perfect, present perfect and past continuous. But when we are describing a repeated past action or a habit in the past, we have certain verb forms that we use to convey specific nuances of the past action.

The <u>Monterosso</u> decision describes the building where the accident occurred:

> Customers were invited to use [a] rear entrance by advertising signs indicating the presence of both enterprises, and ***would find*** the back door unlocked during the hours that either store was open for business. Before reaching either store, a customer ***would pass*** several unmarked doors and openings.

In this quotation from the case, the court uses the form *would + root verb (infinitive – to)* to express a repeated action. It was not just on one day that customers entered the building by the back entrance and saw the door, but over a long period of time.

We also used the verbal form *used to + verb root* to express the past.

> Before computers, many attorneys *used to dictate* letters to their secretaries.

> Before computers, many attorneys *would dictate* letters to their secretaries.

Both sentences describe a repeated action or a habit in the past. But what's the difference? *Would* and *used to* are not always interchangeable. We use *used to* when we want to describe actions or situations in the past and that are finished now. The actions took place over a period of time. We don't use *used to* for actions that took place on one occasion.

> When I was young, we *used to take* a long trip by car to visit by grandparents every summer.

> NOT: When we were on a trip one year, we ~~used to see~~ many other families traveling.

Would is used to express actions that occur again and again or many times in the past.

> When I worked at the law firm, my co-workers *would* always *go* to lunch at McDonalds.

This action is repeated many times in the past, on many days, again and again, so I can use *would*.

We also use the form *was/were always + gerund* to express a habit or repeated action in the past, but the use of "always" implies that the habit was annoying.

> She *was always waiting* until the last minute to start working on her assignments.

Note that when speaking, we often place an exaggerated and extra stress on the word "always" to emphasize the meaning and the repeated-nature of the action. Because English is a stress-based language, we don't stress all words and all syllables equally. Stressing one word over another in a sentence tells the listener what words and ideas are important to the speaker.

Bishop v. TES Realty Trust,
942 N.E.2d 173 (Mass. 2011).

Vocabulary and Legal Terminology

Ceiling plaster: Mixture of lime and sand that is placed on ceilings.

Crack: A line along the surface of something that usually indicates damage.

Leak: To lose liquids or gas.

Bucket: A round container with a handle used to carry water, dirt or other materials.

Statutory interpretation: The process by which courts interpret the meaning of statutes.

Mischief: Harmful behavior.

To bar: To prevent.

To override: To decide against something, using one's authority or power.

Pre-Reading Questions

Before you begin reading, skim the caption and first two paragraphs (synopsis and holdings) and answer the following questions:

1. Is the case in federal or state court?
2. What happened to lead the plaintiff to file the original complaint?
3. What was the relationship between the plaintiff and the defendant?
4. What happened at the district court?
5. Who appealed?
6. What did the appellate court hold and what was the result of that holding?

Comprehension Questions

With a general idea of the case in your mind, you can now read the case. As you are reading and after you finish reading, answer the following questions:

1. What is the issue in this case? _____
2. What did the trial court conclude with regard to the commercial landlord's duties to make repairs to the property that he leased? _____
3. Why did the court vacate the trial court's judgment and send the case back for a new trial?

4. Statutory interpretation involves first looking at the language of the statute itself. Based on the language of §19, why did the court conclude that the statute and its obligations applied to commercial landlords? _____

5. Statutory interpretation also involves looking at the intent of the legislature when the statute was passed. With regard to legislative intent, what supports the conclusion that §19 applied to commercial landlords? _____

6. What other statutes also support this conclusion? _____

7. Why did the court limit the duty of a commercial landlord to repair only when the tenant has provided written notice, as required under §19? _____

8. Do you agree with this decision and the added duty imposed on commercial landlords? Why or why not? _____

9. Is this case useful for our case?
    a. Why or why not? _____
    b. Is it more useful for the plaintiff or the defendant? Why? _____
    c. Can you analogize or distinguish the facts from our case? How and why can the facts and holdings be useful? _____

Grammar Review — Prepositions[242]

Learning prepositions in a foreign language is very difficult. There often is no logical reason why we use one preposition rather than another one. You simply have to memorize the prepositions, their meanings and the words that they go with.

> *Whether the contract was breached **depends on** many factors.*
>
> *The defendant will likely be **liable for** breach of contract.*

Here are two sentences from the Bishop decision that highlight an additional difficulty in properly using prepositions: when prepositions have similar yet different meanings and are easy to confuse.

1. Bishop placed a bucket **beneath** the leak to catch the water and protect the rug from damage.

Under vs. below vs. beneath vs. underneath

You probably know that *beneath* means under, or in a lower position than something else. So the question remains: In this sentence, can I use *under* instead of *beneath*, and what's the difference between these prepositions with similar meanings?

Under is used to express lower positions, most often with three-dimensional objects.

> I put the bucket under the sink.
>
> The dog was sleeping under the bed because it was warm there.

---

[242] In acknowledgment of the importance and difficulty of prepositions and phrases (including phrasal verbs) that deal with prepositions, the following Grammar Review and Language Focus exercises all deal with prepositions: Maxell, Inc. v. Kenney Deans, Inc. (p. 26); Regency Oaks Corp. v. Norman-Spencer McKernan, Inc. (p. 52); Cook v. Rockwell Int'l Corp. et al., v. Nuclear Reg. (p. 76); Van Wyck v. Apsinwall (p. 146); Anest v. Audino (p. 163). You are encouraged to review and complete the exercises for further practice.

Under is also used with expressions such as *under pressure, under stress, under control*, as well as others.

Below indicates a lower position, but with a flat plane.

> The coffin was buried six feet below the ground.

> The woman placed the picture of her children below the picture of her parents.

Below is also used in expressions such *below zero*.

Beneath instead is the same as under, but has a more formal sound to it. For this reason, the court in the Bishop case chose to use *beneath* rather than *under* as legal writing, especially a court decision, always has a more formal register than everyday language.

Underneath has almost the same meaning as under, but the distinction is minimal. Underneath is often used when something is covered by something else:

> The dog was sleeping underneath the covers.

2. When the Legislature has intended to distinguish **between** residential and commercial leases, it has included specific language to that effect.

Between vs. among

Between and among are often confused as the meanings are very similar, and in some languages, the same preposition is used to express what English uses two separate words for.

Between is used when we are talking about distinct, individual items, whether two or twenty.

> He wasn't able to choose between the two books, so he bought them both.

> He wasn't able to choose between the ten books that he thought looked interesting, so he bought them all.

> During the settlement discussions, there was a lot of tension between the union representative, the employee's attorney and the employer's attorney.

> Note that although you probably hear people frequently saying "between you and I," the correct English is "between you and me."

Among, instead, is used when you aren't speaking about separate individuals or items, but instead are speaking about a group.

> There was a lot of interest among the employees to start offering paid vacation.

> He chose to work with a law firm in New York among all the law firms that he applied to.

Chausse v. Coz,
540 N.E.2d 667 (Mass. 1989).

Vocabulary and Legal Terminology

Transfer on its own initiative: When an appellate court decides to review a case of a lower court without a writ of certiorari being filed by a party.

Build-up: An increase in something that occurs over time, such as steam in this case.

To trigger: To cause to set fire or explode.

To press: (here) To emphasize or underscore.

Implied warranty of habitability: Guarantee understood to exist in all residential leases that the tenants can safely live in the leased property.[243]

Pre-Reading Questions

Before you begin reading, skim the caption and first paragraph and answer the following questions:
1. Is the case in federal or state court?
2. What happened to lead the plaintiff to file the original complaint?
3. What was the relationship between the plaintiff and the defendant?
4. What happened at the trial court?
5. Why do you think the supreme court heard and decided this case on its own initiative?
6. What did the supreme court hold?

Comprehension Questions

With a general idea of the case in your mind, you can now read the case. As you are reading and after you finish reading, answer the following questions:
1. Describe the facts that led to the accident that injured the plaintiff. _____
2. Why does the court dedicate considerable space to explaining the accident and what caused it? _____
3. What arguments did the plaintiff make with regard to the defendant's liability? _____
4. What did the lease agreement state with regard to repairs and why is this important for concluding that the defendant was not liable for the plaintiff's injuries?
5. What policy reasons exist for not extending the implied warranty of habitability to commercial landlords and premises? _____
6. Is this case useful for our case?
   a. Why or why not? _____

---

[243] *Habitability*, Gilbert's Pocket Size Law Dictionary (3rd ed. 2014).

b. Is it more useful for the plaintiff or the defendant? Why? _____
c. Can you analogize or distinguish the facts from our case? How and why can the facts and holdings be useful? _____

Language Review — Adverbs[244]

Adverbs are words that define and describe an adjective, verb or another adverb. Look at the following sentences from the Chausse case with the adverbs highlighted:

> The plaintiff argues **briefly** that the lessors should be liable because, under the terms of the lease, the lessors agreed to repair certain defects in the premises.
>
> The plaintiff presses more **vigorously** his claim that we should extend to commercial lessors the obligation that lessors of residential property have to maintain leased premises in a reasonably safe condition.
>
> The Young opinion **explicitly** reserved the question whether its new rule would apply to leased commercial premises.

Here, each adverb describes the verb in the sentence: argues, presses, reserved. The adverb answers the question of "how" the verb was carried out by the subject (the plaintiff or the Young decision).

Many adverbs end in -ly in English, such as those three examples above, as well as many other adverbs you are familiar with such as slowly, carefully, negligently, and quickly.

However, not all adverbs in English end in -ly. There are also what we call *flat adverbs*, adverbs that do not end in -ly.

> Drive slow!
> He works hard.

Flat adverbs include:

> *far, fast, hard, slow, quick, straight, clean, close, deep,* and *fine*[245]

And yes, some of those adverbs are also adjectives. Both of these sentences are correct:

> He was cut really deep and had to have stitches.
> The water is very deep at the middle of the lake.
>
> He traveled very far before he finally took a rest.
> The nearest gas station is very far from here.

Don't be tricked into thinking that *hard* and *hardly* mean the same thing, however.

> *Are you working hard, or hardly working?*

Do you understand the difference between the two questions? What is it?

---

[244] See the Language Focus with the case Merrell-Benco Agency, LLC v. HSBC Bank USA et al. (Section I, Unit 2) on page 25 for additional information about adverbs.

[245] Bonnie Mills, *Do All Adverbs End in "-Ly"?*, QUICKANDDIRTYTIPS.COM, http://www.quickanddirtytips.com/education/grammar/do-all-adverbs-end-in-ly#sthash.kRlQPL5V.dpuf (last visited May 2, 2016).

The Great Atlantic and Pacific Tea Co. v. Yanofsky,
403 N.E.2d 370 (Mass. 1980).

Vocabulary and Legal Terminology

<u>Direct appellate review</u>: An appeal that goes directly from the trial court to the supreme court, skipping the intermediary appellate court.

<u>To estop</u>: To prevent a party from raising a defense or making a claim or from doing something in general.

<u>To mop up</u>: To clean a spill or liquid on the floor with a mop.

<u>Shopping carriages</u>: Also called shopping carts; a basket on wheels used for carrying shopping purchases.

<u>To drip</u>: To let small amounts of liquid fall from something such as a faucet.

<u>Uncontradicted</u>: Undisputed.

Pre-Reading Questions

Before you begin reading, skim the caption and first paragraph and answer the following questions:
1. Is the case in federal or state court?
2. Who are the parties to the case and why are they in court?
3. What was the relationship between the plaintiff and the defendant?
4. What happened at the trial court?
5. Who appealed?
6. What arguments did the defendant/landlord make on appeal?
7. What did the supreme court hold?
8. What does this holding mean with regard to any money that the tenant is owed?

Comprehension Questions

With a general idea of the case in your mind, you can now read the case. As you are reading and after you finish reading, answer the following questions:
1. Describe the facts that led to the accident that injured the plaintiff. What arguments did the plaintiff make with regard to the defendant's liability? _____
_____

2. Did the injured customer have a jury trial? Why did A&P bring a claim after her case was concluded? _____

3. What did the lease agreement state with regard to repairs? _____

4. When a landlord agrees to make repairs to the leased premises or to common areas, what is presumed from that agreement? _____

5. When does a commercial landlord have to indemnify a tenant for injuries a party suffered on the property due to the landlord's negligence? _____

6. When will the landlord be relieved of that duty to indemnify? _____

7. Is this case useful for our case?
   a. Why or why not? _____
   b. Is it more useful for the plaintiff or the defendant? Why? _____
   c. Can you analogize or distinguish the facts from our case? How and why can the facts and holdings be useful? _____

8. In our case, we know that the lease between Gateway West and SDA had no indemnification provision. How does that affect the case and how you determine who might be liable for Julianna's injuries? What other facts might be determinative? _____

Language Focus — Conciseness[246]

Writing concisely or "tightly"[247] is an objective that all writers should have – whether they are writing legal English or "regular" English. Unlike some languages, English values short, tight, and concise sentences. Here are some quotes of famous writers that underscore this:

> "If I had more time I would have written a shorter letter." Blaise Pascal

> "The most valuable of all talents is that of never using two words when one will do." Thomas Jefferson

> "Vigorous writing is concise. A sentence should contain no unnecessary words, a paragraph no unnecessary sentences, for the same reason that a drawing should have

---

[246] The skill of "tightening up" your writing is a very important one for a good writer to develop, so much so that you will find another Language Focus, with similar introductory information, on this same topic in Unit 1 of this same Section of the ESL Workbook (Zellner v. Conrad). For more practice, you can do the exercise presented with the Zellner case. Bryan Garner's book Legal Writing in Plain English is also a good resource with not just extensive explanations about writing more concisely and in plain English, but also practice exercises.

[247] While you might be familiar with the adjective tight to describe clothing that fits closely to the skin, we also use it to describe writing. *Tight writing* is writing that is clear, concise and well organized.

no unnecessary lines and a machine no unnecessary parts. This requires not that the writer make all his sentences short, or that he avoid all detail and treat his subject only in outline, but that every word tell." William Strunk and EB White

Unfortunately, legal writing is often some of the least concise writing out there! You have no doubt read court decisions with long, convoluted sentences. Contracts and statutes have the same problem. It seems that many attorneys think that to sound "lawyerly," they have to write in long sentences with long, technical and unfamiliar words.

Here is an example of a sentence from the Great Atlantic & Pacific. The revised second sentence shows you that with a few changes and edits, an overly wordy and long sentence can be improved to be tighter and more concise.

> In the present case, the lessor knew at the times he renewed the lease that the lessee operated a store frequented by members of the general public, old and young, feeble and firm, who would be bent upon the task of shopping for groceries and other items.

> Here, when the landlord renewed the lease, he knew that the tenant operated a grocery store and that all members of the general public, of all ages and abilities, would shop there.

Which do you think sounds better? Why?

Here is another paragraph, a lot longer, from the same Great Atlantic & Pacific case. Why don't you try your hand at editing it to tighten up the writing?

> Action was brought against lessor by lessee seeking indemnity for money paid to settle personal injury claim. The Superior Court found for lessee, and after review was sought the Supreme Judicial Court, on its own initiative, ordered direct appellate review. The Supreme Judicial Court held that where lease required lessor to make repairs to exterior of building, and lessor was aware of leaky roof which permitted water to accumulate on floor of store, lessor was required to indemnify lessor with settled claim for personal injuries sustained by customer who slipped and fell as result of water being on floor and that evidence sustained finding that lessee was not negligent.

The Great Atlantic and Pacific Tea Co. v. Yanofsky, 403 N.E.2d 370 (Mass. 1980)

Putting All the Sources — Case Law and Statutes — Together

When you have various primary sources that have different but interrelated factors like the cases you have read for this Unit, completing a table comparing those sources can be very helpful in understanding how they are interrelated and how the factors (such as landlord liability and duties) are the same as well as different.

Complete the table, including not only the yes/no answer but also the citation to the case (or cases) and/or the statute that provides and establishes the rule.

	Residential landlord	Commercial landlord	Tenant (commercial or residential – indicate which)
Duty to repair common areas?	Yes, landlord owes a duty of reasonable care to those on property that not subject to risk of unreasonable harm. <u>Young v. Garwacki</u>, 402 N.E.2d 1045 (Mass. 1980).		
Duty to repair areas under tenant's control?		No, unless contractually established. <u>Humphrey v. Byron</u>, 850 N.E.2d 1044 (Mass. 2006).	
Duty of reasonable care to everyone who is lawfully on the premises?			
Implied warranty of habitability?	Yes.		
Duty to repair unsafe conditions not created by tenant upon written notice from tenant?			
Can contractually limit liability for injuries that occur on property?		No. M.G.L.A. 186 §15. Applied to commercial landlords in <u>Bishop v. TES Realty Trust</u>, 942 N.E.2d 2d (Mass. 2011).	

Index

Language or Grammar Focus	Detailed description	Page	Case Name
Adjectives (order of)		p. 153	State v. Rodriquez
Adverbs		p. 18	Merrell-Benco Agency, LLC v. HSBC Bank USA et al.
		p. 290	Chausse v. Coz
Articles (definite and indefinite)		p. 186	Veramark Technologies, Inc. v. Bouk
Business Communication		p. 58	168th Dodge LP v. Rave Reviews Cinemas, LLC
Capital (uppercase) Letters		p. 89	Davoust v. Mitchell
Cases	Analogizing and distinguishing	p. 46	Bazak Int'l Corp. v. Tarrant Apparel Group
	Reading old cases	p. 82	Owens v. Phillips
	Personal experiences affecting reading of	p. 98	Lundgren v. Fultz
	Use of in analysis	p. 108	Udofot v. Seven Eights Liquor
Direct v. Indirect Speech		p. 129	Baldwin v. Shell Oil Co.
English	Latin v. Germanic words	p. 61	Public Service Co. of Colorado v. Van Wyck
	U.S. v. U.K. English	p. 122	Herlihy v. The Metropolitan Museum of Art
	Formality of language	p. 37	Int'l Business Machines Corp. v. Johnson
	Direct v. indirect speech	p. 129	Baldwin v. Shell Oil Co.
	Figures of speech and metaphors	p. 135	Byam v. Collins
	Same word, different meaning	p. 94	Hendricks v. Tubbs

Language or Grammar Focus	Detailed description	Page	Case Name
Figures of Speech and Metaphors		p. 135	Byam v. Collins
Formality of Language		p. 37	Int'l Business Machines Corp. v. Johnson
Idiomatic Expressions	From case	p. 26	Greene v. Hellman
	With bitter and sweet	p. 11	Jensen v. Walsh
	With body parts	p. 167	Shrock v. Meier
	With tools	p. 196	Lucente v. Int'l Business Machines Corp.
Legal Analysis	Analogizing and distinguishing	p. 46	Bazak Int'l Corp. v. Tarrant Apparel Group
	Use of in analysis	p. 108	Udofot v. Seven Eights Liquor
	Standards of review	p. 159	Gifford v. Gallano Farms, LLC
	Citations and sources	p. 178	BDO Seidman v. Hirshberg
	In general in U.S. legal writing	p. 182	Kanan, Corbin, Schupak, Aronow, Inc. v. FD Int'l Ltd.
	Tests used in	p. 216	Mink v. AAA Development Inc.
	Public policy in	p. 244	Bhatia v. Chevron U.S.A., Inc.
	Citations and signals	p. 280	Humphrey v. Byron
Legal English and Legalese	Thereto, Herein, etc.	p. 71	Miller v. Carnation Co.
	Revising complex sentences	p. 43	Kowalchuk v. Stroup
	Revising complex sentences	p. 22	Hallock v. State of New York
	Same word, different meanings	p. 94	Hendricks v. Tubbs
	Revising complex sentences	p. 228	The Kelly Law Firm, P.C. v. An Attorney For You
	Latin words and phrases in	p. 132	Buckley v. Litman
	Translating into «regular» English	p. 267	EEOC Consent Decree in EEOC v. Razzoo's L.P.
Phrasal Verbs		p. 238	American Postal Workers Union v. Postmasters General
		p. 51	Maxell Inc. v. Kenney Deans, Inc.

Language or Grammar Focus	Detailed description	Page	Case Name
Predictive v. Persuasive Language		p. 14	Edinburg Volunteer Fire Co. v. Danko Emergency Equipment, Co.
Prefixes	-Dis and -in	p. 259	Proctor v. Cosolidated Freightways Corp. of Delaware
Prepositions	In phrasal verbs	p. 51	Maxell Inc. v. Kenney Deans, Inc.
	with adjectives and verbs	p. 30	Regency Oaks Corp. v. Norman Spencer McKernan
	In general	p. 69	Cook v. Rockwell Int'l Corp.
	Placement and position of	p. 138	Van Wyck v. Aspinwall
	On, onto, upon, in and into	p. 264	Tiano v. Dillards Dep't Stores, Inc.
	Difficult ones	p. 155	Anest v. Ardino
	Under/beneath/below/underneath and between/among	p. 287	Bishop v. TES Realty Trust
Pronunciation	Of compound words	p. 118	Wood on Behalf of Doe v. Ashford
	verbs vs. nouns	p. 142	State v. Boland
Pronouns	Definite and indefinite	p. 40	Trademark Properties Inc. v. A&E Television Networks
	Relative (and relative clauses)	p. 210	Atkinson v. McLaughlin
Proverbs	Vague use of	p. 147	State v. Sweeney
Punctuation	Periods, Commas, Semicolons and Colons	p. 86	Bonewitz v. Parker
	Hypens, en-dash and em-dash	p. 74	Cobai v. Young
Reading Skills	Inference	p. 163	Azulay, Horn and Seiden, LLC v. Horn
	Reading statutes and long sentences	p. 270	M.G.L.A. § 15 and § 19

Language or Grammar Focus	Detailed description	Page	Case Name
Same Words, Different Meanings		p. 94	Hendricks v. Tubbs
Sentence Structure/ Revising		p. 110	H.B. ex rel. v. Whittemore
		p. 43	Kowalchuk v. Stroup
		p. 22	Hallock v. State of New York
Slang		p. 231	Percle v. SFGL Foods, Inc.
Synonyms (or are they?)	Formality	p. 49	Goff-Hamel v. Obstretricians v. Gynecologists, P.C.
	Cadaver/body/ remains and steal/ rob/burglarize/ shoplift	p. 5	State v. Weber
	To find/to rule/to hold	p. 8	State v. Graham
	To break/to violate/ to breach/to infringe	p. 235	Tempur-Pedic Int'l, Inc. v. Go Satellite, Inc.
	Legal vs. non-legal	p. 247	Burns v. Southern Pac. Transp. Co.
	To rub	p. 101	Bjerke v. Johnson
Suffixes of -ful and -less		p. 222	Ford v. Mentor Worldwide
Transition Words		p. 78	Wernke v. Halas
Will, use of		p. 33	Cleveland Wrecking Co. v. Hercules Const. Corp.
Verbs	Will, use of	p. 33	Cleveland Wrecking Co. v. Hercules Const. Corp.
	Conditional Tense	p. 54	deNourie & Yost Homes, LLC v. Frost
	Subjunctive	p. 1	Soucek v. Banham
	Active v. Passive	p. 66	Hoery v. United States

Language or Grammar Focus	Detailed description	Page	Case Name
	To get and different expressions with	p. 104	Patzwald v. Krey
	To strike and different meanings of	p. 174	Reed, Roberts Associates, Inc. v. Strauman
	Past tenses (past simple, continuous and past perfect)	p. 193	Merrill Lynch, Pierce, Fenner & Smith v. Dunn
	With gerund and infinitives	p. 206	Ashland Management Inc. v. Altair Investments NA, LLC
	Descriptive verbs	p. 225	Gatte v. Ready 4 A Change, LLC
	Frequently confused	p. 242	Anderson v. General Dynamics Convair Aerospace Division
	«Verbing»	p. 253	EEOC v. Townley Engineering & Manufacturing, Co.
	Active v. Passive II	p. 256	Int'l Ass'n of Machinists & Aerospace Workers v. The Boeing Co.
	Irregular	p. 262	Slater v. Douglas County
	Modal verbs	p. 274	Young v. Garwacki
	Describing repeated past actions or habits	p. 284	Monterosso v. Gaudette
Writing and Vocabulary	Precision in word choice	p. 150	State. v. Graffius
	Homophones, Homonyms and Homographs	p. 170	Tully v. McLean
	Parallel constructions	p. 190	Scott, Stackrow & Co. v. Skavina
	Concisenesss in writing	p. 201	Zellner v. Conrad
	Find the mistakes	p. 219	Carrot Bunch Co., Inc. v. Computer Friends, Inc.
	Quotation marks, use of	p. 249	EEOC v. AutoNation USA Corp.
	Concisenesss in writing	p. 292	The Great Atlantic and Pacific Tea Co. v. Yanofsky
	Modal verbs	p. 274	Young v. Garwacki
	Describing repeated past actions or habits	p. 284	Monterosso v. Gaudette